Political Parties in Palestine

Previously published

The Politics of Change in Palestine: State-Building and Nonviolent Resistance (2011)

Politischer Islam in Westafrika. Eine Bestandsaufnahme (2006)
edited by Michael Bröning and Holger Weiss

"Wie jedes andere Land..." Das Deutschlandbild der israelischen Presse 1990–2000 (2004)

Political Parties in Palestine

Leadership and Thought

Michael Bröning

In association with the research group including
Christoph Dinkelaker (head), Judith Althaus, Usama Anthar,
Stefanie Kirster, Helene Kortländer, Henrik Meyer,
Alexander Rüsche, Eva Schreiner

POLITICAL PARTIES IN PALESTINE
Copyright © Michael Bröning, 2013.

All rights reserved.

First published in 2013 by
PALGRAVE MACMILLAN®
in the United States—a division of St. Martin's Press LLC,
175 Fifth Avenue, New York, NY 10010.

Where this book is distributed in the UK, Europe and the rest of the world, this is by Palgrave Macmillan, a division of Macmillan Publishers Limited, registered in England, company number 785998, of Houndmills, Basingstoke, Hampshire RG21 6XS.

Palgrave Macmillan is the global academic imprint of the above companies and has companies and representatives throughout the world.

Palgrave® and Macmillan® are registered trademarks in the United States, the United Kingdom, Europe and other countries.

ISBN: 978–1–137–29692–4

Library of Congress Cataloging-in-Publication Data is available from the Library of Congress.

A catalogue record of the book is available from the British Library.

Design by Newgen Imaging Systems (P) Ltd., Chennai, India.

First edition: February 2013

10 9 8 7 6 5 4 3 2 1

Transferred to Digital Printing in 2013

CONTENTS

List of Tables and Charts		vii
Acknowledgments		ix
List of Abbreviations		xi
One	Political Factions in Palestine: Stagnation, Ambiguity, and Change	1
Two	Hamas: Between Terror and Realpolitik	15
Three	Fatah: From Resistance Movement to Party of State	57
Four	PFLP: Arab Anti-Imperialists	97
Five	PNI: A History of Nonviolence	121
Six	PPP: The PNA's Loyal Opposition	147
Seven	DFLP: Palestinian Marxists and their Coming of Age	173
Timeline of Political Events in the Palestinian Territories		199
Notes		205
Bibliography		213
Index		219

TABLES AND CHARTS

Tables

2.1	Hamas at a glance	16
3.1	Fatah at a glance	58
4.1	The PFLP at a glance	98
5.1	The PNI at a glance	122
6.1	The PPP at a glance	148
7.1	The DFLP at a glance	174

Charts

2.1	Organizational structure of Hamas	25
3.1	Organizational structure of Fatah	59
4.1	Organizational structure of the PFLP	104
5.1	Organizational structure of the PNI	124
6.1	Organizational structure of the PPP	150
7.1	Organizational structure of the DFLP	175

ACKNOWLEDGMENTS

I would like to thank the members of the FES research group for their inputs, ideas, and contributions over the course of the past year. This book would not have seen the light of day without their extensive efforts in field work, research, and drafting of texts. I would also like to thank several Palestinian colleagues and academics in East Jerusalem, Ramallah, and Gaza who provided critical feedback. Furthermore, I am grateful to Palestinian party representatives who kindly granted permission to print excerpts from party programs and who agreed to be interviewed for this project.

Finally, my gratitude also extends to Jolie Chai and Judy Heiblum for their editorial input.

ABBREVIATIONS

AKP	Turkish Justice and Development Party
ANM	Arab Nationalist Movement
DFLP	Democratic Front for the Liberation of Palestine
DoP	Declaration of Principles
FIDA	Palestine Democratic Union
GUPW	General Union of Palestinian Women
HDIP	Health, Development Information and Policy Institute
JCP	Jordan's Communist Party
NGC	National Guidance Committee
NLL	National Liberation League
NSU	Negotiation Support Unit
PCP	Palestine Communist Party
PFLP	Popular Front for the Liberation of Palestine
PGFTU	Palestinian General Federation of Trade Unions
PLC	Palestinian Legislative Council
PLO	Palestine Liberation Organization
PNA	Palestinian National Authority
PNC	Palestinian National Council
PNI	Palestinian National Initiative
PPP	Palestinian People's Party
PPSR	Palestinian Popular Struggle Front
SI	Socialist International
UNLU	United National Leadership of the Uprising
UNRWA	United Nations Relief and Works Agency

CHAPTER ONE

Political Factions in Palestine: Stagnation, Ambiguity, and Change

To a degree, the history of all hitherto existing Palestinian politics is the history of political factionalism. Heterogeneity and ideological pluralism have defined Palestinian political life from its inception, giving rise to a spectrum of different political outlooks that have long been considered unique in the Arab world.[1] Yet, Palestinian political life has been defined not only by ideological heterogeneity, but also as a succession of distinct chronological phases, in which different political factions have at different periods of time laid claims to representing the Palestinian national movement in its totality.[2]

Subsequent to the establishment of the State of Israel in 1948, pan-Arab groups such as the Movement of Arab Nationalists dominated the political scene, which can be defined as the first phase. As joint military attempts by Arab states to counter the founding of the State of Israel proved unsuccessful, the strategic approach of pan-Arabism was increasingly discredited.

The second stage of Palestinian nationalism was largely defined by the dominant role of the Palestinian National Liberation Movement (Fatah). The secular organization was founded in 1959 and rapidly expanded after 1968 to represent an independent Palestinian approach to realizing national aspirations. Fatah would dominate the political landscape for the better part of three decades. While Fatah competed fiercely at times with other secular factions such as the Popular Front for the Liberation of Palestine (PFLP) or the Democratic Front for the Liberation of Palestine (DFLP), these factions were ultimately united under the Palestine Liberation Organization (PLO), a political umbrella recognized as the "sole legitimate representative of the Palestinian people" by the United Nations in 1974, and by the United States and Israel in 1993.[3]

Starting in the 1980s, these PLO factions were increasingly confronted with the rise of alternative groups, which marks the third phase. The challenge from the Islamic Resistance Movement (Hamas) and other militant groups, such as the Islamic Jihad, was based on the perceived failure of secular Palestinian nationalism to realize its strategic objectives and arose against the background of a wider regional resurgence of politicized religion. As such, the rise of Hamas came to define Palestinian nationalism during this third period. Since then, dualism and increased polarization between the secular and the religious camps led, respectively, by Fatah from the one side and Hamas from the other has remained one of the defining features of current-day Palestinian political life.[4]

In many ways, the central role that Palestinian political movements have played throughout decades of conflict is hardly surprising—in particular, from a theoretical perspective. Given the absence of a Palestinian state, political movements such as Fatah—and later Hamas—have fulfilled responsibilities that went far beyond the role of political parties in independent democratic states. Palestinian parties have provided services and rudimentary governance (in the case of Fatah via the PLO, in the case of Hamas via a network of charity organizations, and in the case of leftist factions through nongovernmental organizations), engaged in militant and terrorist operations, and upheld Palestinian political ambitions on the global political agenda.

Movement or Party? The Importance of Being Ambiguous

Notably, most factions that continue to define political life in the Palestinian Territories have until now eschewed the label of political party.[5] Instead, they have chosen to identify as political "movements," or "liberation fronts."[6] This is not merely a semantic particularity but a highly relevant indicator of their self-perception.

The transformation of Palestinian political organizations from *movements* to clearly defined *political parties* remains incomplete. In fact, this reality arguably is a necessity within the Palestinian context, where factions have come to mirror existing inadequacies in the political system of which they form a part.[7]

On a technical level, this is illustrated by the fact that the role of political organizations in the Palestinian National Authority (PNA) has not been officially regulated within a legal framework. While draft laws on the role of political parties have repeatedly been met with internal criticism, the stagnation of the political process since the electoral victory of Hamas in 2006 has blocked the formalization of one set of legal regulations that describes the role and function of political organizations.[8]

This incomplete transformation has challenged political factions in terms of programmatic clarity, procedural processes, and (occasionally) in the safeguarding of organizational homogeneity. However, reluctance to transform has had little to do with aversion to change per se. Instead, for political factions, ambiguity has become an essential element of self-preservation.

As defined in the Oslo Accords concluded in 1993, the authority of the PNA has effectively remained limited to the densely populated Palestinian areas of the West Bank and the Gaza Strip. Against this background, disavowing the wider self-perception of liberation movements would have far-reaching consequences. Redefining "movements" as streamlined political parties would entail restricting ambitions to electoral politics, identifying government responsibility or the role of a "loyal opposition" within the existing political framework as their exclusive political objective. Any such step would essentially confine the scope of political movements to the limitations of the status quo. At the same time, a comprehensive transformation would also include severing ties to the large diaspora of Palestinian refugees. While the diaspora is not represented by the PNA, it plays a central role in the Israeli-Palestinian conflict. Also, in many cases, relations to the diaspora have always been essential in providing political legitimacy and financial support.

Against this background, most Palestinian factions have for the longest period of their development opted for ambiguity. They have, to different degrees, maintained the ideology of political organizations as political *movements*, which thereby transcend the limits dictated by the PNA. At the same time, political organizations have also embraced the functions of political parties within the confines of the Oslo Accords. On this political playing field, the factions seen today have attempted to gather public support for their positions by engaging in activities comparable to that of an opposition party in functioning democratic systems: establishing formalized political platforms, running for public office, and attempting to influence government behavior.[9]

In adopting certain roles of political parties, Palestinian movements have thus become essential players on the domestic level of the PNA, where they have channeled political aspirations into the realm of institutionalized electoral politics. The first elections held in the PNA in 1996 resulted in a sweeping victory of Fatah, a result that certainly reflects the fact that the party's main competitors Hamas, PFLP, DFLP, and Islamic Jihad had chosen to boycott the vote. As a consequence, the newly established Palestinian Legislative Council (PLC) was largely controlled by Fatah. In the resulting political system dominated by Fatah, this proved less than ideal. In the words of political scientist Amal Jamal, the overwhelming importance of Fatah in 1996 caused "a regression in the role of political parties in Palestinian politics."[10]

While this assessment certainly seems correct with regard to the formalized political process of PNA institutions, the absence of competing political forces from within the PNA and the PLO only facilitated fundamental political antagonism from outside of the political system. Growing opposition to Fatah ultimately resulted in Hamas's electoral triumph in the elections for the PLC in 2006, and initiated the above-mentioned third phase characteristic of Palestinian nationalism. The elections marked the forceful return of factionalism to Palestinian politics and caused the establishment of the bipolar party system seen today.

One year later, violent clashes between Fatah and Hamas effectively divided the PNA into two competing power centers. Each was taken over by rivaling political factions: Hamas took control of Gaza while Fatah struggled to retain its hegemonic position as the leading party of state in the West Bank.

While the resulting split once again illustrated the clout of political factionalism within Palestinian politics, this polarization also caused a near-total paralysis of formalized political procedures in the PNA.[11] Combined with the challenges posed by Israeli restrictions on freedom of movement, this schism has at the time of writing caused a wide-ranging stagnation in formalized democratic processes.[12]

Since the founding of the PNA, parliamentary and presidential elections have only been conducted in 1996 and in 2005/2006. Since the split, the postponement of elections and the sidelining of parliamentary procedures through the issuance of executive decrees have become almost a daily routine. In January 2010, scheduled presidential and legislative elections were postponed "due to the inability to conduct them in the southern districts of the nation...for the sake of public interest," as announced in a presidential decree.[13] Since then, attempts to hold elections have been repeatedly blocked by persisting antagonism between Fatah and Hamas.

Taking this into consideration, it seems that while the absence of state institutions prior to the establishment of the PNA has necessarily facilitated the development of influential political movements, the reluctance of political movements to transform into streamlined political parties has in turn weakened the political capacity of the PNA.

The Future of Political Factions

Despite a high level of control exercised by the factions in the West Bank and in Gaza, their primary objective to establish an independent Palestinian state remains unfulfilled. This has prompted some observers to flatly define the current established political factions as a "failed national movement."[14] While this statement might be overly unforgiving, it is clear that the current status quo poses a fundamental structural challenge to legitimacy and appeal of the political establishment in the West Bank *and* in Gaza. This is of particular importance given the success of alternative grassroot movements as witnessed in the uprisings of the Arab Spring.

The ensuing question raised by Palestinian journalist Daoud Kuttab as to whether "all those thousands of active young people [of the Arab revolts] will create or follow a new movement/party?" is certainly pertinent.[15] Taking note of a prominent global trend of voter *dealignment* from political parties in general, concern for the future role of the established political forces in the Palestinian Territories seems justified.

By now, it has become a near-cliché to point out that established political forces played only marginal roles in the ousting of autocratic rulers in Tunisia and Egypt. For many decision-makers in Palestinian political factions, this sidelining of established political movements has been unsettling. This, last but not least, in view of recent opinion polls that indicate a growing disenchantment by Palestinians with *all* conventional political factions. An opinion poll conducted in April 2012 by Near East Consulting found that 43 percent of Palestinians were convinced that neither Fatah nor Hamas were working "in the national interest."[16] The causes for this disenchantment are numerous. To a degree, they can be attributed to internal shortcomings. At the same time, however, it also seems clear that the limits of Palestinian authority as defined in the Oslo Accords has also fundamentally limited the extent to which both the Hamas- and the Fatah-run governments in the West Bank and Gaza have been able to maintain legitimacy through either political achievements vis-a-vis their political ambitions or the provision of services.

Despite this, however, dismissing traditional Palestinian factions as irrelevant for the future course of political life in the Palestinian Territories would be premature. There are several reasons for this: first, on a technical level, the PNA's election law is likely to safeguard a future role for political movements short of a complete dissolution of PNA institutions. The law combines a majority system with strong components of proportional representation and thus in principle strengthens the role of political factions. Recent proposals to amend the law have suggested shifting the balance even further toward strengthening political factions by allocating 75 percent of PLC seats to candidates from party lists.

On a second, more general level of analysis it can be argued that established political factions in the region might have, at first, been sidestepped but eventually emerged strengthened from the turmoil of the Arab Spring. At least in some prominent cases, established oppositional groups gained support in free elections. There are reasons to assume that a similar development would be a likely scenario in the Palestinian Territories.

In this context, it should also not be forgotten that there has been no shortage of attempts to overcome the factual bipolar system by establishing a viable alternative political force. The attempt in 2006 by Salam Fayyad and Hanan Ashrawi to mobilize voters for an alternative Third Way list is one of the most prominent examples although the list only gained two seats in Parliament. While future success for a newly emerging alternative movement can thus by no means be ruled out (and could very well be a likely outcome), such attempts have so far been short-lived and largely unsuccessful. At least for the time being, it seems, the established political factions in the Palestinian Territories are here to stay.

Charting a Political Cartography

Despite their general prominence, political movements in the Palestinian Territories remain surprisingly underdocumented. Existing compilations rarely move beyond short and frequently simplistic synopses failing to describe ideological positions in a more comprehensive manner. While broader analyses of the Palestinian political system and detailed case studies of individual political factions such as Hamas are common, an overview of Palestinian factions in their own right has so far not been attempted.[17] Given the depth and scope of scholarship allocated to other aspects of the Israeli-Palestinian conflict, and the pertinence of political factionalism, this was found to be a serious shortcoming.

Certainly, there are reasons for this blind spot. To start, movements such as Fatah or the DFLP have been viewed as terrorist groups for a long part of their history. Even today, factions such as Hamas or the PFLP are considered foreign terrorist organizations by Israel and most Western governments. As a consequence, several Palestinian factions have opted for less transparency, often operating in clandestine cells underground.

Simultaneously, most Palestinian factions have, rather understandably, prioritized intra-Palestinian discourse over attempts to reach out to the international community in deliberately choosing to address only Arabic-speaking audiences. This has effectively resulted in an imprecise representation of the political framework of Palestinian discourse for outside observers, inaccurately relegating certain parties and movements to a second-tier status while at times misrepresenting ideological outlooks and internal structures.

This explains why, contrary to other political institutions such as the PNA, Palestinian factions have been difficult to study. Facts that are readily available in other contexts, including, for example, the composition of leadership institutions, sources of finance, or in some cases even current political programs, are rare in the Palestinian context.

Against this background, this text attempts to present information on all political movements currently represented in the PLC, aiming to provide a complete overview. While the book covers well-known factions including Fatah and Hamas, it also offers insight into previously unpublished information on lesser-known factions that have at times played an equally vital role in the composition, outlook, and direction of Palestinian political life.

Obviously, this focus on PLC factions has its disadvantages. Significant movements such as the Islamic Jihad or the Hizb ut-Tahrir (Liberation Party) are not examined, as both organizations have rejected and opted out of electoral processes. In addition, otherwise relevant players such as Prime Minister Fayyad or recent protest movements against his policies are also not considered. While it is widely expected that Fayyad will play a future role by establishing a parliamentary list to run in future PLC elections, his dissolved Third Way list from the 2006 legislative elections has not been included. Similarly, the Palestinian Democratic Union (FIDA) of Yasser Abed Rabbo has been omitted as the party did not win a PLC seat despite having cooperated with the DFLP and Palestinian People's Party (PPP) in 2006.

Concerning structure, each chapter focuses on an individual political movement, beginning with an analytical summary of major historical developments. The objective was not a comprehensive analysis of general Palestinian history but rather a short and succinct description of major trends and ideological foundations of each political faction. Short bibliographic recommendations on suggested further readings in English have also been added.

Following this overview, each chapter includes biographies of personalities, given that political life in the Palestinian Territories has long been defined by a high degree of personalization (a process also notable in established Western democracies). These personalities have been selected on the basis of their inherent association with the faction. Biographies attempt to offer a concise description of key events that have determined an individual's public perception in Palestinian political discourse—and in many cases—resulted in the popular appeal of the affiliated political organization.

This section is followed by interviews with persons in different positions of authority in the West Bank and in the Gaza Strip. Each person was questioned in order to provide a wider understanding of different wings from inside each movement. Interviews focus on party leaders who are (in some cases) rarely seen in the larger public forum but nevertheless play an important role in determining policy and ideological positioning. The interviews were not conducted with the intent to confront party leaders with possible programmatic shortcomings (although tough questions were asked) but rather to offer the reader insight into party ideology as presented by decision makers in their own words. Similar sets of questions (and topics) were posed consistently throughout all interviews to better enable a comparative analysis between movements.

To provide further material on current party ideology and political thought, each chapter includes excerpts from current and historical election programs and party communiqués. The excerpts were organized according to four categories: party views on the Israeli-Palestinian conflict, economic development, the state's role vis-a-vis religion, and the general vision of state and society. In some cases, programs were available in English (such as the Hamas Charter, or Fatah's 2009 party platform) while other sources were found in printed material from party activists and translated into English where necessary. The excerpts begin with the most recent statements and subsequently present older (and in some cases outdated documents) to illustrate programmatic developments.

Certainly, the importance of party programs in general can be questioned not only in the Palestinian context. However, while it is understood that party programs are rarely consistently implemented, it was found that formalized programmatic statements do in many cases illustrate an intraparty consensus on important ideological questions. As such, they provide a useful indicator of the scope (and occasionally the limitations) of intraparty discourse.

Finally, each chapter contains organizational charts to illustrate internal procedures. The charts are based on a review of party bylaws and on interviews conducted with party representatives. It should be mentioned that research on this topic proved problematic due to a noticeable reluctance to reveal sensitive details (for instance, concerning electoral processes from within Hamas). Also, occasionally, contradictions between theory and practice were noted, at which point statements by party activists were given priority.

The book as such is the result of a 12-month project conducted by a team of researchers from the Jerusalem office of the Friedrich-Ebert-Stiftung (FES). The FES is a German political foundation affiliated to the Social Democratic Party (SPD) and is represented in the Palestinian Territories in the West Bank and Gaza. While the political cooperation of FES with two sister-parties in the Palestinian Territories (Fatah and the Palestinian National Initiative, PNI) need not be concealed, it is hoped that this affiliation did not influence what is believed to be an objective stocktaking. Likewise, the analysis put forward in the text should not be interpreted as official positions of either the FES or the SPD. Rather, it represents attempts to enrich the debate with critical, impartial, and informative assessments.

This organizational affiliation is particularly relevant in view of the fact that the book offers detailed information on the ideological outlook of groups that have been labeled "terrorist organizations," particularly the PFLP and Hamas. It is understood that this approach may be perceived as offering these groups a forum of expression. However, neglecting organizations such as Hamas would have fundamentally undermined the comprehensive scope of the book.

While the intention is to present a well-informed overview of political factions, the text deliberately avoids engaging and analyzing political controversies of the Israeli-Palestinian conflict. While such disputes certainly exist and are acknowledged in the text (such as differing interpretations of the Camp David Summit of 2000), the reader is encouraged to consult the existing parallel sources of literature for a full academic discussion of controversial historical events. Similarly, the number of references was kept to a minimum with an emphasis on primary sources and verbatim quotes.

Ideology and Pragmatism: A Consensus in the Making?

Unsurprisingly, the ideological positions outlined in the present text illustrate a wide array of conflicting perceptions between different Palestinian factions. Despite deep-rooted ideological differences and occasionally fierce competition, the statements gathered are also indicative of an emerging supraparty consensus and theoretically a common denominator vis-a-vis the Israeli–Palestinian conflict.

As formulated in the National Unity Document agreed upon by 13 Palestinian political factions in Cairo on June 28, 2006, all Palestinian factions have recently, at least in rhetoric, replaced original (often divergent) demands with calls for the establishment of a Palestinian state along the 1967 borders. Notably, this consensus is far from unambiguous. Here, it seems that the very challenges that have forced political factions to reject the role of political *parties* have also caused ambiguities in programmatic positions.

In terms of accepting a Two-State Solution, the political spectrum has by now largely fallen into three distinct camps. The first is represented by Fatah, the left-wing PPP, and the PNI, which have all formally committed themselves to a Palestinian State within the borders of 1967. Fatah, for the first time in its history, formally accepted the Two-State Paradigm in its 2009 party convention in Bethlehem. Similarly, the leftist PNI has formally adopted the Two-State Solution as its overriding programmatic objective while also indicating openness to the prospect of a One-State Solution with equal rights for Palestinians and Israelis should two states prove unattainable. The same holds true for the PPP, which from its founding in 1991 has called for a state along the 1967 borders.

The second camp is composed of the leftists PFLP and the DFLP. Falling short of a formal acceptance of two states in the long run, both movements have in recent years de facto opted for a Palestinian state along the 1967 borders. Yet, they have officially remained committed to the concept of "phased liberation," in which the establishment of a Palestinian state is seen as a prelude to the eventual creation of a single democratic state for Jews and Palestinians. The ideological shift implemented by these PLO factions might seem gradual to the outside observer. However, Palestinian pulpits have marked these changes as significant, at times criticizing the emerging consensus among the PLO factions as a deplorable "lack of differentiation that once was [sic] between the agendas of the PLO factions and its attitudes and visions."[18]

Predictably, the third camp consists of the Islamic Resistance Movement (Hamas), which in programmatic statements strictly adheres to the claim of liberating "all of Palestine." In parallel, however, recent public statements from key Hamas leaders have come a long way from the annihilationist anti-Semitism of the movement's founding years. Effectively, recent statements first and foremost from the movement's diaspora leadership appear close to accepting the Two-State Paradigm in a manner similar to the PFLP and DFLP, calling for the establishment of a Palestinian state on the 1967 borders as a tactical step in the longer process of "liberating" all of historic Palestine.

Taking stock of these positions, it seems that all relevant political factions have by now either embraced the Two-State Solution in formalized programmatic positions or as a short-term objective in public statements by relevant leaders. While this is a remarkable development, enthusiasm that this will boost the prospects for a negotiated solution to the conflict between Israelis and Palestinians in the short run should be curbed. Positions such as those put forward by the PFLP, DFLP, or by important protagonists from within Hamas, on the one hand, clearly indicate ideological progression and increasing pragmatism when compared to original demands. Yet, on the other hand, they remain incompatible with Israeli demands for a peace agreement that stipulates an "end to all claims," and, of course, with the continuing expansion of Israeli settlements in the West Bank.

In parallel, intra-Palestinian trends from outside of established factions threaten to jeopardize any emerging consensus. After all, calls for two states by the political factions have recently been countered by demands for a One-State Solution. According to current opinion polls, such calls have gained public support and are by now shared by up to 26 percent of the Palestinian populace.[19] While Palestinian political factions have thus through the years gradually embraced positions that in theory could facilitate a pragmatic consensus for a political solution, the factions themselves seem to have lost touch with important shifts within their electorate.

This is not the only notable, albeit ambiguous development identified in the research for the book. A second finding purports to demonstrate a growing support from within a wide array of Palestinian political factions for nonviolent activism. Parties such as Fatah, the DFLP, and the PFLP have of late come to formally enshrine support for nonviolent activism in their programmatic statements. At the same time, they have largely—but not exclusively—refrained from engaging in militant acts against Israel. Factions such as the PPP and the PNI that have strictly advocated nonviolence since their founding have felt encouraged by the Arab Spring and appear more committed to nonviolent activism than ever before.

While Palestinian political movements have thus begun to advocate a fundamental change in Palestinian tactics, all but one party (the PNI) have remained committed to perceived rights to "armed resistance."[20] Unsurprisingly, Hamas and the PFLP have maintained the strongest commitment to the use of violence. While recent statements from within Hamas and the PFLP have begun to hail forms of "popular struggle," the movements have notably refrained from qualifying their general support for militancy. In terms of realpolitik, this has translated into restraint: Hamas has recently been keen to respect a fragile cease-fire in Gaza in addition to preventing other militant factions such as the Islamic Jihad from engaging in acts of violence. Whether this approach will prove permanent, however, remains unclear.

Such ambiguous stances concerning the use of violence (or *resistance* in Palestinian parlance) are unacceptable to most current Israeli leaders. Yet, from a Palestinian perspective they often seem logical, legitimate, and quite simply difficult to overcome. As political scientist Yezid Sayigh put it, against the background of dispossession and disempowerment "armed struggle [has] provided the central theme and practice around Palestinian nation-building" for decades.[21]

While formal renouncements of violence would unquestionably be hailed by the international community, any such formalized changes would carry significant political costs in the Palestinian domestic context. Such a repositioning would amount to a comprehensive redefinition of collective political identities constructed on the very notion of resistance. In the case of Hamas, Palestinian academic Khaled Hroub has convincingly described any such endeavors as "political suicide."[22] These political risks for political factions are only exacerbated by the continued absence of a promising diplomatic path to realize political ambitions, which has made the formal renouncing of violence a dangerous undertaking for the majority of Palestinian factions—at least at this point in time.

Against this background, it seems that persisting ambiguities concerning the transformation of political movements, ideological inconsistencies, and differences in political practice are unlikely to be overcome in the near future. While such contradictions certainly do not facilitate a straightforward reading of the status quo, the ambiguities documented in the following chapters also represent opportunities. For despite everything else, they illustrate an impressive level of vigor and political dynamics. In a conflict that has long been characterized by stagnation, this is not to be disregarded.

CHAPTER TWO

Hamas: Between Terror and Realpolitik

The Islamic Resistance Movement at a Crossroad

The Islamic Resistance Movement, better known by its Arabic acronym Hamas (Zeal, Enthusiasm), is perceived as the most influential spoiler of Palestinian–Israeli peace. Hamas rejected the Oslo Accords and has engaged in numerous terrorist operations against Israel. Historically related to the Egyptian Muslim Brotherhood, Hamas is considered a terrorist organization by a majority of Western states, which have not recognized it as a legitimate political force. Nevertheless, Hamas was democratically elected during the Palestinian elections of 2006 and has held power in the Gaza Strip since defeating Fatah in a military confrontation there in June 2007. Since this time, parts of Hamas have adopted a more statesmanlike stance, focusing on institution-building and governing in the coastal strip (Table 2.1).

Hamas was founded in the Gaza Strip at the beginning of the first *intifada*. From the outset the organization attempted to represent an alternative not only to the status quo of Israeli administration of the Palestinian Territories, but also to the secular institutions of Palestinian political life as represented by Fatah and other factions of the Palestine Liberation Organization (PLO). Until today, internal resistance and outside pressures have kept Hamas outside of the PLO.

Table 2.1 Hamas at a glance

Official name	: Hamas / Islamic Resistance Movement *(Harakat al-Muqawama al-Islamiya)*
Year founded	: 1987
PLO membership since	: –
PLC members 1996	: – (boycotted; seven seats won by Hamas-affiliated individual candidates)
PLC members 2006	: 76 (Change and Reform list)
Ideological orientation	: Islamist / affiliated to the Muslim Brotherhood
Leadership base	: Political Bureau: Damascus (until 2012). Currently, Doha (Qatar) and Cairo (Egypt). Hamas-led PNA branch: Gaza City (since 2007)

Many of its founders, including Sheikh Ahmed Yassin, were previously active in the Islamic Association (*al-Mujama'a al-Islami*), which maintained a network of mosques and social institutions throughout the Palestinian Territories. Until the outbreak of the first *intifada* in 1987, these networks, which in their early years refrained from instigating violence, were left free to operate by Israel, whose security establishment considered Islamic movements a stabilizing counterweight to the militant secular factions of the PLO.

Hamas has always had close ties with the *Sunni* Muslim Brotherhood. The Brotherhood originated in Egypt in the late 1920s and quickly spread to other Arab societies. The Brotherhood established a presence in Palestine during the 1940s under the leadership of Amin al-Husseini. After fighting alongside Arab armies during the 1948 war, members of the Muslim Brotherhood adopted a quietist position, focusing on social, educational, charitable, and religious activism. It was only during the first *intifada* that Brotherhood activists again began to advocate for political involvement, calling for support in the uprising.

The result of such calls was the founding of Hamas as "one of the wings of the Muslim Brotherhood in Palestine," as stated in the Hamas Charter written by a confidant of Ahmed Yassin in 1988.[1] In the ensuing years, Hamas ceased to describe itself merely as one wing of the Brotherhood, declaring instead that Hamas and the Brotherhood were one and the same. Because Hamas initially grew out of the Muslim Brotherhood's social and charitable networks, which extended throughout the Palestinian Territories, it has had deep roots in Palestinian society—particularly in the more conservative Gaza Strip.

Hamas's stated goal in its Charter was "to raise the banner of Allah on every inch of Palestine." Unlike secular national movements such as Fatah and the Popular Front for the Liberation of Palestine (PFLP), Hamas took as its starting point the conviction that all of historical Palestine was an Islamic endowment that could not be surrendered and, as stated in the Charter, was "consecrated for future Muslim generations until Judgment Day."

The Charter calls for the establishment of an Islamic state in Palestine, which includes Israel, the West Bank, and Gaza, and proclaims that "Allah is the target, the Prophet its model, and the Quran its constitution." The document contains numerous anti-Semitic references, outlines an uncompromising Islamist agenda, rejects any notion of a negotiated solution of the conflict, and considers any contact with Israel as a "waste of time."[2] For many years, the Hamas Charter shaped the movement's international and domestic image and is among the several reasons the West has refused to grant Hamas political recognition.

Whereas Hamas once wore this rejection as a badge of pride, which distinguished it from the factions organized in the PLO, in recent years it has sought broader international recognition and cooperation. The party's slow integration into the Palestinian political system has been accompanied by an attempt to downplay the importance of the Hamas Charter, by elaborating on a series of programmatic statements that leave the crude anti-Semitism of the Charter largely behind. The head of Hamas's political bureau, Khaled Meshal, has repeatedly stated that the document is no longer the movement's political manifesto and that "the Charter should not be regarded as the fundamental ideological frame of reference." Similarly, Mahmoud Ahmad al-Ramahi, a member of Hamas and the secretary general of the Palestinian Legislative Council (PLC), said in 2007 that the Charter "should not be confused with the Holy *Qur'an*."[3]

Militant forces from within Hamas made their public debut in 1989, when Hamas claimed responsibility for the killing of two Israeli soldiers. Prior to this attack, Hamas's violent operations had been limited to what it considered acts of retaliation against perceived collaborators with Israel. The attack on Israeli soldiers brought an end to Israel's tolerance of the movement: Hamas leader Ahmed Yassin was arrested and sentenced to life in prison. Also, in Jordan, the movement faced difficulties. One year later, Hamas was formally declared illegal in the Hashemite Kingdom. In 1992, Israel deported over 400 Hamas and Islamic Jihad militants to Israeli-occupied southern Lebanon. These actions, however, did not achieve Israel's desired effect. Rather than resulting in further isolation and obscurity, the Islamic Resistance Movement received unprecedented media exposure and an opportunity to establish connections with representatives of other Palestinian factions. In Lebanon, Hamas increased the flow of financial support mainly from the Gulf States. Ever since, Hamas has received substantial funding from private donors in the Gulf States as well as from Iran and Syria. Also, the numbers of activists willing to join the movement increased significantly. This subsequently had repercussions on the formalization of the movement's institutions.

Between 1990 and 1993 Hamas established formalized institutions such as a political bureau and administrative branches charged with organizational and mobilization tasks. In 1991, the movement also established an official military wing, the Izz ad-Din al-Qassam Brigades, named after a religious scholar who co-led militant actions against the British Mandate. The Qassam Brigades have conducted numerous terror attacks, including suicide operations, against Israeli civilians and have frequently targeted the Israeli military in Israel and the Palestinian Territories. Hamas's position has been that such attacks are a legitimate response to the Israeli military's killing of Hamas leaders and to the suffering of Palestinian civilians. In addition, violent operations were at times supported by a substantial part of Palestinian society, which felt that the use of violence was the only tool with which Palestinians could exert pressure on Israel.

Hamas's rejection of the Oslo Accords signed between the PLO and Israel in 1993 was comprehensive. As Hamas remained out of the PLO, the movement was not included in the diplomatic processes leading to Oslo. Hamas leaders rejected the accords because they were not only convinced that the negotiation process was deeply flawed, but also adamantly argued against recognizing Israel's legitimacy. Hamas's rejectionist stance positioned the movement as the main opposition to Fatah, which came to be associated with the increasingly unpopular Oslo Process. Hamas prided itself on refusing to compromise and effectively acted as an umbrella organization, channeling and fusing growing fundamental opposition to the status quo.

Consequently, Hamas, as a movement, boycotted PNA elections in 1996, because possible participation in the electoral process was seen as legitimizing the Oslo Process. Nevertheless, in the 1996 legislative elections, seven Hamas-affiliated individuals gained seats in the Palestinian Legislative Council (PLC). Against the background of diplomatic stagnation between the PLO and Israel, Hamas prospered politically as Oslo failed to bring about the establishment of a Palestinian state. Hamas leaders such as Khaled Meshal, Ahmed Yassin, and Mahmoud al-Zahar were widely perceived by Palestinians as offering a convincing alternative narrative with the potential to overcome the status quo. Also, Hamas leaders were personally perceived as incorruptible, whereas the PNA leadership and Fatah were associated with nepotism, personal greed, and a mordant diplomatic process.

Israel, often with the cooperation of PNA security forces, stepped up its campaign against Hamas leaders, carrying out arrests and the so-called targeted killings after the establishment of the PNA. In 1996, Yahya Ayyash, a leader of the Qassam Brigades in the West Bank, was assassinated. An attempt on the life of Khaled Meshal (head of Hamas political bureau) in Amman the following year failed, and severely strained Israeli–Jordanian relations.

The escalating violence of the second *intifada* brought Hamas notably closer to the political mainstream of Palestinian politics and on frequent occasions closed ranks between Hamas and PLO factions. In the eyes of many Palestinians, the faltering negotiation process with Israel seemed to justify Hamas's early rejectionism. During the uprising, the Qassam Brigades, like other Palestinian militant groups, intensified terrorist activities targeting Israeli civilians. One such attack was the August 19, 2003 Shmuel HaNavi bus bombing, for which the Qassam Brigades took credit. Nineteen Israeli civilians were killed. As a result, the Israeli army continued to eliminate senior Hamas leaders, including Ismail Abu Shanab in 2003, a prominent Hamas official considered by many to be a moderate force within the movement.

In January 2004, Hamas Gaza leader and co-founder Abdel Aziz al-Rantisi announced the cessation of "armed resistance" in the framework of a truce, or *hudna*, of limited duration. Explaining that it was "difficult to liberate all our land at this stage," Rantisi proclaimed that Hamas would "accept a state in the West Bank, including East Jerusalem, and the Gaza Strip."[4] The cease-fire did not hold for long. Hamas did not end all violence and Israel did not cease its targeted killings. In 2004 Ahmed Yassin and Abdel Aziz al-Rantisi were both assassinated.

The next generation of Hamas leaders, however, agreed to another cease-fire with Israel in July 2004, marking the continuation of a certain moderating trend within Hamas. Secret Qatari mediation secured Hamas's decision to halt suicide attacks, a position the movement holds to this day.[5] Hamas also gradually changed its position with regard to participation in Palestinian electoral politics. The party ran in the 2005 municipal elections and won seats in more than half of the municipal councils, gaining a majority of seats in one-third of all municipalities. Certainly, for a movement that had started out on a platform of fundamental political rejectionism, this decision to enter into established institutionalized politics was significant and signaled a coming to terms with political realities. Further integration into the established political system was continued by Hamas's internationally backed decision to run in the 2006 PLC elections.

In advance of the elections, Hamas published an election platform that described "armed resistance" as a legitimate strategy to "end the occupation" but in other ways differed substantially from its 1988 Charter: anti-Semitic polemic was omitted; calls for the destruction of the State of Israel were left out. The document also devoted considerable space to describing the necessity of establishing democratic institutions, separating the three branches of government, and guaranteeing public freedoms and citizens' rights. Also, the program called for a "minimum wage" and for establishing "labor unions and occupational societies."[6] Notably the platform was put forward by an electoral list that operated under the headline "Change and Reform."

To the surprise of most foreign observers (and many within Hamas), the Change and Reform list won the 2006 elections, gaining 76 of 132 seats in the PLC. Hamas's long-standing opposition to the Oslo Process, its conservative religious positions, its extensive network of charity organizations, and the growing dissatisfaction of many Palestinians with Fatah, proved decisive in bringing the movement to power. However, a closer look at the election also indicates that Hamas's professional electoral campaign greatly contributed to the Hamas victory: PLC seats were allocated based on a complex electoral system in which Palestinians cast two ballots: one for a party list (in which candidates had been selected by the party) and one directly for individual politicians in their local districts. While Hamas's party list won only three percent more popular votes than Fatah's, the Islamic movement's direct candidates succeeded in defeating their Fatah rivals in many districts.

Shortly after the 2006 election results were announced, Hamas co-founder Mahmoud al-Zahar (who also served as a foreign minister in the first Hamas government) said that the movement would agree to a "long-term *hudna* or long-term truce" in exchange for an "independent state on the area occupied [in] 1967."[7] For the international community, this did not go far enough. The Middle East Quartet (comprised of the United States, the EU, the UN, and Russia) created three conditions, known as the "quartet principles" that a Hamas-led government would have to meet in order to avoid financial and diplomatic isolation: adhere to previous Israeli–Palestinian agreements, recognize the State of Israel's right to exist, and unconditionally renounce violence. Hamas refused. On February 3, Khaled Meshal not only reiterated the idea of a long-term truce but also unambiguously declared in an article in the Ramallah based *al-Hayat al-Jadida* that Hamas would "never recognize the legitimacy of the Zionist state that was established on our land."

Hamas's noncompliance with quartet demands was perceived as counter-productive by the international community. For Hamas, however, an acceptance of the "quartet principles" would have meant relinquishing the party's unique position of a "resistance movement" following an unprecedented electoral victory. Embracing the "quartet principles" essentially would have been interpreted as surrendering to international demands. In the words of one Palestinian observer, demanding recognition of the principles in the eyes of Hamas would amount to calling upon the movement to commit "voluntary political suicide." Hamas's refusal to do so meant the freezing of aid for the PNA and a political boycott of the Hamas-led government.

The economic strain on the West Bank and Gaza aggravated the animosity between Hamas and Fatah. Fatah affiliates, who dominated the public sector, challenged the authority of the new government by refusing to follow instructions issued by the Hamas-led cabinet. International aid was redirected to the office of President Mahmoud Abbas, and authority over PNA security forces was transferred from the government to the president. Tensions between Fatah and Hamas soon erupted into bloody clashes, in Gaza and the West Bank.

In June 2006, Israeli shelling of a Gaza beach is widely believed to have killed eight Palestinian civilians. While the Israeli military denied responsibility, Hamas declared the previous cease-fire over and launched heavy rocket attacks against civilians in southern Israel. That same month, Palestinian militants from Gaza launched a cross-border raid in which Israeli soldier Gilad Shalit was abducted and two of his fellow soldiers were killed. The Israeli military's response was Operation Summer Rain, in which 11 Israelis and around 400 Palestinians lost their lives. Israel arrested several dozen Hamas officials, including 8 cabinet ministers and 20 PLC members, severely weakening the party's ability to fulfill its democratic mandate.

A tentative rapprochement between the Palestinian factions Fatah and Hamas took place in 2007. The Saudi-brokered Mecca Agreement, based on the National Unity Document of the Prisoners, brought Hamas closer but did not meet the Quartet's conditions, This, however, temporarily halted clashes between Hamas and Fatah. The two factions formed a National Unity Government headed by Hamas leader

Ismail Haniya. The program of the 2007 Unity Government conditioned "halting resistance" on "ending the occupation and achieving freedom, return, and independence." In terms of prospects for a "final agreement" with Israel, the government called for ratification by a "new Palestinian National Council" or a "general referendum."[8]

Less than three months later, tensions between Fatah and Hamas escalated once again. In a move described by Hamas supporters as forestalling a US- and Israel-sponsored Fatah coup, the Islamic movement took control of the Gaza Strip. During several days of heavy clashes, documented war crimes by both Hamas and Fatah occurred, drawing widespread condemnation.

The repercussions of the Hamas takeover in Gaza were tremendous. Israel and Egypt initiated a land, sea, and air blockade, which degraded already desperate living conditions and limited freedom of movement in Gaza. For the first time in modern history, an offshoot of the Muslim Brotherhood had gained complete control over a territory and established an authoritarian regime. Hamas took over the existing PNA institutions, collected taxes, provided social services, and engaged in formalized political planning.

While certainly not an "Islamic Caliphate," as some critics claimed, Gaza under Hamas was subject to a highly conservative, repressive rule, and the movement instituted a noticeable Islamization of public life and a harsh clamp-down against public dissent as represented in Gaza's media sector. At times, such policies also brought the Hamas government on a collision course with the United Nations Relief and Works Agency (UNRWA), which offers vital services and programs to Palestinian refugees in Gaza. Some of these policies were highly unpopular even in the socially conservative Gaza strip. This, in part, explains why calls from within Gaza for the reestablishment of Palestinian unity between Gaza and the West Bank have become more common.

At the same time, the taking over of Gaza also had repercussions for Hamas as a movement. Confronted with the task of administering the coastal strip, the leadership was challenged with synchronizing ideological convictions with the practicalities of day-to-day political administration. The ensuing clash between ideology and political facts on the ground has so far mostly been resolved by resorting to political pragmatism and *realpolitik*. Thus, for instance, clauses from the Hamas Charter stipulating that "the law governing the land of Palestine is the Islamic Sharia law" were not implemented.[9]

State institutions such as cabinet meetings and parliamentary sessions continued in Gaza, but without representation from anti-Hamas forces. Other factions were allowed only limited freedom of expression. Fatah's party activities were banned, although Fatah PLC members continued low-key activities in their capacity as PLC members from their personal PLC offices. The Popular Front for the Liberation of Palestine (PFLP), Democratic Front for the Liberation of Palestine (DFLP), and the Palestinian National Initiative (PNI), in contrast, were able to remain nominally active.

The suppression of Fatah in Gaza was mirrored in the West Bank, where Hamas members and supporters faced persecution and arrest by the PNA and Israeli authorities. Thousands of Hamas sympathizers were dismissed from the public sector in the West Bank as were tens of thousands of Fatah-affiliated government employees in Gaza. The majority of Hamas's charitable organizations in the West Bank were either disbanded or co-opted by the PNA or Fatah loyalists.

The years 2008–2009 brought another, deadlier, armed confrontation between Hamas and Israel. In Operation Cast Lead, 13 Israelis and some 1,400 Palestinians lost their lives. As in previous escalations, each side accused the other of breaching the cease-fire agreed upon just months earlier. In the course of the war, a substantial part of Gaza was targeted. However, the Israeli army did not accomplish its goal of severely weakening Hamas. The movement's leadership maintained its control of the Gaza Strip and has since this time, largely but not completely been able to rein in armed groups such as Islamic Jihad and grassroots Popular Resistance Committees that have repeatedly violated the de facto cease-fire.

Politically, since taking over sole responsibility for governing Gaza in 2007, the movement adopted a more state-building stance, focusing on developing institutions in the coastal strip. Comparing historical platforms such as the Hamas Charter to more recent statements such as the program of the National Unity Government from 2007, or the 2011–2012 development plan of the Gaza Ministry of Planning, an embracing of pragmatist politics as opposed to earlier religious rhetoric can be observed. Thus, the development plan put forward by the Hamas-run Gaza Ministry of Planning in 2010 discussed "main objectives" and formalized "sub-objectives" in terms of "improving economic and living conditions, realizing a comprehensive, balanced and fair social development, maintaining security, strengthening the rule of law and good governance, and developing infrastructure and service productivity."[10]

In terms of ideology, Hamas has repeatedly affirmed its readiness for a long-term cease-fire in exchange for the founding of a

Palestinian state alongside Israel's pre-1967 borders. However, despite years of administering in the Gaza Strip, Hamas has not officially recognized Israel or formally renounced violence. Within Hamas, such ideological compromises are often rejected by pointing at the historical experience of the PLO, which recognized the State of Israel in 1993 but failed to bring about the establishment of a Palestinian state in return.

Since 2007, Hamas's rule of Gaza and the tension between ideology and realpolitik have given rise to political ambiguity on several levels. While calls for "armed resistance" are constantly issued by members of Hamas from Gaza, an unofficial cease-fire between the movement and Israel has by and large continued to hold despite repeated clashes in and around Gaza triggered by the Islamic Jihad and the Popular Resistance Committees. Hamas forces in Gaza have repeatedly arrested militants who threatened the cease-fire.

As a role model for the movement, some leading Hamas figures have on several occasions mentioned the Turkish Justice and Development Party (AKP). This, however, is not an ambition shared by all. Hamas is governed by a multifaceted organizational structure, comprising different wings and a complex interplay of institutions (see chart 2.1). Throughout the years, Hamas leaders have reiterated the homogeneity of the movement although Hamas's leadership is fragmented, with officials in exile, Gaza, the West Bank, and Israeli prisons. The most influential figures from each group convene in the movement's overarching *Shoura* council, which is regularly selected in secret intraparty elections. Recently, tensions between the different leaderships have escalated in the aftermath of the Arab Spring, which has encouraged the exiled branch to embrace further moderation, while emboldening the Gaza leadership to stand its ground in the ongoing confrontation with the PNA in Ramallah.

The trigger for this was the 2011 regime change in Cairo. The Gaza leadership at first reacted nervously to the emerging uprising in Egypt. In Gaza, economic stagnation, widespread poverty, and unpopular policies of suppressing and curbing civil liberties had severely tainted Hamas's previous appeal as an inviting alternative to Fatah. Faced with unrest in Cairo, the Gaza leadership thus feared that their rule in the coastal strip would be similarly swept away in a popular uprising. While public discontent with Hamas in Gaza has not decreased in recent months, Hamas rule has nevertheless stabilized. Hamas in Gaza has benefitted from the fact that regime change in important Arab states has ended the movement's days of near-total isolation.

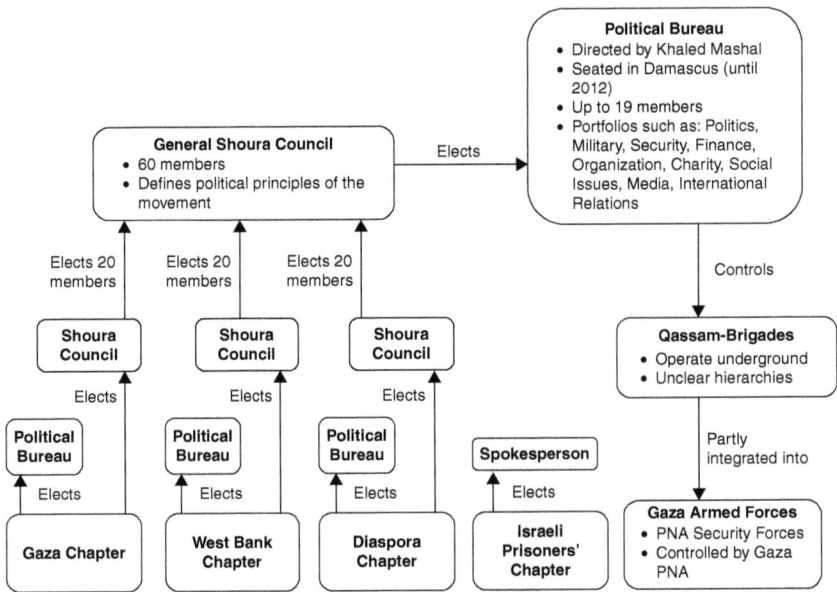

Chart 2.1 Organizational structure of Hamas.

Although most Western governments continued to consider Hamas a terrorist organization, in Arab capitals, political embargos gave way to engagement. In December 2011, Gaza prime minister Ismail Haniya embarked on a Mediterranean tour that included Tunis, Cairo, and Istanbul. In mid-February 2012, the Gaza prime minister was warmly received in Qatar, Bahrain, and Iran. Notably, Haniya's diplomatic tour garnered not only recognition for Hamas as a movement, but also recognition for the more uncompromising wing of Hamas represented by the Gaza leadership. The Gaza prime minister took every opportunity to criticize "futile" peace negotiations, and, in Tehran, he pledged that Hamas's "resistance" would continue "until all Palestinian land has been liberated."[11]

Divisions within Hamas became apparent in May 2011, when Hamas's "outside" leadership, represented by Meshal, and Fatah's Abbas signed a reconciliation document in Cairo. The agreement committed Hamas to a transitional unity government, a cessation of violence, and the acceptance of a Palestinian state on the 1967 borders. Meshal also agreed to grant Abbas a one-year mandate for negotiations with Israel. Furthermore, a reform process of the PLO was to be initiated with the objective to eventually include Hamas in the organization. The Cairo Agreement was obstructed by Hamas's Gaza leadership, which refused to share power with Fatah partly based on the conviction that the ongoing shunning of Hamas by Western states and Israel would prevent the movement from gaining strength in the West Bank. Months later, Gaza's leaders brokered a deal to free hundreds of Palestinian prisoners in exchange for Israeli soldier Gilad Shalit, further elevating the Gaza leadership's standing.

Tensions within Hamas continued to escalate in February 2012, when Meshal signed another unity agreement with Fatah in Qatar. The agreement committed both Palestinian movements to a transitional government under Mahmoud Abbas's leadership as president *and* prime minister. Like the Cairo Agreement, the Doha Declaration was rejected by Hamas's Gaza leadership, which was not included in the prior negotiations. More than just a power struggle between Hamas leaders, the conflict around reconciliation pointed to a struggle over the future course of Hamas as a movement.

Meshal's desire to reconcile with Fatah and meet at least some key demands of the international community for moderation could be explained in part by the popular revolt against President Bashar al-Assad in Syria. Until 2012, Assad had hosted Hamas's overall political bureau in Damascus. With the outbreak of the revolt, Hamas was under pressure to side with the regime. As Syrian violence against the *Sunni*-dominated opposition escalated, Hamas's Damascus leadership left Syria. Some of its leaders moved to Doha (Qatar), others to Cairo. This stance also alienated Syria's ally, Iran, which responded to Hamas's reluctance to support Assad by reducing its financial support, which was estimated at nearly 150 million USD annually. This was a loss to Hamas's Damascus leadership not just in funding, but also in influence within the movement: the leadership in the Diaspora had always been responsible for securing financing; with that role diminished, the balance of power within the movement further shifted to Gaza.

At the time of writing attempts to bring about national reconciliation between Fatah and Hamas continued. Palestinian observers, however, viewed its chances of success skeptically. Whether Hamas as a whole will follow its political bureau in conciliatory steps remains to be seen. For now, it seems possible that the hard-line forces within the movement—first and foremost in Gaza—will block any movement toward reconciliation with Fatah or rapprochement with Israel.

The stance of Hamas regarding the implementation of the Cairo and Doha Agreements depends to a large extent on the internal elections within the movement. Elections within Hamas are traditionally carried out for political bureaus and *Shoura* councils in Gaza, the West Bank, the Diaspora, and within Israeli detention facilities. In the first half of 2012, elections for the local political bureau and *Shoura* Council only proceeded in the Gaza Strip.

The elections were conducted clandestinely due to fear of Israeli obstruction. Hamas leaders decided neither to announce the dates of elections, nor to officially release results. However, press reports indicated despite the lack of transparency in election protocol that Ismail Haniya's position was elevated by his successful election as head of the political bureau in the Gaza Strip. Supporters of Meshal, however, were reported to have lost some backing. Relative moderates such as former Deputy Foreign Ministers Ahmad Yousef and Ghazi Hamad only gained seats in the Gaza *Shoura* Council, but not in the political bureau. Noteworthy is the fact that two representatives of the Qassam Brigades, Ahmed Jabari and Marwan Issa, were elected to the political bureau in Gaza.

This development points to a significant increase in the military wing's position within Hamas in Gaza. While the Qassam Brigades were previously mostly loyal to Meshal, it remains to be seen if they will act more independently following Meshal's apparent loss of influence. Also undecided at the time of writing was the question of Hamas's overall leadership: specifically Khaled Meshal's future role in the movement and the prospects for joint elections orchestrated by Hamas and Fatah.

Concerning the future prospects of Hamas, predictions are near-impossible. Since its founding, the movement has benefitted from a stance that positions Hamas as an ideologically comprehensive and radical alternative to the status quo. They have enjoyed broad support not unlike other Islamist movements in the region. However, differing from representatives of politicized religion elsewhere, Hamas as a political alternative has already been put to the test. So far, ruling Gaza has certainly resulted in a tangible demystification of the movement in the Palestinian Territories. Against this background, the future political appeal of Hamas will depend to a large extent on whether the movement will be able to deliver concrete political results. This, in turn, is likely to depend on how far Hamas will come to terms with political realities on the ground without alienating the traditional support base and jeopardizing the unity of the movement.[12]

Ahmed Yassin

Co-founder and spiritual leader of Hamas, Ahmed Yassin, was in his fifties and already in poor health when he attracted international attention as a prime challenger to the leadership of Yasir Arafat.

Ahmed Yassin was born in 1938 in the coastal village of al-Jura, near Gaza City. In the 1948 war, his family fled to Gaza's al-Shati refugee camp. During his youth, Yassin was injured in a sporting accident and damage to his spine left him a quadriplegic. Confined to a wheelchair, he was educated largely at home, although he attended the renowned al-Azhar University in Cairo for some time. According to most accounts, it was in Cairo that Yassin became convinced that "the land Palestine is an Islamic *waqf*" (endowment), as the Hamas Charter would later describe and therefore a land that could not be surrendered.[13] It was also in Egypt that Yassin became active in the Muslim Brotherhood, an affiliation for which he was briefly detained during the presidency of Gamal Abdel Nasser.

Yassin's teaching career was hampered by his physical disability and weakening eyesight. It was not until 1964 that he was able to find employment as a teacher of Arabic and Islamic faith although he was forced to enter early retirement 20 years later. Already as a young man Yassin had begun to give widely attended weekly sermons and had gained influence as a political activist in the Gaza Strip. He not only preached in favor of a *jihad* to "liberate Palestine" but initially also emphasized forms of nonviolent struggle, in an effort to counter secularism, which he held responsible for the perceived stagnation of the Islamic World. In 1973, "the Sheikh" (as he was often called) started the Islamic Center (*al-Mujama' al-Islami*), which founded the territory's Islamic University among other religious institutions.

In the 1980s, Yassin and his followers began to embrace active *jihad*, adding violent operations against the Israeli military in the West Bank and Gaza to their social and religious activities. When, in 1984, 60 rifles were discovered in a mosque built by Yassin's *al-Mujama' al-Islami*, he was sentenced to 13 years in an Israeli prison. However, Yassin was released one year later in a prisoner swap and was allowed to remain politically active.

Yassin gained international notoriety after the outbreak of the first *intifada* in 1987, which prompted him to co-found Hamas as the movement's spiritual leader. He adopted inflammatory rhetoric opposing any compromise with Israel and called instead for "armed struggle" as the sole path to "liberation." He rejected the Oslo Process, which he labeled a "disgraceful capitulation" and a "great deception."[14]

In 1989, Yassin was arrested following an attack on Israeli soldiers, for which Hamas claimed responsibility. He was sentenced to life in prison for founding Hamas and for inciting violence. In 1997, he was again set free in a prisoner swap following Israel's failed attempt to assassinate Khaled Meshal in Jordan. Upon his release, Yassin made the unprecedented offer of a decade-long cease-fire in exchange for the withdrawal of Israeli troops and settlers from Gaza, the West Bank, and East Jerusalem and accepting the Palestinian "right to return." In July 2000, he stated: "If Israel withdraws completely from the West Bank and Gaza and it removes all of its settlements, I will make a truce with it."[15]

However, in the absence of such an agreement, Yassin called for the use of violence, including suicide bombings, against Israel. When Ariel Sharon was elected prime minister of Israel during the second *intifada*, his government initiated a strategy of "targeted assassinations" of militant Palestinian leaders. Accusing Yassin of personally ordering terrorist operations, Israeli authorities openly discussed killing Yassin. A first assassination attempt in September 2003 failed. On March 22, 2004, Yassin was killed, along with nine others, outside a Gaza mosque. Sharon declared that Israel had thus eliminated "the greatest arch-murderer of Palestinian terrorism."[16] The assassination was condemned widely, most notably by then UN secretary general Kofi Annan, who stated that "extrajudicial killings are against international law" and called on the Government of Israel "to immediately end this practice."[17] The PNA declared three official days of mourning following his death as tens of thousands of Palestinians took to the streets for his funeral.

Khaled Meshal

At the time of writing, Khaled Meshal was the head of Hamas's political bureau and one of its most prominent leaders. Until 2012, he was based in Syria, from where he worked to secure the Islamic movement's financial and political support. In 2011 and 2012, Meshal emerged as a force of relative moderation within Hamas, pushing for reconciliation with the Fatah movement and calling for a Palestinian state alongside Israel's pre-1967 borders.

Born in 1956, Khaled Meshal was 11 years old when the Six Day War broke out, forcing his family to relocate from his native village, Silwad, near Ramallah, to Kuwait. Meshal's father was a village imam and raised his 11 children according to strict religious principles. As a high-school student, Meshal joined the Muslim Brotherhood and was engaged in religious activism. At the Kuwait University, where he studied physics, he headed the Islamic list within the local General Union of Palestinian Students. After graduating in 1978, Meshal established the Islamic League for Palestinian Students to represent the interests of a growing number of Islamists in the Palestinian Diaspora.

Meshal taught physics at secondary schools in Kuwait until 1984, at which point he began devoting time to establishing an organization to unite disparate Islamic currents inside the Palestinian Territories and abroad. Following Hamas's founding in 1987, Meshal led the movement's Kuwaiti section, but initially did not otherwise play a highly visible role. The political spotlight was on the West Bank and Gaza during the first *intifada* and Meshal followed these events from the sidelines. This changed, however, when in 1990 Meshal, like numerous other Palestinians in his country of residence, was forced to move to Jordan after the Iraqi invasion of Kuwait. In the Hashemite Kingdom, Meshal became Hamas's leading fundraiser, establishing close links with regional powers such as Syria, Iran, and Saudi Arabia, all of which increased their financial and logistical support for Hamas. In 1996, Meshal was elected chairman of Hamas's political bureau after former chairman Musa Abu Marzouk was arrested in New York by US authorities.

Israeli authorities watched Meshal's rise warily, accusing him of supplying Hamas with the means to carry out terror attacks against civilians. In 1997, Mossad agents disguised as tourists poisoned Meshal in Amman. Before they could leave the country, the Israeli agents were arrested by the Jordanian police, and King Hussein heavily pressured Israeli prime minister Benyamin Netanyahu to supply the antidote and, as a result, saved Meshal's life.

However, two years later, claiming that Meshal's activities disrupted peaceful relations between Israel and Jordan, the Jordanian leadership forced him to leave. After residing briefly in Qatar, Meshal settled in Syria in 2001. Following the assassinations of Hamas's founding members Ahmed Yassin and Abdel Aziz al-Rantisi, he emerged as Hamas's undisputed top official and in this position directed the course of the movement in the first decade of the new millennium.

In 2011, Meshal's reputation in the Palestinian Territories became increasingly controversial. He embraced more moderate political positions, representing a force of change within Hamas. In the process, some in Gaza's leadership have come to see him as a rogue figure, willing to compromise key aspects of Hamas's political agenda in order to accommodate the international community. Meshal has officially and on several occasions offered Israel a long-term truce in return for a Palestinian state in the West Bank, the Gaza Strip, and East Jerusalem, and for recognition of the right of return for Palestinian refugees. He has also sought to distance himself from the 1988 Hamas Charter. Yet, Meshal continued to consider "armed resistance" legitimate. This position has prevented him from being embraced by Western decision makers.

In 2011 and 2012, Meshal was also the driving force behind attempts to find a compromise with Fatah. In May 2011 he signed the Cairo Agreement, stipulating the joint establishment by Hamas and Fatah of a transitional government to prepare for new PLC elections. However, the agreement's implementation was obstructed, mainly by Hamas leaders in Gaza. Without consulting Hamas's leadership in Gaza, Meshal proceeded to sign the Doha Declaration of February 2012, which again aimed to install a transitional unity government backed by Hamas and Fatah, this time under the leadership of President Abbas, who would also serve as prime minister.

Meshal backed his gambit with an unconcealed threat to resign as head of Hamas's political bureau should the movement's Gaza leadership refuse to support him. At the time of writing, Meshal's future seemed uncertain. As of 2012, Mashal appeared to have lost some backing within Hamas. The Gaza leadership refused to fall in line with his initiative to sign the Cairo and Doha Agreements and to push for reconciliation with Fatah. Against this background, it is not clear if Meshal intends to remain at the movement's head and indeed if he would be able to hold his ground against rivals such as Haniya or his predecessor, Musa Mohammed Abu Marzouk, as head of the political bureau. Some observers speculate that Mashal might pursue other options, possibly emerging as the head of a newly established Palestinian branch of the Muslim Brotherhood, or as a leader of a new Islamist political party under the umbrella of the PLO.

Ismail Haniya

Depending on one's perspective, Ismail Haniya is either a radical terrorist or the legitimate prime minister of the PNA. The former student leader came to the political fore due to the Islamic movement's gradual move toward political engagement—a step Haniya co-initiated. Following the legislative elections in 2006, Haniya was often described as a Hamas moderate, a label recently called into question following his expression of more uncompromising positions in an escalating power struggle with Khaled Meshal.

The son of refugees from the vicinity of Ashqelon, who fled to the Gaza Strip during the 1948 war, Ismail Haniya was born in al-Shati refugee camp in 1962. To this day, he resides in a simple home within the camp, a symbol of humility much lauded by his supporters. Haniya attended United Nations Relief and Works Agency (UNRWA) schools and later enrolled at the religious Azhar Institute in Gaza City. While a student of Arabic literature at the Islamic University in Gaza, Haniya became politically active in the university's Islamic bloc. In 1985, about one year before graduating, Haniya was elected head of the university's student council.

During the first *intifada*, Haniya participated in protests and assisted in developing Hamas's social network. He would spend most of the first *intifada* in Israeli prisons: a six-month term in 1988 was followed by a three-year term in 1989. It was in Israeli custody that he became a close aide of Hamas's co-founder and spiritual leader Ahmed Yassin.

Upon Haniya's release in 1992, he was deported to southern Lebanon. He returned to the Gaza Strip in 1993 and focused initially on academic pursuits and was that year appointed dean of the Islamic University in Gaza. He also served, until 2000, as chairman of the Islamic Society. Haniya unsuccessfully lobbied for Hamas's participation in the 1996 PLC elections and even announced his intention to run for office as an independent candidate.

When Ahmed Yassin was released from prison in 1997, he made Haniya his top aide and bureau chief. Haniya later acted as Hamas's representative to the PNA, earning a reputation as a pragmatist with outstanding administrative skills. Haniya was involved in cease-fire talks between several Palestinian factions and Israel in mid-2003. Within Hamas, Haniya benefited from his close relationship with spiritual leader of Hamas, Yassin. His increasing prominence made him a target of the Israeli army, which resulted in an attempted assassination in September 2003. Following the 2004 assassination of Yassin and his successor, Abd al-Aziz al-Rantisi, Hamas did not reveal the identity of its leaders in the Gaza Strip. It is assumed, however, that Haniya was appointed to the movement's leadership along with Mahmoud al-Zahar and Sayid Siam, the minister of the interior of the 2007 Unity Government, who was killed by an Israeli airstrike during the Gaza War of 2008 and 2009.

In 2006, Haniya led the movement's Change and Reform list to victory in the PLC election. Winning 76 out of 132 seats, Hamas was granted the mandate to form a new government. However, doing so would prove difficult. After weeks of negotiations with its rival, Fatah, and other factions, Haniya became prime minister of a cabinet composed primarily of Hamas members and technocrats. Among his first steps as prime minister was to seek channels of dialogue with the United States and the EU. He unsuccessfully tried to reverse the Middle East Quartet's decision to cut funding to the Hamas-led PNA. While stressing Hamas's desire for formal relations with the West and its readiness to enter negotiations with international mediators on the Israeli–Palestinian conflict, he refused to disavow the legitimacy of "armed resistance" and to formally recognize Israel.

In June 2007, fighting between Fatah and Hamas ended in Hamas's takeover of the Gaza Strip. PNA president Mahmoud Abbas dismissed Haniya as prime minister. The ensuing split created two Palestinian entities with rival governments: the Gaza branch headed by Haniya and the West Bank branch headed by Abbas and the technocrat he appointed as prime minister, Salam Fayyad. An international political and financial boycott was imposed on the Gaza Strip and an Israeli and Egyptian blockade was enforced. Despite these hardships and the Gaza War of 2008–2009, Haniya managed to establish a functioning, authoritarian *quasi*-state apparatus.

In contrast to Khaled Mashal, who from 2011 onwards tried to steer Hamas toward reconciliation with Fatah, Haniya embraced a more radical political posture. On the one hand, he announced in December 2010 that Hamas "accepts a Palestinian state on the borders of 1967, with Jerusalem as its capital, the release of Palestinian prisoners, and the resolution of the issue of refugees," as long as the Palestinian people were in favor of such a scenario.[18] This position was also formulated in the program of the National Unity Government of 2007. On the other hand, in December 2011, Haniya announced before tens of thousands of supporters in Gaza that "armed resistance and armed struggle are the strategic way to liberate the Palestinian land from the sea to the river,"[19] and suggested Hamas merge with the die-hard militant group Islamic Jihad. In addition, in 2012, Haniya praised Osama Bin Laden, calling him a "holy warrior" and condemned his killing.[20] Such praise was surprising in light of the Haniya government's hostility to al-Qaeda and its suppression of its emulators in the Gaza Strip. The shift has been explained as Haniya's attempt to shore up his standing in the face of attempts to establish a unity government in which he would not serve as prime minister.

Starting in 2011, Haniya sought to solidify his authority in Gaza by embarking on international tours to countries including Sudan, Tunisia, Egypt, Turkey, Kuwait, Qatar, and Iran. In the course of these trips, the Gaza prime minister criticized "futile" peace negotiations with Israel, and, in Tehran, pledged that Hamas's "resistance" would continue and that "all occupied lands will eventually be liberated from Israeli occupation."[21]

Following the departure of Hamas's exiled leadership from Damascus in 2012, Haniya also broke with the Assad regime, praising the Syrian opposition in a sermon delivered at Cairo's prestigious al-Azhar mosque. This political shift, however, seemed not so much rooted in a change of heart but rather in pressure from Egypt, which had stopped fuel shipments to the Gaza Strip to pressure Haniya away from his alliance with Bashar al-Assad.

In May 2012 internal elections within Hamas were conducted in Gaza. Observers agree that the preliminary results of the elections strengthened Haniya's standing within Hamas.

As prime minister of the de facto government in Gaza, Haniya has unquestionably held a key position in Gaza throughout the past years. He was, despite this, not described as a central figure in the movement's overall leadership. The elections partially carried out in 2012 cemented Haniya's position as head of the Gaza political bureau of Hamas, a pivotal position within the movement and the first key Hamas leader openly holding this position since the assassinations of Ahmed Yassin and Abd al-Aziz al-Rantisi.

★ ★ ★

Interviews with Hamas Decision Makers

The following interviews were conducted with representatives of Hamas in Gaza and the West Bank. Ahmad Yousef has until 2007 served as a close advisor to Gaza prime minister Ismael Haniya and for a time acted as Gaza's de facto foreign minister, when the post was left vacant. In 2006, he co-authored the election program of Hamas's Change and

Reform list and is perceived as a Hamas moderate who is known for attempts to reach out to the international community. Yousef's relations to Haniya have recently soured, as Haniya increasingly embraced hard-line positions. In 2012, Yousef was elected to Hamas's *Shoura* council in Gaza.

A different wing from within Hamas in Gaza is represented by Huda Naim, who is a member of the PLC for Hamas and one of its youngest (and few female) representatives. Huda Naim represents a more uncompromising wing of Hamas within Gaza and prior to her political career was political active in the universities.

Hamas in the West Bank is represented by Nasser Abdel Jawad. Jawad gained a PLC seat on Hamas's Change and Reform list in 2006 and previously served more than 15 years in Israeli detention. The interview was conducted shortly before Israeli forces arrested Jawad again and put him into administrative detention on June 28, 2011.

Interview with Ahmed Yousef, Former Deputy Foreign Minister of the Gaza PNA

How would you characterize the Hamas movement today?

Hamas is a national liberation party with an Islamic nature. As part of the Muslim Brotherhood Movement, we are Islamists who seek the liberation of Palestine. That is why the Palestinian people have confidence in us. Hamas accepts responsibility for liberating Palestine while Israel refuses its responsibility for five million dispersed people. The party represents the Palestinians' ambitions, even in exile. We advocate two different kinds of causes: common causes of all Palestinians and special causes of Hamas.

Hamas is a diverse movement. But what makes us unique is our approach to tradition and modernity at the same time. And while other parties are associated with corruption, Hamas has maintained its transparent structures and close relations to the people through its comprehensive vision that has a strong social focus.

What are Hamas's positions on the prospects for peace and coexistence with Israel?

Hamas has different visions for different time frames. Our current causes are the commitment to the present cease-fire, the release of political prisoners, and the end to the blockade of the Gaza Strip. Our medium-term vision is to create a Palestinian state within the borders of 1967 on the basis of a *hudna* (cease-fire). This is the roadmap for realizing a solution to the Israeli–Palestinian conflict.

If Hamas's "medium-term vision" is a Palestinian state on the borders of 1967, what is your long-term objective?

Our position is the foundation of a Palestinian state on the borders of 1967 with Jerusalem as its capital and a just solution for the refugees in accordance with the UN resolution 194. Concerning the relations with the State of Israel after the founding of the Palestinian state, different factors such as demography, realpolitik, and geography will have to be taken into account. Options include a One-State Solution, a binational state, a federal solution, or a confederation. We will leave such decisions to the coming Palestinian generations.

The Hamas Charter from 1988 contains several anti-Semitic passages. Does it represent the views of the movement today?

In my article Hamas Charter: Vision, Fact and Fiction, I contextualized the Charter and its limited relevance to Hamas today. The 2006 election program, Ismail Haniya's government inaugural speech, and our recent party programs are by now the main points of reference.

If that is the case, why has Hamas never abrogated the Charter?

In 1988, the Charter was used for the purpose of mobilization in order to act against the occupation and to fulfill our historical rights. Contrary to what many people believe, the Charter is not our official platform. It is merely a document that has not even been ratified by a formal decision. It is part of the historical literature of Hamas. That is the reason why it has never been formally abrogated.

Has the decision to enter politics changed Hamas's perspective on violence?

Hamas believes that there is a legitimate right to resistance. However, the circumstances should determine the quality of resistance. If nonviolent struggle brings about international support and an end to the occupation, we will opt for nonviolence. Recently, Palestinian groups have opted to adapt nonviolent struggle to give the international community the opportunity to fulfill its obligations and its responsibility concerning the fulfillment of Palestinian rights.

Initially, Hamas did not have any intention to engage in politics. The main goal was to educate the Palestinian people according to our ideology. But from about 2004 onwards, we decided to engage in municipal elections. The electoral successes gradually shifted Hamas's focus from ideology to realpolitik and, at present, our strategy is based on political analysis.

Hamas operations have killed scores of civilians. Does Hamas regret the use of violence?

Resistance is a legitimate right. I do not think that any nation has managed to liberate itself from colonial oppression without resorting to violence. As long as there is occupation, there will be resistance.

Can you comment on the current political system in Gaza?

It is quite a unique system. We try to be a full-fledged government but due to the siege and the occupation we do not have all the governing instruments. For example, our foreign relations are almost nonexistent. Sometimes governing feels like acting as a charity organization or a silo government that guarantees that the population survives rather than representing the executive of an entity.

Are there strong contacts to Islamists in Israel?

Naturally there is sympathy between us and Islamists within Palestine of 1948 since we are Palestinian brothers. For example, we respect Raed Salah (the head of the Islamic Movement in Israel) as an icon of resistance advocating for protecting Jerusalem's holy places as his main cause—both Christian and Muslim. Both we and his Islamic Movement in Palestine of 1948 refer to a moderate interpretation of Islamic ideology, similar to that of the Turkish AKP. And both movements emerged from the Muslim Brotherhood. But there is no organic connection with the Islamists in Palestine of 1948. Salah's Islamic Movement has gradually shifted its attention to the West Bank and Gaza because they are not accepted as equal citizens in Israel.

How would you describe Hamas's relations with the Islamic Jihad?

The Islamic Jihad emerged from the Muslim Brotherhood in Gaza before Hamas was founded and with regard to the struggle against Israel their strategy differed from ours. While the Islamic Jihad was ready to fight Israel without foreign support, Hamas's leader Sheikh Ahmed Yassin opted to wait for support by strong Islamic countries. In the mid-1990s we were, for example, hoping that an Islamist Movement would take over power in Egypt. During that time, there were attempts to unite with Islamic Jihad and even though these attempts were not successful, we are today close partners. Due to our common vision of fighting for liberation, we do not consider Islamic Jihad an oppositional group.

Your hope that the influence of the Muslim Brotherhood in Egypt would increase has come true since the ousting of Hosni Mubarak. What is the impact on Palestine?

Until recently, countries were either defined as part of the US system or as part of the Iranian system. The catalyzing events in Egypt, Libya, and Tunisia will accelerate the process of ending this bi-polarization and a new fabric and a new approach will emerge. The new governments know that the Palestinian question is the mother of all conflicts and therefore everybody will try to please the Palestinians by raising funds, humanitarian aid and—in the Egyptian case—by opening the borders to Gaza. Egypt as the Arab backbone will distance itself from Israel. Turkey has also come back to the Arab side after the Gaza Flotilla events (the Mavi Marmara convoy that attempted to breach the Gaza blockade in 2010). Adding Iran to Egypt and Turkey, Palestine can count on the three main regional powers in the future.

The Arab Spring proves that time is on our side. The United States must rethink its support for Israel because of its strategic interests. The United States will be forced to pursue a balanced policy in the Middle East, and Israel will become more and more isolated. For the moment, the United States has lost its credibility after vetoing the UN Resolution on Settlements in February 2011; this is especially true because hopes were high due to President Obama's Cairo speech and his pressure on Hosni Mubarak to resign. This US stance was truly a great policy.

The Doha Declaration signed by Khaled Meshal and Mahmoud Abbas in February 2012 has caused tensions between Haniya and Meshal. Is Hamas confronted with a split?

Hamas as a movement is governed by the *Shoura* council. The current discussions are a healthy development. The fact that Hamas has opted for increased openness and transparency has opened space for public debate and for different positions. Some see this as signs of a split. I do not agree. In reality, such differences of opinion merely reflect different schools of thought.

Interview with Huda Naim, Member of the PLC, Gaza

What is Hamas's solution for the conflict with Israel?

Hamas is willing to accept the Two-State Solution. But there are important conditions attached to this acceptance. Our commitment to two states is based on the condition that we will not recognize Israel's right to exist. We also demand the right of Palestinian refugees to return. In return for accepting these conditions, we are prepared to offer Israel a long-term cease-fire. Our position is based on our conviction that historical Palestine is the rightful home of Palestinians. We are aware of the fact that the current balance of power favors the forces of occupation. That is why we are willing to accept the formula of two states with the above-mentioned conditions.

You are certainly aware that Israel is unlikely to voluntarily accept this. Is this a realistic objective?

We are prepared to wait. Time is on our side. The time will come in which the equation of power will not be in favor of Israel. In general, we believe that we are entitled to use any means necessary to achieve our goals. We believe in resistance and we will continue to oppose the occupation also with violent means. It is simple: For Israel, the occupation has to come with a price tag. By resisting Israel, we are making Israel pay a price. However, we also believe that popular resistance and diplomatic initiatives can play important roles.

As concerning global politics, we are only too aware of Western double standards and of Western collaboration with Israel. It is outrageously unfair that we as the victims of the conflict are constantly asked to make concessions for the solution of the conflict. The West recognizes that our territories were occupied in 1967. But what have Western powers done do remedy this injustice? What has Israel done to end the occupation?

If that is your assessment—what are the prospects for finding a solution in peace negotiations with Israel?

In principle, we do not have anything against negotiations as such. That is why we also negotiated with Israel in the past, for instance over the release of Gilad Shalit. The all-important question, however, is the character of negotiations. Are both negotiating partners operating on a level playing field?

Whatever negotiations have been conducted between the PNA, the PLO, and Israel in the past does not merit the label negotiations. Those were not negotiations but dictates. Since the start of these so-called negotiations, 20 years have passed and these processes have brought about no benefits for Palestinians. Instead, these negotiations have provided Israel with a political cover for the continuation of the occupation and for the continuation of its settlement policies. In view of the fact that we have already wasted 20 years, we simply do not believe in negotiations that are conducted between unequal partners.

Would a Palestinian state ever recognize a state for the Jewish people?

The concept of a Jewish state runs contrary to the ideals of a modern, civil state. However, isn't this, what the international community demands from every group that aspires for statehood? Once again, the State of Israel is allowed to be the exception to the general rule that is valid for everybody else. Israel is allowed to define itself as nationalistic and religious state based on Jewish religion. That is despite the fact that Israel as a matter of fact embraces apartheid and rejects the norms of civility and democracy that are expected from any other state.

You reject what you call a "religious state" in Israel. But in the 2006 election program Hamas called for the implementation of Sharia in Palestine? Is this not a contradiction?

We as Hamas believe in a democratic state with an Islamic base and an Islamic background. We fundamentally believe in democracy as the means to achieve and hand-over political power. At the same time, we consider democracy a product of modernity. Again, we have no problems at all with democracy as such. But democracy cannot be allowed to violate Islamic principles.

Speaking of Democracy in the Arab World, what has changed for Hamas since the Arab Spring?

The Arab Spring has changed the equation of power on many levels. We are absolutely sure that all Arab societies are fundamentally in tune with legitimate Palestinian demands. The old Arab regimes that have now been removed from power were among the prime defenders of the status quo. Not only did they refuse to support legitimate Palestinian demands, they in many cases prevented the realization of our national rights. They simply provided Israel with a political cover. Now, against the background of the Arab Spring, we feel that we are getting closer to the realization of our dream.

But one of the most important consequences of the Arab Spring was the fact that Arabs have sent a powerful message to the world that Islamists are not radicals who deserve to be shunned. Since the Arab Spring removed the old regimes and paved the way for Islamists to ascent to power, Islamist actors have been widely acknowledged as legitimate partners of the West. Western leaders have now started to recognize and negotiate with Islamists. This only confirms our views and our dreams. Actually, the Arab Spring has reminded us that we are not dreaming.

Interview with Nassir Abdel Jawad, Member of the Palestinian Legislative Council

In what ways do you consider Hamas different from Islamist groups such as Islamic Jihad?

In terms of ideology and the religious focus there is no difference between Hamas and these groups. But there are important differences in terms of strategy. Islamic Jihad is promoting exclusively military resistance, which Hamas does not. And these other parties have a rather narrow agenda, which does not contain too many issues. Hamas is rooted in a comprehensive system of thought and theory encompassing economics, media, social, and other issues. In the way Hamas is dealing with the main Palestinian issues like the refugees and Jerusalem, the movement demonstrates its uniqueness.

How does Hamas see itself? Is it an Islamist or an Arab or a national Palestinian movement?

Hamas is all of those things—it engages in many circles. The first circle is the Palestinian cause which Hamas wants to serve in various aspects. The second circle is the Arab nations and the third circle is the worldwide Islamic *umma*.

This concept of "circles" is also mentioned in the Hamas Charter. Does the Charter still represent the overall program of Hamas?

Of course not. Hamas is pragmatic, not static. The movement has developed. Our theory stays the same, but we continue to develop our strategy. It has to develop—this is what the Palestinian people want.

How would a Hamas-ruled Palestine deal with religious minorities like Christians or Jews or with secular groups such as communists?

Looking at Hamas's social and political program one sees that there is no problem with factions or minorities. In Hamas-ruled Palestine there would be a constitution, and minorities would be protected by special courts. Under the Muslim rule of the Caliphate there were no problems between Muslims, Christians, and Jews for hundreds of years. Limits are of course set where national security is concerned, and maybe communism would pose a problem.

What is Hamas's situation in the West Bank?

There are many problems and complaints. The main reason for this lies in foreign interventions by Israel and the United States, which fight Hamas and now add to the increasing violation of human rights in the West Bank.

How closely does Hamas in the West Bank follow events in Gaza? Is Gaza a first "experiment" and how would you evaluate it?

I am not in Gaza but my contacts in Gaza tell me that the situation under Hamas rule has improved in various fields, including the economy. The people of Gaza were in a miserable situation before, and now, for instance, corruption has lessened. But of course, it is still a situation of siege.

What are the means and methods Hamas intends to use to create an independent Palestinian state?

Hamas will obviously do everything to free Palestine. Armed resistance is one strategy against the occupation and I believe it is legitimate. But at the same time, international human rights agreements have to be respected. Hamas is a pragmatic movement. So the question of how to resist depends on the specific situation.

Could Hamas engage in constructive dialogue with the State of Israel?

There is no problem for Hamas to deal with any country, and of course there can be dialogue with enemies. But I do not understand why the West is hesitating to talk to us and why Hamas is on a terror list. Hamas is not responsible for 9/11 or any such terror attacks.

Would a unified multiethnic Palestinian–Israeli state be an option for the party?

This is very difficult. Israel does not favor this option because it would destroy the idea of a Jewish homeland. On the Palestinian side, there is no problem and Hamas will accept any resolution that is accepted by the Palestinian people.

How would you describe the role of women in Hamas?

In Hamas there were many female candidates in the 2006 elections and it is no problem for them to be active in the movement. There are many women in the municipalities, in particular. Traditionally, there was a separation, but today men and women share a common space. Of course, there are moral rules to take into account for both men and women.

How do you see the work of Prime Minister Salam Fayyad? In which way would a Hamas government differ, particularly with respect to economic policies?
Salam Fayyad is an American, and the biggest asset he has is money. Without that money he would not represent anything. His party only has two seats in the PLC (the Third Way, dissolved shortly after the 2006 elections). In economic aspects he has been doing a good job but not in many other fields. For instance, he committed a great crime against the Palestinian people in releasing government employees in the West Bank, who are now in a miserable situation. Those who have voted for Hamas are also prevented from finding a job in the private sector. So, Salam Fayyad has destroyed the Palestinian community. People were arrested and tortured. Fayyad opened schools but he closed welfare organizations in the West Bank—orphanages and the like—because they were Islamic institutions.

★ ★ ★

Excerpts of Hamas Programmatic Documents

The following excerpts are taken from the 2011–2012 development plan developed by the Gaza Ministry of Planning in November 2010,[22] the program of the National Unity Government from 2007,[23] the election program of the Hamas-affiliated Change and Reform list from 2006,[24] and from the Hamas Charter from 1988.[25]

View of Israeli–Palestinian Conflict

Program of the National Unity Government (March 2007):
"1.1- The government affirms that the key to security and stability in the region depends on ending the Israeli occupation of the Palestinian territories and recognizing the right to self-determination of the Palestinian people; the government will work with the international community for the sake of ending the occupation and regaining the legitimate rights of the Palestinian people so that we can build a solid basis for peace, security and prosperity in the region.

1.2- The government shall abide to protect the higher national interests of the Palestinian people and protect their rights and preserve and develop their accomplishments and work on achieving their national goals as ratified by the resolutions of the PNC meetings and the Articles of the Basic Law and the national conciliation document and the resolutions of the Arab summits and based on this, the government shall respect the international legitimacy resolutions and the agreements that were signed by the PLO.

1.3- The government shall abide by rejecting the so-called state with temporary borders because this idea is based on taking away from the legitimate rights of the Palestinian people.

1.4- To cling to the right of the Palestinian refugees and right of return to their lands and properties.

1.5- To work diligently for the sake of liberating the heroic prisoners from the Israeli occupation prisons.

1.6- To confront the measures of the occupation on the ground in terms of the assassinations, arrests, and incursions. The government shall grant special importance to the city of Jerusalem to confront the Israeli policies pertaining to the people, lands and holy sites of Jerusalem....

2.1- The government affirms that peace and stability in the region depends on ending all forms of occupation of the Palestinian territories and removing the apartheid wall and settlements and halt of the Judaization of Jerusalem and policies of annexation and restore the rights to their owners.

2.2- The government affirms that resistance is a legitimate right of the Palestinian people as granted by the international norms and charters; our Palestinian people have the right to defend themselves in face of any Israeli aggression, and believes that halting resistance depends on ending the occupation and achieving freedom, return and independence.

2.3- Despite this, the government, through national conciliation, will work on consolidating the calm and expanding it to become a comprehensive reciprocal truce happening at the same time between both sides and this should be in return for Israel halting its occupation measures on the ground in terms of assassinations, arrests, incursions and home demolitions and leveling of lands and the digging works in Jerusalem and it should work on removing the checkpoints and reopening the crossings and lifting all the restrictions on movement and the release of prisoners.

2.4- The government affirms what came in the national conciliation document on the issue of the administration of the negotiations which is the jurisdiction of the PLO and the President of the PNA on the basis of clinging to the Palestinian national goals and towards achieving these goals, so that any offer on any final agreement should be presented to the new Palestinian National Council for ratification or to hold a general referendum to have the Palestinian people inside and abroad and to have a law that organizes the referendum.

2.5- The government shall support the exerted efforts and shall encourage the relevant parties to accelerate and end the case of the Israeli soldier in the context of an honorable prisoners exchange deal."

Election Platform of Change and Reform List (2006):
"Islam is the solution and is our path to changes and reform. Our platform is our way to enhance the building of the society which was destroyed by the occupation. The safeguarding of resistance and its agenda is the way to strengthen national and Islamic unity—on the way to comprehensive national liberation. This is the platform of the whole people and homeland.

- Historic Palestine is part of the Arab and Islamic land and its ownership by the Palestinian people is a right that does not diminish over time. No military or legal measures will change that right.
- The Palestinian people, wherever they reside, constitute a single and united people and form an integral part of the Arab and Muslim nation. The Palestinian people are still living a phase of national liberation, and thus they have the right to strive to recover their rights and end the occupation using all means, including armed struggle. We have to make all our resources available to support our people and defeat the occupation and establish a Palestinian state with Jerusalem as its capital.
- The right of return of all Palestinian refugees and displaced persons to their land and properties, and the right to self-determination and all other national rights are inalienable and cannot be bargained away for any political concessions.
- We uphold the indigenous and inalienable rights of our people to our land, Jerusalem, our holy places, our water resources, borders, and a fully sovereign independent Palestinian state with Jerusalem as its capital.
- Reinforcing and protecting Palestinian national unity is one of the priorities of the Palestinian national action.

- The issue of the prisoners is at the top of the Palestinian agenda.
- Change and Reform will continue to resist the erection of the Racist Wall and it will seek its destruction."

Hamas Charter (1988):

"Allah is its target, the Prophet is its model, the *Koran* its constitution: *Jihad* is its path and death for the sake of Allah is the loftiest of its wishes.

The Islamic Resistance Movement's program is Islam.... It strives to raise the banner of Allah over every inch of Palestine, for under the wing of Islam followers of all religions can coexist in security and safety where their lives, possessions and rights are concerned. In the absence of Islam, strife will be rife, oppression spreads, evil prevails and schisms and wars will break out.

The Islamic Resistance Movement is one of the wings of Moslem Brotherhood in Palestine.... It is characterized by its deep understanding, accurate comprehension and its complete embrace of all Islamic concepts of all aspects of life, culture, creed, politics, economics, education, society, justice and judgment, the spreading of Islam, education, art, information, science of the occult and conversion to Islam.

In all that, they fear Allah and raise the banner of *Jihad* in the face of the oppressors, so that they would rid the land and the people of their uncleanliness, vileness and evils.

Initiatives, and so-called peaceful solutions and international conferences, are in contradiction to the principles of the Islamic Resistance Movement. Abusing any part of Palestine is abuse directed against part of religion. Nationalism of the Islamic Resistance Movement is part of its religion. Its members have been fed on that. For the sake of hoisting the banner of Allah over their homeland they fight. (Quranic Verse) *'Allah will be prominent, but most people do not know.'*

Now and then the call goes out for the convening of an international conference to look for ways of solving the [Palestinian] question. Some accept, others reject the idea, for this or other reason, with one stipulation or more for consent to convening the conference and participating in it. Knowing the parties constituting these conferences, their past and present attitudes towards Moslem problems, the Islamic Resistance Movement does not consider these conferences capable of realising the demands, restoring the rights or doing justice to the oppressed. These conferences are only ways of setting the infidels in the land of the Moslems as arbitrators. When did the infidels do justice to the believers?

[Quranic Verse] '*But the Jews will not be pleased with thee, neither the Christians, until thou follow their religion; say, The direction of Allah is the true direction. And verily if thou follow their desires, after the knowledge which hath been given thee, thou shalt find no patron or protector against Allah.*' (The Cow-verse 120).

There is no solution for the Palestinian question except through *Jihad*. Initiatives, proposals and international conferences are all a waste of time and vain endeavors. The Palestinian people know better than to consent to having their future, rights and fate toyed with. As in said in the honorable *Hadith*.

... The question of the liberation of Palestine is bound to three circles: the Palestinian circle, the Arab circle and the Islamic circle. Each of these circles has its role in the struggle against Zionism. Each has its duties, and it is a horrible mistake and a sign of deep ignorance to overlook any of these circles. Palestine is an Islamic land which has the first of the two *qiblas* [direction to which Moslems turn in praying], the third of the holy [Islamic] sanctuaries, and the point of departure for Mohamed's midnight journey to the seven heavens [Jerusalem].

[Quranic Verse] '*Praise be unto him who transported his servant by night, from the sacred temple of Mecca to the farther temple of Jerusalem, the circuit of which we have blessed, that we might show him some of our signs; for Allah is he who heareth, and seeth.*' (The Night-Journey-verse 1).

...

The day that enemies usurp part of Moslem land, *Jihad* becomes the individual duty of every Moslem. In face of the Jews' usurpation of Palestine, it is compulsory that the banner of *Jihad* be raised. To do this requires the diffusion of Islamic consciousness among the masses, both on the regional, Arab and Islamic levels. It is necessary to instill the spirit of *Jihad* in the heart of the nation so that they would confront the enemies and join the ranks of the fighters.

It is necessary to instill in the minds of the Moslem generations that the Palestinian problem is a religious problem, and should be dealt with on this basis. Palestine contains Islamic holy sites. In it there is al-Aqsa Mosque which is bound to the great Mosque in Mecca in an inseparable bond as long as heaven and earth speak of *Isra*' [Mohammed's midnight journey to the seven heavens] and *Mi'raj* [Mohammed's ascension to the seven heavens from Jerusalem].

...

The Islamic Resistance Movement believes that the land of Palestine is an Islamic *Waqf* consecrated for future Moslem generations until

Judgment Day. It, or any part of it, should not be squandered: it, or any part of it, should not be given up. Neither a single Arab country nor all Arab countries, neither any king or president, nor all the kings and presidents, neither any organization nor all of them, be they Palestinian or Arab, possess the right to do that. Palestine is an Islamic *Waqf* land consecrated for Moslem generations until Judgment Day. This being so, who could claim to have the right to represent Moslem generations till Judgment Day?"

Economic Development

Development Plan 2011–2012 Gaza Ministry of Planning (2010):
"The Development Plan aims to achieve several key objectives: (1.) Improving economic and living conditions, (2.) realizing a comprehensive, balanced and fair social development, (3.) maintaining security, strengthening the rule of law and good governance, and (4.) developing infrastructure and service productivity. Sectorial objectives:

Program on improving economic and living conditions: Main objective: Improving economic and living conditions. Sub-objectives:

1. strengthening the local capacity of the Palestinian economy by focusing on replacing imports, and on strengthening the role of the private sector to consolidate and develop local markets
2. rehabilitating and protecting sources of agricultural productivity in order to provide food security
3. increasing job opportunities and sources of income
4. protection of the Palestinian environment in the context of sustainable development
5. identifying the needs and priorities of national development.

...

Infrastructure Program: General objective: Development of service infrastructure, increasing productivity and urban development. Sub-objectives:

1. repairing the damage caused by the Israeli aggression and reconstructing Gaza
2. developing the energy sector
3. protecting the Palestinian environment in the context of sustainable development

4. improving the services of the telecommunications sector and of postal services and information technology
5. the development of the transportation sector
6. protecting the limited water resources and finding suitable alternatives
7. improving environmental conditions and the general health of the citizens (water, sewage, solid waste)
8. creating a sustainable urban development
9. enhancing the contribution of the private sector in infrastructure development
10. developing the capacity of government institutions related to infrastructure."

Program of the National Unity Government (March 2007):
"6.1- The government shall work on ending the siege imposed on our Palestinian people through the programs and relations and to activate the regional and international frameworks to alleviate the suffering of our Palestinian people.

6.2- The government shall give priority to upgrade and advance the national economy and encourage the economic and trade sectors with the Arab and Islamic world and encourage economic and trade relations with the European Union and the rest of the world.

6.3- To move to protect the consumer and encourage the private sector and provide the proper climate for its activities and lay down the sound rules for government work and its official institutions and the institutions of the private sector and end monopoly. The government shall work on providing the proper climate and protection and stability of investment projects.

6.4- The government shall work on respecting the principles of free economy in a manner that meets with our values and norms and in a manner that serves the Palestinian development and protect the private sector and encourage investment and fight unemployment and poverty and reinforce the productive economic sectors and reconstruct the infrastructure and develop the industrial zone and the housing and technology sectors."

Election Platform of Change and Reform List (2006):
"On the economic level, the economy and monetary system should be independent from the Zionist entity and its economic and monetary

system. The Change and Reform list will mint Palestinian currency; self-sufficiency is an ultimate objective to be worked for through a number of measures. International economic agreements will be reconsidered and revised so as to serve the interests of the Palestinian people, chief among them:

- the Paris Protocol
- the Free Trade Agreement with the USA
- Partnership Agreement with the EU
- the Economic Agreement with Egypt and Jordan.

The economic and trade relations with the Arab and Islamic world should be developed. The Palestinian economy should be helped to disengage itself from the dependency on the Israeli economy. Income tax laws must be reconsidered and reformed. Labor unions and occupational societies will be encouraged and developed; a minimum wage should be established to guarantee a decent standard of living for all, wages and salaries should be linked to an official index.

Roads must be modernized; movement among cities and villages should be emphasized and smooth; opening of free crossings between the Palestinian territory and Jordan and Egypt. Any foreign interference is rejected; the port and the airport are to be reopened."

State's Role vis-a-vis Religion

Election Platform of Change and Reform List (2006):
"True Islam with its civilized achievements and political, economic, social, and legal aspects is our frame of reference and our way of life. Islamic *Sharia* law should be the principal source of legislation in Palestine. The three branches, legislative, executive and judicial are to be separated. Palestinian *Waqf* [religious endowment] is to be safeguarded, be it Muslim or Christian.

Out of our conviction of the vitality of building a well-rounded Palestinian individual, the Change and Reform list attaches great importance to education which will keep abreast of modern innovations. Islam of course will be the core of the Palestinian education philosophy. Reforms are to be introduced to the current education system."

Hamas Charter (1988):
"The Islamic Resistance Movement is a humanistic movement. It takes care of human rights and is guided by Islamic tolerance when dealing

with the followers of other religions. It does not antagonize anyone of them except if it is antagonized by it or stands in its way to hamper its moves and waste its efforts.

Under the wing of Islam, it is possible for the followers of the three religions—Islam, Christianity and Judaism—to coexist in peace and quiet with each other. Peace and quiet would not be possible except under the wing of Islam. Past and present history is the best witness to that.

It is the duty of the followers of other religions to stop disputing the sovereignty of Islam in this region, because the day these followers should take over there will be nothing but carnage, displacement and terror....

Islam confers upon everyone his legitimate rights. Islam prevents the incursion on other people's rights. The Zionist Nazi activities against our people will not last for long. "For the state of injustice lasts but one day, while the state of justice lasts till Doomsday."

[Quranic Verse] *'As to those who have not borne arms against you on account of religion, nor turned you out of your dwellings, Allah forbiddeth you not to deal kindly with them, and to behave justly towards them; for Allah loveth those who act justly.'* (The Tried-verse 8)."

Vision of State and Society

Development Plan 2011–2012 Gaza Ministry of Planning (2010):
"Program of improving social development: Main objective: Achieving comprehensive, balanced and fair social development. Sub-objectives:

1. developing Palestinian society culturally and educationally
2. providing comprehensive health development requirements
3. strengthening the resilience of the border areas
4. supporting humanitarian and human development of marginalized groups
5. advancing of society religiously and socially...

Program on Security and Good Governance: Main objective: Maintaining security and strengthening the rule of law and good governance. Sub-objectives:

1. continuing security sector reforms
2. developing the judicial system and enhancing its independence

3. ensuring transparency and accountability
4. enhancing reform processes in public administration and the civil service
5. promoting Palestinian rights and Palestinian positions in international media in support of political positions, strengthening the Palestinian and the Arab and Muslim Palestinian society and ensuring access to a pluralistic environment ensuring freedom of opinion and the promotion of democracy."

Program of the National Unity Government (March 2007):
"The national unity government realizes the internal difficult conditions and believes that its top priority at the coming phase is to control the current security conditions and in order to achieve this; the government shall depend in its program on the following:

3.1- to form a higher national security council that represents the terms of reference to all security services and the framework that organizes their work and define their policies, and request from the PLC to finalize the law pertaining to the national security higher council

3.2- to structure the security services and build them on professional basis and work to provide their needs and reduce the partisan considerations and move them away from political polarizations and conflicts and consolidate in them the loyalty to the homeland and have them abide by executing the decisions of their political leadership and to make sure that the personnel working in these services commit themselves to the tasks commissioned to them

3.3- to work on activating the laws that have been ratified by the PLC with regards to the security institution

3.4- to set up a comprehensive security plan to end all forms of chaos and security chaos and aggressions and protect and prevent any bloodshed and honor of families and funds and public and private properties and control the weapons and provide security to the citizen and work on ending the oppression inflicted on the people through the rule of law and support the police to perform its duties in the best manner

4.1- The government shall work in full cooperation with the judicial authority to secure the reform and activation and protection of the judicial apparatus with all its institutions in a manner that can enable it to perform its duties in the context of achieving justice and fighting corruption and abiding by the rule of the law and implement the law with transparency and integrity on everybody without any interference from any party.

4.2- The government affirms that it works according to the Basic Law which organizes the relations between the three authorities on the basis of separating between the authorities and respect the authorities granted to the Presidency and to the government according to law and order.

4.3- The government shall assist the president in performing his various duties and will make sure to cooperate fully with the Presidency institution and the constitutional institutions and work with the PLC and the juridical authorities towards developing the Palestinian political system on the basis of having a unified strong national authority....

5.4- The government shall work on reinforcing the principle of citizenship through equality in rights and duties and equal opportunities and consolidate social justice in appointments and recruitments in the various ministries and institutions and end all forms of political favoritism in civil and security recruitments.

5.5- The government affirms its respect to the principle of political pluralism and protection of public freedoms and reinforce the values of *Shoura* and democracy and protect the human rights and consolidate the principle of justice and equality and protect the free press and freedom of expression and abide by peaceful transfer of power and authorities and conclude the elections at the local councils within the next six months God willing.

5.6- The government shall abide by providing a dignified life to the Palestinian citizen and provide the requirements of life and social welfare and meet the health needs and develop the health facilities and expand health insurance and improve the situation of the hospitals and clinics and work on tackling the phenomena of poverty and unemployment through providing job opportunities and development projects and social securities and the social welfare program; the government shall grant special care to the education and higher education and shall encourage scientific research and provide its needs.

5.7- To care for the sectors of laborers, farmers, fishermen and the sectors of youths and women so that women can assume the status they deserve based on their sacrifices and to secure to them participation in the decision making process and to contribute

in the building process in all institutions and ministries and at various fields. . . .
7.3- within the context of reform, the government shall seek to fight corruption and reinforce the values of integrity and transparency and refrain from abusing public funds and we will give the matter of administrative development and to develop a sound working mechanism based on the principles of modern administration which can assist in implementing this strategy according to the requirements and needs of the Palestinian society."

Election Platform of Change and Reform List (2006):
"The Change and Reform list seeks the construction of a developed Palestinian Civil society based on pluralism; the Palestinian political order should be such as to help achieve Palestinian national rights.

The rights of minorities are to be protected on the basis of good citizenship; public funds are for all; the prisoners and wounded are the embodiment of sacrifice and should be accorded full care.

Women's rights will be guaranteed so that they can contribute to the building of society, socially, economically and politically. Women's organizations should be encouraged. The Change and Reform List enumerates the actions that they should take to raise the status of women. Youth care is among the aims to be achieved by Change and Reform- talents among the young are to be tapped and encouraged.

Culture and media play a vital role in shaping the mentality and thought of citizens, and building up of the nation's personality. Freedom of thinking, expression and fairness and safeguarding the youth from external corruptible influence are chief among the Change and Reform List concerns. Official media should work for enhancing the people's steadfastness and resistance."

Hamas Charter (1987):
"This is the law governing the land of Palestine in the Islamic Sharia [law] and the same goes for any land the Moslems have conquered by force, because during the times of [Islamic] conquests, the Moslems consecrated these lands to Moslem generations till the Day of Judgement.

The Moslem woman has a role no less important than that of the Moslem man in the battle of liberation. She is the maker of men. Her role in guiding and educating the new generations is great. The enemies have realised the importance of her role. They consider that if they are able to direct and bring her up they way they wish, far from Islam, they would have won the battle. That is why you find them giving these attempts constant attention through information campaigns, films, and the school curriculum, using for that purpose their lackeys who are infiltrated through Zionist organizations under various names and shapes, such as Freemasons, Rotary Clubs, espionage groups and others, which are all nothing more than cells of subversion and saboteurs. These organizations have ample resources that enable them to play their role in societies for the purpose of achieving the Zionist targets and to deepen the concepts that would serve the enemy. These organizations operate in the absence of Islam and its estrangement among its people. The Islamic peoples should perform their role in confronting the conspiracies of these saboteurs. The day Islam is in control of guiding the affairs of life, these organizations, hostile to humanity and Islam, will be obliterated.

Woman in the home of the fighting family, whether she is a mother or a sister, plays the most important role in looking after the family, rearing the children and imbuing them with moral values and thoughts derived from Islam. She has to teach them to perform the religious duties in preparation for the role of fighting awaiting them. That is why it is necessary to pay great attention to schools and the curriculum followed in educating Moslem girls, so that they would grow up to be good mothers, aware of their role in the battle of liberation.

She has to be of sufficient knowledge and understanding where the performance of housekeeping matters are concerned, because economy and avoidance of waste of the family budget, is one of the requirements for the ability to continue moving forward in the difficult conditions surrounding us. She should put before her eyes the fact that the money available to her is just like blood which should never flow except through the veins so that both children and grown-ups could continue to live....

It is necessary that scientists, educators and teachers, information and media people, as well as the educated masses, especially the youth and sheikhs of the Islamic movements, should take part in the operation of awakening [the masses]. It is important that basic changes be made in the school curriculum, to cleanse it of the traces of ideological invasion that affected it as a result of the orientalists and missionaries who infiltrated the region following the defeat of the Crusaders at the hands of Salah al-Din [Saladin]. The Crusaders realised that it was impossible to defeat the Moslems without first having ideological invasion pave the way by upsetting their thoughts, disfiguring their heritage and violating their ideals. Only then could they invade with soldiers. This, in its turn, paved the way for the imperialistic invasion that made Allenby declare on entering Jerusalem: 'Only now have the Crusades ended.' General Guru stood at Salah al-Din's grave and said: 'We have returned, O Salah al-Din.' Imperialism has helped towards the strengthening of ideological invasion, deepening, and still does, its roots. All this has paved the way towards the loss of Palestine."

CHAPTER THREE

Fatah: From Resistance Movement to Party of State

Charting Fatah's Transition

For many Palestinians, the Palestinian National Liberation Movement (Fatah) is not just one of several political movements but the embodiment of secular Palestinian nationalism per se. Fatah activists, and in particular their long-time leader Yasir Arafat, have become global symbols of the Palestinian cause and have thus been associated with its achievements and shortcomings.

Fatah (the reverse acronym is translated as opening, conquest) is the largest faction of the Palestine Liberation Organization (PLO), the "sole legitimate representative of the Palestinian people," and has defined Palestinian policies both in acts of "armed resistance" and in negotiations with Israel through its role in the PLO (table 3.1).

Since the establishment of the Palestinian National Authority (PNA), Fatah has also dominated political life in the Palestinian Territories as the de facto party of state, since—as the Fatah program from 2009 describes somewhat euphemistically, "Fatah assumed most of [the Palestinian Territories's] leading and administrative responsibilities."[1] The overlap is such that it has been at times difficult to distinguish Fatah's institutions from the other established forums of Palestinian political life, the PNA and the PLO. A nominally left-wing party, Fatah is a full member of the Socialist

Table 3.1 Fatah at a glance

Official name	: Fatah / Palestinian National Liberation Movement (*Harakat al-Tahrir al-Watani al-Filastini*)
Year founded	: 1959 in Kuwait
PLO membership since	: 1967
PLC members 1996	: 71
PLC members 2006	: 45
Ideological orientation	: Full member party of the Socialist International (SI)
Leadership base	: Ramallah (previously Kuwait, East Jerusalem, Amman, Beirut, Tunis, and Gaza)

International (the global organization of social democratic, socialist, and labor parties, SI) although the movement has always identified itself as transcending narrow ideological allegiances. Discussions about abstract points of policy have traditionally been eschewed by Fatah in favor of forming a broad-based national movement dedicated to serving what has been perceived as the Palestinian national interest.

Fatah was founded in 1959 in Kuwait by Palestinian graduates of Cairo University. In contrast to the pan-Arab ideologies flourishing at that time, Fatah focused exclusively on Palestinian activism and held that the much celebrated ideal of pan-Arab unity should not be a precondition but the consequence of the "complete liberation of Palestine," as stipulated in Fatah's 1964 Constitution.[2] This notion was further captivated by the slogan "Palestine is the road to Arab unity." Pursuing a specifically Palestinian path to realizing national ambitions, the movement strived to act independently from surrounding Arab states. Fatah (and later also the PLO under Fatah's leadership) worked to gain financial and political independence from Arab regimes by cultivating a network of wealthy Palestinian donors in the Diaspora. This source of funding allowed Fatah, based in Syria from 1962 onwards, to finance the training of guerilla fighters for its military wing, *al-Assifa* (the Storm).

To many Palestinians, Fatah would become *the* icon of their national aspirations. When Israel's defeat of Arab armies in the 1967 Six Day War dealt a severe blow to pan-Arab ambitions, Fatah seized the opportunity to advance an alternative approach to achieving Palestinian independence. As the *New York Times* captures in Yasir Arafat's obituary from November 11, 2004, the Arab defeat gave Fatah's leaders "a chance to become heroes to Arabs desperately in need of some."

FATAH: RESISTANCE MOVEMENT TO PARTY OF STATE 59

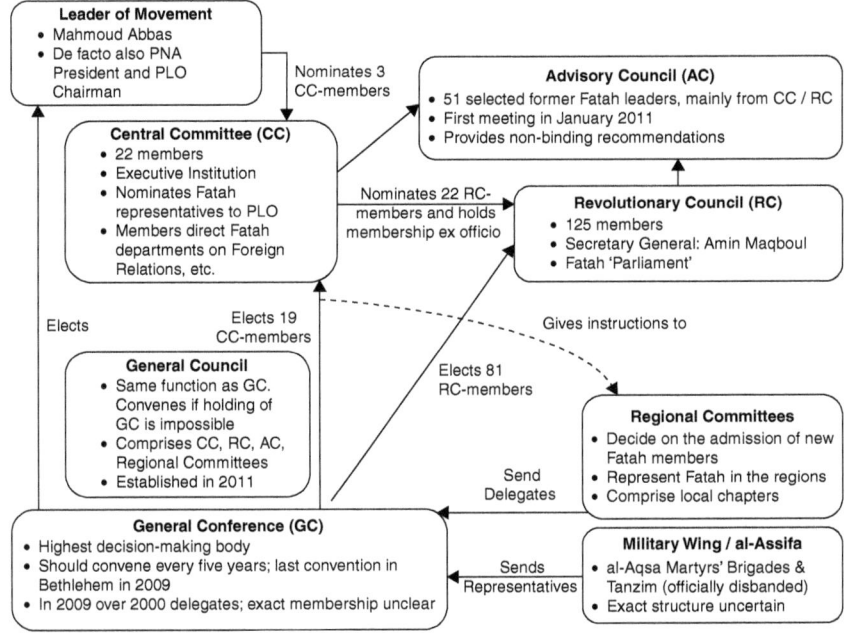

Chart 3.1 Organizational structure of Fatah.

In the 1960s, Fatah engaged in guerilla warfare against the Israeli army and in terrorist operations in historic Palestine. While initially the organization was mainly a network of underground cells, in the mid-1960s Fatah also co-established formalized civil society organizations such as a Trade Union Confederation (later merged with competing confederations from other leftist parties to form the Palestinian General Federation of Trade Unions, PGFTU) and the General Union of Palestinian Women (GUPW). Both organizations have remained closely aligned with Fatah. Also in the mid-1960s, Fatah formalized internal decision-making procedures, in which institutions such as the Central Committee (founded in 1963) played a leading role (see chart 3.1).

As stated in its 1964 Constitution, Fatah's goal was "the complete liberation of Palestine and eradication of Zionist political, military, and cultural existence."[3] The movement established clandestine headquarters in Nablus in 1967, but repeated skirmishes and rising casualties prompted the Israeli military to oust Fatah from the Palestinian Territories within a matter of months. The expulsion of Fatah to Jordan marked the beginning of nearly three decades during which the movement operated almost exclusively from exile. Somewhat ironically, exiling Fatah from the Palestinian Territories later paved the way for gains in public support.

Fatah at that time was but one among several groups of Palestinian *fedayeen* (those who sacrifice) militants confronting Israel. But the movement's reputation skyrocketed after the 1968 Battle of Karameh, named after the Jordanian border town where Fatah's fighters inflicted substantial casualties on Israeli forces. The celebrated success of the Karameh battle was soon followed by the appointment of Fatah leader Yasir Arafat as chairman of the PLO, which Fatah had joined in 1967. During the fifth session of the Palestinian National Council (the PLO's Parliament, PNC) in Cairo in 1969, Fatah effectively gained control of the organization, which had from the outset been perceived as a competitor.

The PLO (founded by an initiative of the Arab League in 1964) had been politically weakened by the Arab defeat of 1967 and the ensuing resignation of its first chairman Ahmad Shukairy. Fatah enhanced its position in the organization and became the leading force of Palestinian armed resistance. Foreign support began to increase. In addition to Palestinian support from the Diaspora, Fatah received substantial financing from Kuwait and Saudi Arabia and gained important moral support and recognition from Egyptian president Gamal Abdel Nasser. Also following Karameh, Jordan's King Hussein permitted the movement to establish official institutions in the Hashemite Kingdom. It was not long, however, before tensions between the Jordanian monarchy and the PLO leadership emerged. Accusing the movement of creating a de facto state on Jordanian territory, King Hussein ordered his troops to expel the PLO factions in a violent crackdown in 1970, a period later known as Black September.

Fatah and the PLO moved their headquarters to Lebanon, from where the Palestinian factions continued their guerilla operations against Israel. While the headquarters were based in Beirut, the PLO's main stronghold was located in the southern part of the country. Fatah became a major player in the Lebanese civil war, suffering several internal splits. The ousting of PLO factions from Jordan so severely weakened Fatah's main competitors from the Popular Front for the Liberation of Palestine (PFLP) and the Democratic Front for the Liberation of Palestine (DFLP) that Fatah was able to secure itself even more firmly as the leading Palestinian faction within the PLO. In 1974 the PLO formally accepted the so-called Ten Point Program, which called for the establishment of a Palestinian authority on any "liberated" part of the Palestinian Territory. While this signaled a noteworthy ideological shift toward at least a temporary acceptance of a Two-State Solution, it obviously fell short of meeting Israeli demands. In Israel and many Western countries, the Ten Point Program was perceived as a thinly veiled attempt to call for the destruction of Israel at a later point in time.

In 1982, Israel invaded Lebanon to eradicate the PLO factions. An internationally brokered deal safeguarded Fatah's eventual relocation to Tunis. While most Fatah institutions were moved to North Africa, some branches were also relocated to Iraq initializing amiable relations between Fatah and Iraq. Nevertheless, a substantial number of Fatah guerillas remained located in Lebanon. One year later, in 1983, a split from within Fatah in Lebanon occurred that led to the establishment of a Syrian backed but ultimately negligible breakaway faction called Fatah al-Intifada.

In remote Tunisia, Fatah and the PLO found themselves on the sidelines of Palestinian activism. In February 1985, Arafat thus concluded the controversial Amman accord, which signaled reconciliation between the PLO and Jordan by calling for a confederation of Palestine and Jordan. This compromise however proved short-lived. Political momentum soon shifted to the West Bank and Gaza. Exiled Fatah leaders were surprised by the first *intifada*, a popular uprising that began in Palestinian refugee camps in 1987. The means of activism including mass demonstrations, general strikes, and incidents of rock throwing were unknown to the guerilla strategies so far undertaken by Fatah. The *intifada* was led by local community councils and the United National Leadership of the Uprising (UNLU). Fatah, like other Palestinian factions, was represented by several local officials, but its leadership in Tunis initially played only a complementary role.

The first *intifada* helped initiate the Israeli–Palestinian negotiations at the 1991 Madrid Peace Conference, and formally ended in 1993 with the signing of the Oslo Accords. Signed by the PLO, the Oslo Accords stipulated the establishment of the Palestinian National Authority (PNA) and at the same time signaled a growing ambiguity from within Fatah, which as a political movement in its own right maintained a more radical approach toward Israel than the PLO. As head of the PLO, Arafat officially recognized "the right of the State of Israel to exist in peace and security" in a letter to the Israeli prime minister Yitzhak Rabin. Also, the PLO's parliament, the PNC, met in Gaza in April 1996 and amended its National Charter "by cancelling the articles that are contrary to the letters exchanged by the PLO and the Government of Israel."[4] Although there is some controversy surrounding whether the Charter was actually changed or simply "frozen," the PLO effectively adopted a new policy vis-a-vis Israel.

In contrast, Fatah's programmatic stance as an independent unit within the PLO remained uncompromising. Officially, Fatah was steadfastly committed to the "complete liberation of Palestine" until its sixth General Conference in 2009 while groups affiliated with Fatah continued to join forces with militant factions, including Hamas and Islamic Jihad, who maintained an adamant opposition to the Oslo Accords. This dissonance between action and rhetoric cost Fatah dearly in credibility and accountability at home and abroad.

After the signing of the Oslo Accords, leading Fatah cadres were allowed to return to the West Bank and Gaza. As head of Fatah and the PLO, Yasir Arafat was given a hero's welcome by thousands of Palestinians in Gaza, where he established his PNA headquarters. Yet the celebrated return of Fatah's exiles also gave rise to tensions with established Fatah cadres on the ground. This so-called young guard had been a driving force behind the *intifada* but now found itself sidelined by the political and military leadership of exiled Fatah members who had not played a key role in the uprising.

The return of Fatah's leadership to the Palestinian Territories marked the beginning of Fatah's transformation from an armed resistance movement to the de facto party of state in the Palestinian Territories. The first elections for the Palestinian Legislative Council (PLC) were held in 1996 and resulted in a landslide victory for Fatah, gaining 71 out of 88 PLC seats. Although Fatah's political victory was secured following decisions by Hamas, the PFLP, and the DFLP to boycott the elections, the organization was widely supported. Fatah was perceived as promoting the national project of state-building and could offer its supporters access to positions of influence in the newly established PNA institutions. Also, Fatah was much better organized than any competing political force. In the first Palestinian cabinet, 18 out of 20 ministers were Fatah-affiliated and in the second, Fatah maintained an overwhelming majority.

Fatah was thus directly associated with the accomplishments and shortcomings of the PNA, including the authority's much-reviled security cooperation with Israeli armed forces. Claims of widespread corruption and nepotism within the PNA and Fatah spread, as did Israeli settlement activities. Many Palestinians increasingly directed their frustration against Fatah. As the main conductor of negotiations with Israel through the PLO, Fatah's popularity and legitimacy increasingly depended on political accomplishments and tangible results from the negotiations. The failure of the 2000 Camp David summit, for which both sides squarely laid blame on the other, thus severely undermined Fatah's standing among Palestinians.

When the leader of the Israeli opposition Ariel Sharon paid a controversial visit to the Temple Mount / *Haram al-Sharif* on September 28, 2000, tensions escalated resulting in the outbreak of the second or *al-Aqsa intifada*.

Politically, Fatah increasingly suffered from internal ideological contradictions as an all-encompassing resistance movement and an essential party of state in the PNA. While it engaged in negotiations with Israel via the PLO and also controlled the PNA as a political party, many of its affiliated groups and its main military organization, the al-Aqsa Martyrs' Brigades, remained keen to challenge Israel militarily. Repeated attacks against Israeli military and civilian targets continued with the al-Aqsa Martyrs' Brigades, at times openly cooperating with Hamas and Islamic Jihad. The Government of Israel accused Fatah's leadership of deliberately orchestrating unrest. Assessments of the extent to which the second *intifada* was instigated by Fatah's leadership greatly differ. US Senator George Mitchell, who headed a task force requested to assess the reasons for the outbreak of violence, came to the conclusion that the Palestinian leadership under Arafat was not personally responsible. It was found that there was "no basis on which to conclude that there was a deliberate plan by the PNA to initiate a campaign of violence at the first opportunity... However, there is also no evidence on which to conclude that the PNA made a consistent effort to contain the demonstrations and control the violence once it began."[5] Notably, Mitchell's assessment only focused on Arafat and the PNA, failing to consider the wider role played by Fatah as a movement.

The second *intifada* again heightened existing tensions within Fatah. Formal hierarchies and long-established leadership institutions such as the Central Committee were challenged by militant Fatah affiliates and especially by younger *intifada* activists. Political rivalries blossomed between the Central Committee and *ad hoc* groups of younger activists. Soon institutions such as the Central Committee and the Revolutionary Council (RC)—by and large Fatah's parliament—ceased to operate in an orderly manner: While the Central Committee, composed of Arafat associates, still convened—often before important PLC sessions—the RC effectively stopped consultations between 2000 and 2004.

As violence escalated in the early months of the second *intifada*, Fatah largely deteriorated into a conglomeration of armed groups.

Fatah-affiliated forces battled the Israeli military, conducting terrorist operations against Israeli civilians, and confronting perceived Palestinian "collaborators," rival Palestinian factions and occasionally PNA security forces. This period also witnessed several lethal clashes between Fatah-affiliated armed factions, including occasional infighting with the al-Aqsa Martyrs' Brigades.

The chaotic situation gradually improved when the Palestinian basic law was amended to allow for the appointment of Mahmoud Abbas as the first prime minister in April 2003, following intense pressure by the United States to reform the PNA and weaken Yasir Arafat. Abbas and his Minister of State for Security Mohammad Dahlan began to disband Fatah's militias as well as other armed groups. Ultimately, Abbas resigned from his post due to tensions with Arafat and was replaced by Ahmad Qurei. After the death of Yasir Arafat in November 2004, he was elected Palestinian president in 2005.

Subsequently, the remaining militant Fatah groups officially disbanded or were integrated into the PNA security apparatus. However, while formal militias including the Tanzim militants led by Marwan Barghouthi or the al-Aqsa Martyrs' Brigades loosely coordinated under the broader *al-Assifa* were factually dissolved, activists and members of these organizations remained active, sporadically resurfacing in the years to come. This was a stark reminder of Fatah's roots as a resistance movement and the organization's unresolved transformation to a political party. The lawless period of the second *intifada* came to an end in March 2005 when 13 Palestinian factions, including Hamas, agreed to a truce with Israel. Abbas had succeeded in bringing the violence of the second *intifada* to a close.

Many Palestinians, however, were unable to disentangle Fatah from the years of corruption, nepotism, internal dissent, undemocratic one-party rule, and political failures of the peace negotiations. A considerable number of Fatah sympathizers also opposed Abbas's policy of engaging and cooperating with Israel. As widespread discontent with the PNA and the faltering negotiation process persisted, Fatah was defeated in the 2006 parliamentary elections.

Certainly, a poorly run election campaign only exacerbated existing turmoil and the party was unable to put forth a single united list. In parallel, Hamas's Change and Reform list ran a well-organized campaign, winning a clear majority of 74 seats compared to Fatah's 45. Western powers, however, refused to recognize the Hamas-led government, and brief but bitter clashes between Hamas and Fatah cadres erupted in the Gaza Strip and in 2007, this resulted in a political split between the West Bank and Gaza. In the West Bank, President Abbas installed a government of "technocrats" officially unaffiliated to Fatah. The movement, however, remained the dominant political force with supporters in key positions of administration in the governorates and the security apparatus.

While Fatah as a party was not part of the "technocratic" government of 2009, several West Bank ministries including the Ministry of Local Government (Khaled al-Qawasmeh), the Ministry of National Economy (Hassan Abu Libdeh), the Ministry of State (Maher Ghneim), the Ministry of the Interior (Said Abu Ali), the Ministry of Prisoners Affairs (Issa Qaraqe), the Ministry of Women Affairs (Rabiha Diab), the Ministry of Transportation (Saadi al-Krunz), and the Ministry of Public Works and Housing (Muhammad Shtayyeh) were led by Fatah party members. In turn, Gaza was ruled by Fatah's chief rival, Hamas.

Fatah's defeat at the polls and expulsion from Gaza dealt severe blows to its legitimacy. Mahmoud Abbas was in dire need of at least symbolic successes and a renewal of his political mandate. With another round of PLC elections, both unfeasible and politically risky, the president focused on reforming Fatah. The party had not held a general conference, Fatah's highest decision-making body, in more than two decades, with leadership positions being filled by executive appointments rather than through elections. By 2003, Fatah was a weakened shell of its former past: 17 of the 22 members of the Central Committee remained living while only 12 resided permanently in the Palestinian Territories, and a number suffered from serious medical conditions, which effectively prevented any actual participation in political affairs. Most members of the committee were beyond the age of 65. The situation in the Revolutionary Council was similar; members had typically been appointed by Arafat and lacked grassroots political support. Meetings took place irregularly if at all. Nevertheless, when Abbas announced that Fatah's long overdue sixth General Conference would be held in Bethlehem in 2009 he was met with strong opposition from the remaining leadership in Tunis and homegrown opponents who feared for their positions.

At the sixth General Conference, party members took several concrete steps toward renewing Fatah and toward transforming the movement into a more streamlined political party focusing first and foremost on the PNA. A new party program was adopted that, while it did not abrogate "armed struggle," emphasized nonviolent means of resistance. The new political platform asserts that "the Palestinian people's right to practice armed resistance against the military occupation of their land remains a constant right confirmed by international law." But the program further stipulates that "Fatah has always rejected targeting civilians anywhere" and points out that "the selection of struggle methods...depends on the necessities of safeguarding the calculations of power equations." The new Fatah program commends nonviolent resistance as practiced in several locations in the West Bank and for the first time unambiguously calls for the establishment of a Palestinian state alongside Israel's pre-1967 borders. Unlike the Declaration of Principles (DoP) signed by the PLO, however, the movement's program does not formally recognize the State of Israel and unequivocally "rejects the call to recognize Israel as a 'Jewish State'."[6]

At the conference, Fatah also updated its Internal Charter from 1964, which deals with the institutional prerogatives of the movement and defines the roles and responsibilities of party institutions. In its 2009 version several controversial statements were deleted, including the following, which in 1964 defined Fatah's position on Israel and armed resistance:

- Article (7) The Zionist Movement is racial, colonial, and aggressive in ideology, goals, organization, and method.
- Article (8) The Israeli existence in Palestine is a Zionist invasion with a colonial expansive base, and it is a natural ally to colonialism and international imperialism.
- Article (12) Complete liberation of Palestine, and eradication of Zionist economic, political, military, and cultural existence is a goal of the movement.[7]

Clearly, elections in Bethlehem did not meet international standards of transparency. Delegates were elected *and* appointed from the top, votes were sold, and some successful candidates were silently removed from their elected positions.

However, despite these shortcomings, the congress changed the face of Fatah's leadership, bringing a new generation of activists into positions of power. In the Central Committee, 14 of 17 previous members were replaced with representatives from a younger generation.

Notably, Hamas refused to grant exit visas to Fatah delegates from Gaza, and the Palestinian Diaspora was barely represented at the conference. The new leadership hailed mostly from the West Bank, putting an end to years of internal power struggles between the "old" and the "young guard," the "outside" and "inside" leadership. This resulted in a severe weakening of influence from Fatah's Diaspora and brought

Fatah closer to a streamlined political party focusing exclusively on its role in the PNA. Notably, the convention also revitalized defunct party institutions and relevant inner-party organizations restarted convening for regular meetings immediately after the congress.

While the conference was generally but not exclusively received positively in the Palestinian Territories, improving Fatah's reputation among Palestinians continued to depend on actual political results outside the party's internal proceedings. Fatah's leadership continued to fail to make progress in negotiations with Israel, despite indications that the organization was prepared to make far-reaching compromises. In parallel, expansions of Israeli settlements continued. In 2011, *al-Jazeera* published the leaked Palestine Papers, which detailed the closed-door discussions between PLO and Israeli negotiators. Mahmoud Abbas and Fatah's inner circle were widely criticized by both Islamist and secular opposition figures for "selling out" Palestinian rights.

To the detriment of many Fatah leaders, positive developments in the West Bank such as significant economic growth between the end of the second *intifada* and 2011 and the process of institution-building initiated by the politically independent prime minister Salam Fayyad have typically not been associated with Fatah. What has been associated with the party is the quasi-authoritarian rule of Fatah-affiliated security services in the West Bank. Since 2006, the PNA in Ramallah has governed mostly by presidential decree. Its elected institutions, such as the PLC, have stopped convening due to the division with Hamas, and the PNA suffers from a notable lack of democratic legitimacy.

Also, Fatah and Abbas came under criticism for failing to resolve the breach with Hamas. Inspired by the events of the Arab Spring, thousands of Palestinians, most of them young, took to the streets at the beginning of 2011 to protest the national division, outspokenly criticizing the two parties' refusal to reconcile. The reconciliation agreements signed between Fatah and Hamas in Cairo in May 2011 and Doha in 2012 remained, at the time of writing, unimplemented. The parties' inability to agree on the terms of a national unity government and eventual legislative elections attested to their reluctance to seriously consider divisions of power and accept the risk of an eventual loss of influence following new elections.

Even at the municipality level, the holding of elections has proved difficult. In 2011, Fatah failed to come up with unified candidate lists for scheduled local elections. Reminiscent of the chaos prior to the 2006 elections, Fatah candidates were vying against other Fatah candidates for desirable positions. The party ultimately chose, again, to push for a postponement of the elections—a sober reminder of the internal challenges that continue to plague Fatah as a political party.

In May 2012, President Mahmoud Abbas swore in a new cabinet in the West Bank. While the new government under an extension of Premier Salam Fayyad's term was perceived as widening the gap between West Bank and Gaza, the new government also significantly bolstered the role of Fatah in the PNA. The 2012 cabinet was composed of 13 Fatah-affiliated ministers (from a total of 26 cabinet members). The posts of cabinet secretary (Naim Abu al-Humos), minister of the environment (Yousef Abu Safieh), minister of the interior (Said Abu Ali), minister of local governance (Khaled al-Qawasmeh), minister of public work and Housing (Maher Ghneim), minister of women's affairs (Rabeha Diab), minister of prisoner's affairs (Issa Qaraqe), minister of the economy (Jawad al-Naji), minister of tourism (Rula Maayah), minister of Jerusalem affairs (Adnan Husseini), minister of justice (Ali Muhanna), minister of agriculture (Waleed Assaf), and minister of transportation (Ali Abu Zuhri) were filled by Fatah members. The comprehensive cabinet reshuffle essentially put an end to years of "technocratic" governments that operated largely without formalized Fatah representation in the West Bank. Most PNA governors in the West Bank also maintained affiliation to Fatah, once again underlining the position of Fatah as the de facto party of state in the West Bank.

This, however, is anything but a comfortable position. While close affiliation of Fatah with the West Bank PNA and the PLO certainly allows the party to generate and benefit from loyalty based on patronage, it also comes at a steep price to political legitimacy. The limitations of PNA sovereignty and the continued lack of progress in a negotiated solution to the conflict with Israel have prevented Fatah from fulfilling its fundamental political mandate of bringing about Palestinian independence. This poses a long-term strategic challenge for Fatah and remains the key obstacle to genuine political approval.[8]

Yasir Arafat

To describe Yasir Arafat as "controversial" would be an understatement. "Terrorist," "President," and Nobel laureate; there exists no shortage of conflicting political labels. In the Palestinian Territories, Arafat's status has been less ambiguous. His role has been compared to that of a national secular saint.

According to most accounts, Yasir Arafat was born in Cairo in 1929. As a student at the Fuad University (today Cairo University), Arafat was exposed to Arab nationalism and was allegedly involved in smuggling weapons into Mandate-era Palestine. When the Arab–Israeli war of 1948 broke out, he purportedly joined ranks with the Egyptian Muslim Brotherhood in the Gaza Strip. Following the Arab defeat, Arafat returned to Cairo and obtained a degree in civil engineering. Between 1952 and 1956, he headed the General Union of Palestinian Students, and he served in the Egyptian army during the 1956 Suez Crisis.

By the time he moved to Kuwait, Arafat had given up on the widespread view at the time that only pan-Arab forces could achieve the "complete liberation of Palestine," as the Fatah Constitution of 1964 would later describe.[9] Instead, Arafat was convinced that Palestinians should take up their own struggle, independent of the Arab states and should bring about Arab unity through the realization of Palestinian "liberation." Along with Salah Khalaf and Khalil al-Wazir (Abu Jihad), he established a Palestinian refugee organization — a precursor to Fatah. According to contemporaries, Arafat exercised strong control over the organization from the very beginning.

Starting in 1964/1965, Fatah commandos carried out a number of guerilla attacks in Israel, some of which were allegedly led by Arafat himself. Immediately following the defeat of Arab armies in the 1967 Six Day War, Arafat seized the opportunity to relocate to the occupied West Bank and set up Fatah offices in different locations in the West Bank and Jerusalem. Fatah's self-confident and confrontational stance vis-a-vis Israel attracted new supporters and earned Arafat international recognition. In 1967 PLO chairman Yahia Hammuda formally requested that Fatah join the PLO, and Egyptian president Gamal Abdel Nasser conferred status and legitimacy on Arafat by recognizing him as the Palestinian leader.

Large-scale Israeli military operations in response to Fatah's guerrilla tactics in the West Bank soon compelled Arafat to relocate to Jordan, where Fatah's achievements in the 1968 Battle of Karameh rendered him a hero among many Palestinians. Whether he actually fought in Karameh, though, remains subject of speculation. The global attention the battle garnered gave such a boost to Fatah that Arafat soon appeared on the cover of *Time* magazine and, in 1969, succeeded Hammuda as the PLO's chairman, an office Arafat held until his death in 2004.

In Jordan, the PLO under Arafat began to establish state-like institutions that challenged King Hussein's authority. To quell growing tensions, the King of Jordan offered Arafat the post of prime minister but was rebuffed. Meanwhile, Palestinian operations targeting Israel continued to be launched from Jordanian soil, endangering a precarious calm between Jordan and Israel. King Hussein's response was the Black September, which forced Arafat to reestablish the PLO in Lebanon.

With the relocation to Lebanon, militants close to Fatah started to carry out terrorist attacks in Western countries. Groups such as the Black September Organization, which gained notoriety for its attack on Israeli athletes during the 1972 Olympic Games in Munich, were initially part of Fatah (Black September and its affiliated splinter group the Fatah Revolutionary Council were expelled from the PLO in 1974). Arafat failed to condemn some of these actions, occasionally sending conflicting messages to English- and Arabic-speaking audiences. This resulted in allegations that Fatah had orchestrated the violence and damaged Arafat's reputation in the West. Many Palestinians, though, praised Arafat for successfully bringing attention to the Palestinian cause.

In 1974 the PLO issued the Ten Point Program, which stipulated the establishment of an "independent combatant national authority for the people over every part of Palestinian territory that is liberated."[10] That same year, Arafat gave a now famous speech before the plenary session of the UN General Assembly in which his metaphor of "bearing an olive branch and a freedom fighter's gun" effectively appealed to the global public not to "let the olive branch fall from his hand."[11] The speech was met with a surge of international empathy for Palestinian political ambitions with the UN General Assembly recognizing "the right of the Palestinian people to sovereignty and national independence" and the PLO gaining observer status at the international organization.

On the ground in the Palestinian Territories, however, the situation deteriorated. Arafat and the PLO were forced in August of 1982 to flee Lebanon to Tunis after two months of Israeli bombardment. In 1985, Arafat survived an attack of the Israeli airforce on the PLO headquarters in Tunis, which further heightened his fame among Palestinians. However, exile in Tunisia resulted in a notable loss of influence over developments in the West Bank and Gaza.

It was Arafat's desire to reestablish his primacy within Palestinian politics that, many believe, motivated him to begin to pursue diplomatic engagement with Israel. In 1988 Arafat again addressed the UN General Assembly, acknowledging "Israel's right to exist in peace and security," and condemning "terrorism in all its forms."[12] Notably, the United

States refused to grant Arafat a visa to address the General Assembly in New York and his speech was therefore held in Geneva rather than New York. Arafat's formal commitment to a Two-State Solution was acclaimed in the West and paved the way for Israeli–Palestinian peace negotiations first in Madrid and subsequently in Oslo.

Despite Arafat's mollified rhetoric, he remained controversial. During the Second Gulf War, he declared his solidarity with Saddam Hussein. In acknowledgment of long-standing Iraqi support for Palestinians, Arafat opposed Western military intervention against Iraq. The consequences were grave: several Arab states discontinued their financial support of the PLO and hundreds of thousands of Palestinians were forced to leave Gulf States such as Kuwait, where they had found employment and reestablished their lives.

Arafat's amiable relations with Iraq did not prevent the Israeli government from entering into secret negotiations with the PLO leadership in 1993. The signing of the Oslo Accords allowed for Arafat's triumphant return to the Palestinian Territories on July 1, 1994 following 25 years in exile. While the actual documents were signed by Mahmoud Abbas on behalf of the PLO, Arafat received credit for the Oslo Accords. In 1994 he was awarded the Nobel Peace Prize along with Israeli prime minister Yitzhak Rabin and then foreign minister Shimon Peres.

However, in the ensuing years Arafat's leadership met with less and less international praise. In 1996, Arafat was democratically elected President of the PNA with 88 percent of the total vote. This impressive victory, however, was qualified by the fact that major opponents such as Hamas boycotted the vote. Arafat used his position as head of the PLO and newly established PNA to create a paternalistic, nontransparent, and often corrupt political system not unlike other one-party regimes in the Middle East. Formalized political procedures were routinely circumvented, democratic decisions ignored and opponents were co-opted or sidelined.

Somewhat ironically, Arafat's style of leadership, which included consistent attempts to fragment oppositional groups, had through years of exile protected his position and (some would argue) the very survival of Fatah. Now, this style of governance severely hampered the establishment of a functioning democratic political system. Fatah was increasingly viewed as corrupt and nepotistic. In 1999, several prominent Palestinian intellectuals and political leaders accused the PNA of being "corrupt and unjust" and were summarily arrested by Palestinian security forces.

Criticism of Arafat did not stem solely from mismanagement of the PNA. Relations with Israel failed to provide Arafat with diplomatic gains that could be translated into much needed political capital. The result was a growing disparity between Palestinians' personal affection for Arafat and their disillusionment with the movement that he led.

The Camp David peace talks in 2000 and the last-ditch efforts to strike a deal at Taba in 2001 gave rise to further controversy. According to Israeli and American accounts, Arafat refused to embrace a peace offer made by Prime Minister Ehud Barak and was accused by US president Bill Clinton of having turned his presidency into a political "failure." In Arafat's view, however, Barak's offer was unacceptable and far from generous as it did not allow for full sovereignty of a Palestinian state. The diplomatic failure contributed to the intensification of the second *intifada*.

This furthermore triggered heightened animosity as the Israeli Army accused Arafat of coordinating the eruption of violence, confining him to his headquarters in Ramallah. For weeks, he remained in the basement of his government compound as the building was held under siege. Israeli prime minister Sharon ordered him to leave the Palestinian Territories, at which point Arafat rebuffed, asserting that he would "rather die than surrender."[13] US president George W. Bush accused Arafat of having "never played a role of someone who can be trusted," declared him irrelevant and called for an alternative Palestinian leadership.[14] Arafat was eventually forced to cede much of his power, when he bowed to US demands to hand over important presidential prerogatives to a newly established office of prime minister, a post filled by Mahmoud Abbas, who until then had been second in command in the PLO.

In October 2004, Arafat was medically evacuated to the Percy Military Teaching Hospital in France to undergo medical treatment; he passed away on November 11, 2004. Among Palestinians, rumors quickly spread that his death had not resulted from natural causes. He is currently buried adjacent to his former headquarters in Ramallah, until his resting place can be transferred to Jerusalem, as was his wish.

Arafat's death resulted in a power vacuum in Palestinian politics that has only recently been partially filled by Mahmoud Abbas. In death, as in life, he remains a controversial figure, but undeniably a powerful unifying force for Palestinians around the world. For many, he remains a much admired and humble leader and the very symbol of the Palestinian pursuit of independence.

Mahmoud Abbas

After the death of Yasir Arafat in 2004, Mahmoud Abbas took over as president of the PNA, chairman of the PLO, and leader of Fatah. Long perceived as indecisive and prone to falter under pressure, in 2011 Abbas boosted his popularity among Palestinians by applying for UN membership for the State of Palestine in defiance of heavy international pressure.

Mahmoud Abbas was born in Safed in the Northern Galilee in 1935 and is among the first generation of Fatah activists. In 1948, Abbas fled to Syria and became politically active in the mid-1950s. He lived for a time in Qatar, where he gained experience working as an officer in the civil service and established a wide political network of Palestinian activists in the Gulf. Abbas gradually became an influential figure within Fatah and the PLO, first as a fundraiser prior to being appointed head of the PLO's Department for National and International Relations in 1980.

Abbas completed a controversial doctoral dissertation entitled "The Secret Relationship between Nazism and Zionism" in Moscow in 1982. Despite this inflammatory academic work, he was known as a pragmatist and established dialogues with Jewish left-wing movements. These contacts proved vital when Israeli–Palestinian peace talks were launched in the early 1990s. In 1988 the PLO Executive Committee appointed Abbas chairman of the Occupied Territories portfolio, and in 1996 he was elected secretary general of the PLO's Executive Committee, emerging as Yasir Arafat's deputy. In this capacity, Abbas co-signed the Declaration of Principles in September 1993 on behalf of the PLO, a credit often mistakenly assigned to Yasir Arafat. An unflagging supporter of the Oslo Process, Abbas is intimately associated by Palestinians with the accords and their outcomes.

Abbas did not arrive at the first tier of Palestinian politics until the second *intifada*. The United States and Israel were increasingly unwilling to deal with PNA president Yasir Arafat and pressured him to create the office of the prime minister for the PNA to dilute his influence. To take up the new post, Abbas in March 2003 was called back to the West Bank from Tunis, where Arafat had sent him three years earlier. With the support from the Minister of State for Security, Mohammad Dahlan, Abbas attempted to restore a Palestinian monopoly of power in the areas under his control by corralling armed militias.

As prime minister, Abbas from the outset publicly condemned terrorist operations and focused on diplomatic initiatives such as the US-backed Road Map for Peace of 2003. However, less than half a year into his term, Abbas resigned and was replaced by Ahmad Qurei. Abbas justified his resignation by pointing at the persisting diplomatic stalemate. However, a relentless power struggle with Arafat is widely believed to be the main reason for this decision.

When Yasir Arafat died in November 2004, Fatah's Central Committee in the absence of party elections declared Abbas "leader of Fatah," despite the fact that such an office was not defined in Fatah's Internal Charter. He was elected president of the PNA in January 2005, winning 62 percent of the vote (Hamas and the PFLP had boycotted the elections). Abbas scored an early success when a March 2005 informal truce between Israel and 13 Palestinian factions effectively ended the second *intifada*.

As Abbas gained popularity in the West, he increasingly lost standing and legitimacy among Palestinians. Responding to internal pressure from Fatah following the party's poor showing in the 2006 legislative elections, Abbas convened Fatah's sixth General Conference in 2009. Here, Abbas managed to solidify his leadership position within the movement and "freed himself from the ghost of Arafat," as one Palestinian observer described. However, the longer a substantial breakthrough in peace negotiations with Israel remained unattainable, the louder voices of internal Palestinian criticism for the president grew. Opposition to Abbas reached a peak following the Gaza War of 2008–2009.

In October 2009, Abbas bowed to US pressure and agreed to postpone a UN debate on the Goldstone Report, which accused the Israeli army and Hamas militants of war crimes and crimes against humanity. Many Palestinians saw this as tantamount to collaborating with Israel. A little over a year later, in early 2011, widespread anger was sparked again among Palestinians when the so-called Palestine Papers, leaked by *al-Jazeera*, revealed that Abbas and his chief negotiator Saeb Erekat had been willing to cede large parts of the West Bank and East Jerusalem to Israel. More importantly, Abbas seemed ready to accept a dramatic compromise concerning the number of refugees who would be allowed to return to Israel.

Abbas now took, to the surprise of many, a more uncompromising stance, ruling out negotiations with Israel as long as settlement construction continued in the Palestinian Territories. His resolve to apply for UN membership in September 2011 resulted in a significant, temporary surge in domestic popularity, as well as an increase in criticism from Israel. In December 2011, Israeli foreign minister Avigdor Lieberman argued that Abbas "proves time after time that he is not a partner for anything."[15]

Abbas's tenure as president of the PNA has been clouded by a lack of internal democracy, corruption allegations against his sons, repeated military clashes between Israel and Hamas, and (first and foremost) by the hostile division between Hamas and Fatah. The reconciliation agreement signed by Abbas and Khaled Mashal in Cairo in May 2011 and reaffirmed in Doha in February 2012 is intended to end the split and result in Palestinian elections. These elections are crucial to Abbas's legitimacy, particularly given the expiration of his democratic mandate in 2009. Abbas himself has repeatedly stated that he will not run for reelection. It remains to be seen if he will follow through on this pronouncement particularly given that Fatah's Revolutionary Council voted unanimously in February 2012 to nominate Mahmoud Abbas as Fatah's presidential candidate in the next elections.

Marwan Barghouthi

Marwan Barghouthi is arguably the most popular of Fatah's "young guard." He was a prominent leader of the second intifada and is serving five consecutive life sentences for involvement in the murder of five Israeli citizens. His imprisonment has prompted some supporters to refer to him as "Palestine's Mandela." Despite his incarceration, Barghouthi continues to play a prominent role in Palestinian domestic politics and in 2009 was elected to Fatah's Central Committee.

Born in 1958 (or 1959 according to some accounts) in the West Bank village of Kobar, Marwan Barghouthi joined Fatah as a teenager, co-founded Fatah's youth wing, Shabibe, and was first arrested by Israeli authorities on charges of being a member of an armed Palestinian group in 1976. Numerous arrests were to follow.

In 1983, Barghouthi began studying history and political science at Birzeit University near Ramallah and in October 1984 married Fadwa Ibrahim who would later on occasion serve as his informal spokesperson. Barghouthi headed Birzeit's Student Council, a position from which he gradually emerged as a leading member of Fatah's "young guard." Unlike Fatah's founding figures, who had been exiled for decades, these young leaders were deeply rooted in the West Bank and Gaza.

Barghouthi was one of the orchestrators of the first *intifada* in the West Bank, during which he was arrested and deported to Jordan. From Amman and later from exile in Tunisia, Barghouthi continued to coordinate *intifada* operations. Based on his reputation as a charismatic and personally committed activist, he was the youngest party leader ever elected to the Fatah Revolutionary Council.

In 1994, Barghouthi returned to the West Bank, a move that was made possible by the signing of the Oslo Accords. Two weeks after his return he was appointed Fatah's secretary general in the West Bank. There, Barghouthi established the West Bank Fatah Higher Committee, which focused on transforming Fatah into a political party with strong links to civil society. Barghouthi organized more than 150 local and district internal Fatah elections and repeatedly called for the long-delayed sixth General Conference. Unsurprisingly, this heightened tensions between Barghouthi and influential members of Fatah's "old guard," who were wary of democratic procedures that could very well jeopardize their positions. In the 1996 PLC elections, Barghouthi was omitted from Fatah's electoral list but nevertheless won a seat as an independent candidate representing the Ramallah district.

Following his election to the PLC, Barghouthi gained further popularity by focusing on grassroots activism and openly expressing dissatisfaction with the established PNA leadership. As early as 1998, Barghouthi argued for a national unity government to include Hamas. He called for investigations into charges of PNA corruption and human rights abuses by the president's security services. However, his relationship with Yasir Arafat has persistently been a matter of some contention. Reports of Arafat's attempts to sideline Barghouthi conflict with the public statements of praise. Many Fatah members are convinced that Arafat considered Barghouthi a possible successor.

As with many Palestinians, Barghouthi's initial support of the Oslo Accords eventually gave way to doubts and ultimately rejection. In the early 1990s he established close contacts with Israeli activists and decision makers, mostly from the left. By 1998, however, he vocally and publicly supported Two-State Solution, but began expressing concern that the Oslo approach would not lead to Palestinian statehood. He questioned the fundamental fact concerning whether Israel was willing to reach a negotiated settlement. In an op-ed in the January 2002 edition of the *Washington Post*, Barghouthi expressed his disillusionment with the Peace Process, stating that he had "no faith in the United States," promised "to resist the Israeli occupation" and to "fight for freedom." He wrote that "if Palestinians are expected to negotiate under occupation, then Israel must be expected to negotiate as we resist that occupation."[16] He called on the PLO leadership to cease all negotiations with Israel until all settlement construction halted.

As settlement activities continued under the Labor and the Likud-led governments of Israel, Barghouthi advocated for a more confrontational approach toward Israel and became one of the most active leaders of the second *intifada*. Appointed the head of the West Bank Steering Committee coordinating the uprising, he gave speeches at demonstrations and funerals and advocated in the media for the Palestinian cause. More importantly, he also led the Fatah-affiliated Tanzim militant group, which engaged in attacks against the Israeli military and attacks on Israeli settlements in the West Bank. He accused Israelis and Palestinians who called for renewed negotiations of being naïve, and condemned Israelis for "killing people on the ground day by day" while continuing to live "a secure life in Tel Aviv."[17]

Thus, for many Israelis, Barghouthi became the face of the second *intifada*. Israel retaliated by firing missiles at his convoy in April 2001, sending Barghouthi underground. Six weeks later, a warrant was issued for his arrest. The Israeli army claimed he was the founder and leader of Fatah's al-Aqsa Martyrs' Brigades, which had carried out several attacks on Israeli soldiers and civilians, a charge Barghouthi denied. In August 2002, Barghouti was arrested and tried. In a court proceeding Barghouthi denounced as a "show trial," a statement supported by the Inter-Parliamentary Union (an international organization representing national parliaments from 157 countries), which described the trial as "unfair," Barghouti was sentenced to five consecutive life terms in June 2004.[18]

Barghouthi remains an influential voice in Palestinian politics despite his incarceration. He played a key role in persuading the leadership of Hamas and Islamic Jihad to agree to a temporary ceasefire with Israel in July 2004. He was also one of the architects of and signatories to the National Conciliation Document of the Prisoners. Signed by members of all major Palestinian factions in May 2006, the document was meant to pave the way to a national unity government. In 2011, Barghouthi called the US intention to veto the Palestinian bid for membership at the UN an act of "terrorism," and has repeatedly called for a popular (nonviolent) uprising against the Israeli occupation of the West Bank.[19]

Barghouthi completed his PhD in political science under incarceration. His doctoral dissertation discusses the functions and challenges of the PLC. Prior to the 2006 legislative elections, Barghouthi declared that he would not run on Fatah's list, which was selected by the Central Committee.

He instead announced that he would join an independent list of the "young guard" known as *al-Mustaqbal* (The Future), which comprised prominent Fatah leaders such as Mohammad Dahlan. A split within Fatah was finally prevented by Mahmoud Abbas, who agreed to put forth a list headed by Barghouthi. Barghouthi's significant base of support secured him a seat in Fatah's Central Committee during the party's sixth General Conference in 2009, although popularity did not extend to his associates, who were mostly shut out of positions of influence.

Although Hamas leader Khaled Mashal promised to reject proposed prisoner-swaps that did not include Barghouthi, in October 2011, when 1,027 Palestinian prisoners were exchanged for captured Israeli soldier Gilad Shalit, Barghouthi remained at Nafha Prison in the Negev, where he continues to serve his sentence.

Barghouthi is thought to be one of the few Palestinian leaders who could unite the disparate Palestinian factions and is the only Fatah leader aside from Abbas who, according to numerous polls, could win a presidential election at present. However, the pursuit of these political aspirations depends on securing Barghouthi's early release from prison.

★ ★ ★

Interviews with Fatah Decision Makers

The following interviews were held with a cross section of Fatah's current leadership. Nabil Shaath is a senior member of Fatah's Central Committee. He has held numerous cabinet positions in the PNA including foreign minister (2003 to 2005), a short stint as acting prime minister (December 2005), and has represented Palestinians as chief negotiator in numerous rounds of negotiations with Israel. He is considered a close confidant of President Mahmoud Abbas.

In contrast, Sabri Saidam represents the "young guard" of Fatah. He previously served as PNA minister of telecommunications (2005–2006) and as a presidential advisor in the same field. In Fatah's sixth General Conference 2009, Saidam gained a seat in the Revolutionary Council. He currently serves as the council's deputy secretary general. In March 2011, Saidam participated in an event commemorating Fatah militant Dalal Mughrabi who participated in the 1978 Coastal Road Massacre and was subsequently accused of praising terrorism.

Amal Hamad is a leading Fatah activist from Gaza and one of the few women in an elevated leadership position within Fatah. In 2012 she was elected to replace Mohammad Dahlan as a member of the Central Committee. Previously, she served as second deputy secretary general of the Revolutionary Council. She is currently the youngest and only female member of the Central Committee.

Interview with Nabil Shaath, Member of Fatah's Central Committee

In what ways is Fatah a unique force within Palestinian politics?
Fatah differs from all other Palestinian parties in the way it was formed, has acted and in the way it has delivered on its promises. It started as a liberation movement that was inspired by the Vietnamese and Algerian anticolonial movements, and has been the only movement to succeed in uniting rightist and leftist activists focusing on the common struggle against the occupation. This can be seen in the original leadership that consisted of members of the Muslim Brotherhood, the pan-Arab Baath Party, and the Palestinian left.

Over the years, Fatah came to be seen as *the* national Palestinian movement, although it still considers itself part of the Arab nation. In its authoritarian regional environment, Fatah has from the very beginning been developing internal democratic structures, electing its main bodies like the Central Committee. The focus on the liberation of Palestine called for the development of an elaborate ideology. At present, I would describe Fatah as an Arab Social Democratic Party. Although Islam always played an influential role within Fatah, the movement opted for a secular ideology willing to embrace Christians and Jews as well.

Fatah is often associated with corruption and nontransparent structures. How has the party responded to these charges?
The shortcomings were caused by the political circumstances between 1989 and 2009. In the past two decades, the Palestinians witnessed grave instability caused by the years of hope in the course of the Oslo process and the disappointments that followed. Fatah was fully preoccupied with repressive Israeli policies such as the virtual imprisonment of Yasir Arafat in his Ramallah headquarters. Because of its responsibilities within the Palestinian National Authority, Fatah neglected its own political program and structure.

However, the major reason why Fatah has been associated with corruption recently was the infiltration of the movement by "security" forces. These semi-independent groups were responsible for 90 percent of the corruption. To rein in the security forces and to separate them from civil institutions have been Fatah's main achievements in the past years. The sixth General Conference in Bethlehem added to this positive development.

How would you describe the results of the General Conference?

The conference marked the return of elective democracy to Fatah. By electing a new Central Committee and a new Revolutionary Council, the movement regained its democratic legitimacy. Fatah's political and organizational programs were modernized and have steered the party into a new direction.

How does Fatah assess the prospects for a Two-State Solution?

Even at the end of the 1960s, I dreamed of a secular Jewish–Christian–Muslim binational state. The idea is not far-fetched—just look at South Africa after the end of the Apartheid regime. I was the one to write a manifesto advocating this concept but only very few Jewish Israelis were—and until today are—accepting such a scenario. For them, this is a "demographic bomb." That is the reason why there is no other option but a Two-State Solution. After establishing two states, we could possibly enter into negotiations on forming one binational state. But as stated in our party platform: Fatah works for the establishment of a Palestinian state on the 1967 borders.

What is Fatah's stance on nonviolent resistance?

Nonviolent resistance was applied in Palestine between 1982 and 1988 even though most people did not refer to an elaborated theory of nonviolence. In Fatah's current party program, this method of resistance has been institutionalized as one of the movement's doctrines. Adopting nonviolent resistance or popular resistance after armed resistance proved unsuccessful shows Fatah's creativity and flexibility in terms of its strategies to overcome the occupation.

How does Fatah view the repercussions of the Arab Spring and particularly regime change in Cairo?

A stronger and a more progressive Egypt is likely to help our bargaining power with Israel in any future negotiations. That seems clear. Also, regime change in Cairo could well help in bringing about a more constructive Israeli position in core questions. It is rather simple: A disunited Egypt will not be helpful. Of course, many questions are still unanswered: Will Israel lose Egypt? Will that perhaps make its leadership less inclined to compromise? Essentially, our perception is defined by a mixture of joy and concerns.

Interview with Sabri Saidam, Deputy Secretary General of the Revolutionary Council

How did the General Congress in Bethlehem in 2009 address Fatah's internal divisions?

Considering the size of the movement the question of how to command and control different streams within Fatah is difficult to solve. This has given way to corruption and illnesses that have been clinging to the body of Fatah. Fatah has also been shaken by the political divide within Palestinian ranks. Although there have been different opinions and even infightings, there has never been a political division of the Palestinian Resistance Movement. So after years in the waiting, the General Congress finally took place. At the same time, we must differentiate between nostalgia and the reality on the ground. The results have fallen short of expectations and demands of our people.

How does Fatah attempt to build political confidence?

One of the measures was the decision not to give in to US pressure and return to the negotiation table without a settlement freeze. Another one was to tackle corruption through the establishment of investigatory committees, one of them dealing with Mohammad Dahlan's former Fatah leader in the Gaza Strip. We also question critically why, for example, local elections have not been held on time. In this respect, my colleagues in the Fatah Revolutionary Council and I are adamant to report any findings to our supporters and to the nation at large—and always in a transparent way.

Reconciliation efforts between Hamas and Fatah are also a way to regain trust among Palestinians. We will reconfirm our commitment to press the UN Security Council on reaffirming previously passed resolutions on the illegality of settlements. The recognition of a Palestinian state, mainly by Latin American countries, is a sign of trust from the outside world in this respect.

What is Fatah's solution to the Israeli–Palestinian conflict?

Our party platform calls for the "right to establish a sovereign and independent state on the land occupied by Israel in 1967." However, what is happening on the ground annihilates the chances of establishing an independent Palestinian state. A state is not only about identity but also about contiguity. And there will not be any solution without overcoming the internal divide in Palestine, without bridging the gap between Hamas and Fatah. The reconciliation process is not yet concluded.

Fatah members from Gaza are underrepresented in institutions like the Central Committee and the Revolutionary Council. Has the movement given up on Gaza?

Not at all. There has never been representation in Fatah based on geography. The people elected in the General Conference were not elected according to proportions. Fatah's situation in Gaza was extremely difficult before the reconciliation agreement in Cairo, when there was a total ban of the movement. No public meetings were allowed so the public profile of parties other than Hamas disappeared. Therefore one might get the impression that Fatah is not present in Gaza. Certainly Gaza is constantly on our agenda, and much of the discussion in the Revolutionary Council centers around it.

How does Fatah assess the prospects of nonviolent resistance?

I have to admit that most Palestinian factions had doubts as to whether popular struggle will yield any positive results. But the existing successes have led many Palestinians to reconsider popular struggle as an important mode of resistance. Fatah cannot claim to be the founder of popular resistance but we can now claim to be part of it.

Another such mode of resistance is the boycott of settlement products. The PNA passed a law boycotting such products. These nonviolent and peaceful forms also seem to have won the support of the international community. Perhaps the reason that nonviolent resistance has gone so far is because it is nonfactional and not part of one single party.

But you personally have been accused of praising terrorism. Is armed resistance still a viable strategy for Fatah?

I do not think armed resistance is a viable strategy. That said, I cannot deny that a large sector of Palestinian society considers armed resistance one of many options, believing that Israel will only give in to military pressure.

Do exiled politicians within Fatah still play a leading role?

I would personally like to see them play a role but frankly speaking they do not. There have been recent expressions of discontent among some cadres in Jordan but they do not carry enough weight to cause any alarm within Fatah. The reason is the fact that the Palestinian Diaspora has been marginalized since the PLO moved back to Palestine.

How does Fatah perceive Prime Minister Salam Fayyad?

There is a huge debate about Fayyad within Fatah. The widespread perception within the movement is that Fatah is blamed for anything bad happening, whereas any success is attributed to Fayyad. This causes considerable dismay since we are offering a political umbrella and our blessing to this government which also benefits from our structures.

Another issue is that Fatah has always maintained the necessity of simultaneous liberation and development. The Fayyad government has reversed the priorities in favor of development, which makes his entire project questionable. For many years we have focused on development—with the help of European and American tax payers—but these efforts were literally bulldozed by the Israeli military in repeated phases of confrontation. So development without political progress is worthless.

In general, Fayyad is a competent man who has achieved successes in the West Bank. But the fact that the positive results are restricted to the West Bank while East Jerusalem and Gaza are neglected aggravates tensions.

What is the current role of Fatah's Revolutionary Council?

The debates within the Revolutionary Council qualify the body to be a kind of Fatah Parliament. The Revolutionary Council leaves no stone unturned—all important matters are discussed frankly. The problem is not the discussions or resolutions adopted by the Revolutionary Council but the implementation of its recommendations by the Central Committee.

The relationship between the two bodies is really competitive. While in the past, the Central Committee decisions were never questioned by the Revolutionary Council, this has changed tremendously since the General Congress in 2009. There is much heated debate about the role of the Central Committee since in theory, according to Fatah's constitution, the Revolutionary Council is the movement's highest authority the moment it opens its session. In this respect we need further reforms within Fatah.

Can you elaborate on the role of women within the movement?

There is intense debate in the Revolutionary Council about this. Most members argue that women should not accept quotas but rise in the hierarchy solely through their qualifications and abilities. Although I oppose quotas for women since regional quotas for Gaza and the West Bank are more important in my eyes, I am happy with women receiving proportional representation in line with the ratio of men and women who attended the General Congress in 2009. Out of the 2,300 party members who attended, only 50 or 60 were women. So, 12 female members in the Revolutionary Council in total are not bad, although of course not wholly satisfactory.

Palestine has a lot of striking examples of women in leading positions. Take the female ministers in the Fayyad government. Take Lana Abu Hijla who heads the Cooperative Housing Foundation or Huda Awwad who leads the Central Bureau of Statistics, one of the most reputable Palestinian institutions. I think Palestine is ready for a female prime minister, maybe even a female president.

Does Fatah cooperate with Israeli Palestinian parties?

For a long time Palestinians in Israel and Palestinians in the West Bank and Gaza considered their cause to be unconnected. It was only quite recently that Israeli Palestinians have realized that events in the West Bank and Gaza cannot be isolated from their own experiences in Israel. They are feeling the heat. Many realize that Palestinian unity is necessary to secure the survival of Palestinian Israelis who face severe legal discrimination and the threat of expulsion.

It is no secret that some Israeli Arab activists have even tried to mediate between Fatah and Hamas, for example, the leader of the Islamic Movement in Israel, Raed Salah. The cooperation between Palestinians in Israel and in the Palestinian territories will definitely become stronger and more important.

Interview with Amal Hamad, Member of the Central Committee, Gaza

What changes did the sixth General Conference bring for Fatah?

The program adopted in the sixth Congress foresaw the changes taking place in the region now. All national questions were attended to and the mechanisms of resistance were defined. All issues were dealt with: Jerusalem, borders, water, prisoners, etc. At the same time, the mechanism changed, and it is no longer limited to violent resistance but also includes nonviolent resistance campaigns. Now the focus is on popular resistance initiatives. The most important question is that of true national reconciliation. After reconciliation we will have better chances to deal with the occupation. We will be able to have elections and to use our basic rights.

Fatah has often been associated with inner-party struggle and corruption. Did the Congress succeed in rebuilding confidence in Fatah?

The Congress was the basis for Fatah's renewal, bringing up internal anticorruption laws, a system of checks and balances, better transparency, and the right of inquiry. The Revolutionary Council can put pressure on the Central Committee and can even call a motion of no-confidence if it so wishes. As Fatah, there are many steps we can use to rebuild trust. In the West Bank, conditions have really improved, and our branches in Lebanon and Syria have new leaders, which is good for the movement. Yet, in Gaza, we cannot be very creative—it is just not in our hands.

In Gaza we are not allowed to engage in any public activities. We tried on Arafat Day and also on the anniversary of the foundation of Fatah, but it was all refused until the signing of the unity deal in Cairo.

Gaza is underrepresented in the bodies of Fatah. Do you feel neglected?

Honestly, yes. We are neglected at many levels.

The Fatah program has undergone significant modifications—in how far do these represent a change in substance?

There has to be constant renewal. The only thing permanent in the world is change. Renewal is not only about words, it is about action. This is what we strongly believe. And this is our strategy: Address the UN Security Council with a bid for Palestinian statehood and carry on with demonstrations and the settlement boycott.

For Fatah, what are the prospects for renewing negotiations?

We still believe in negotiations, but we will not negotiate forever. We will see how far negotiating takes us, but I do not think there is any reason to question our current strategy. We strive for a state within the borders of 1967 and if that is not possible we want one democratic secular state for Jews and Arabs to live in.

And how does this position differ from that of Hamas?

There are several differences between Hamas and Fatah. In our case, this is a purely national strategy. With regard to Hamas, Iran and Syria are pulling the strings. Hamas does not have a firm position—they will say one thing one day and then the complete opposite the next. We do have firm stands. We believe in human rights, in the majority system, and the peaceful transfer of power. Hamas does not. We believe in the freedom of women. If the Muslim Brotherhood in Egypt takes over, Gaza will become an Islamic state.

What is the current situation for women in Fatah?

There is a quota now reserving 20 percent of positions at all levels of Fatah for women. In the next elections this will be implemented.

Fatah lost the 2006 elections.

What does the concept of opposition mean to Fatah?
The mandate of the PLC has long expired by now, so it is futile to talk about winners and losers. The best solution would be a national unity government. There is a tendency to blame Fatah for everything negative that happens. But Fatah has to be credited for the positive dynamics as well.

★ ★ ★

Excerpts of Fatah Programmatic Documents

The following excerpts are from the most recent Political Platform of Fatah, ratified during the sixth General Conference in 2009.[20] To explicate Fatah's programmatic evolution, excerpts are also taken from the Fatah "Constitution" of 1964, the movement's first formal comprehensive programmatic statement.[21] The document was valid until 2009, when it was replaced by a new set of bylaws that do not discuss political positions. For the PLC elections in 2006, Fatah did not present a comprehensive political program as a platform for the Fatah list but represented merely a stump program of the Fatah Higher Committee.

View on the Israeli–Palestinian Conflict

Political Platform of Fatah (2009):
"The liberation of the homeland is the central axis of the Fatah Movement's struggle, including the right of the Palestinian people to self-determination as an inalienable right. This right cannot be lost by attrition since it was recognized and confirmed by the international community. This includes the right to establish its own sovereign and independent state with Jerusalem as its capital on the liberated Palestinian land occupied by Israel since June 4, 1967, the right of the refugees to return and to compensation, based on the United Nations Charter and the UN General Assembly Resolution 194. In the short run, it focuses on confronting the settlements, the Judaization of Jerusalem, the siege imposed on our territories, putting an end to the occupation of our cities and villages as a step towards achieving our strategic goals.

Our central goal remains to defeat the occupation, liberate the homeland, establish our independent state with Jerusalem as its capital, and ensure the right of refugees to return and to compensation. Our interim tasks to be accomplished for the achievement of these goals include: Confronting the settler occupation, preserving the land and holy places and their Arab character, especially in Jerusalem; working for the release of prisoners, steadfastly upholding our principles in difficult times, and mobilizing different forms of struggle to defeat the occupation, rectifying the course of negotiations without being confined solely to it, or accepting a futile continuation of it. We have to try to achieve progress through negotiations towards our goals, exploring alternative strategic means of struggle if the Peace Process fails in its current form. We have to keep on building our own strength in order to carry on the struggle. We must strive to translate these directives into detailed interim tasks in order to achieve our objectives in the next stage; which will be presented as follows:

1. Principles: Continued commitment to national principles, self-determination and the establishment of the independent Palestinian state with Jerusalem as its capital.
2. Refugees: Fatah Movement is committed to the following:
   - Working hard to achieve the right of refugees for return, compensation and restitution of properties while maintaining the unity of the refugees' cause regardless of their location, including the refugees inside the Green Line. Fatah supports the need to preserve the refugee camps as a political witness to the plight of the refugees who have been deprived of returning to their homes pending the resolution of their cause. Fatah will strive to preserve UNRWA as an international address for the rights of the refugees until their return to their homes and country. Working to improve the conditions of the refugees and their camps is a national necessity.
   - Rejecting forced implantation of our refugees away from their homeland to an alternative homeland. No settlement '*Tawteen*' in Lebanon and no substitute homeland '*Watan Badil*' for the Palestinians in Jordan are acceptable.
3. Detainees: We commit ourselves to strive to liberate all Palestinian prisoners and never to sign any final peace agreement without the freedom of every one of them.
4. Right to resist: Fatah adheres to the right of the Palestinian people to resist the occupation by all legitimate means, including the right to use arms. Such a right is guaranteed by international law as long as the occupation, settlement, and the denial of our inalienable rights continue.

5. Forms of struggle in the current stage: Fatah adopts all forms of legitimate struggle while remaining committed to the option of peace, without being restricted to negotiations only. The forms of this struggle, which can be successfully used in the current stage to support negotiations and reactivate them, or substitute them if they do not deliver may include:
   - Mobilizing popular nonviolent struggle against settlement activities as expressed in its successful present model in Bil'in and Ni'lin against the Wall, and to the struggle to rescue Jerusalem and prevent its Judaization. Our mission is to mobilize all citizens to take part in those activities, to mobilize Arab and international participation support from the Authority and its agencies, and to urge leaders to take part in its most important activities.
   - Creating new forms of struggle and resistance through grassroots initiatives and those of Fatah cadres in the framework of our people's determination to resist and stand firm protected by international law and international guarantees.
   - Boycotting Israeli products at home and abroad through popular movement, particularly those goods for which there is a local substitute. Performing new forms of civil disobedience against the occupation and launching an international campaign to boycott Israel, its products, and its institutions, benefiting from the experience of South Africa against Apartheid.
   - Exploring strategic alternatives if progress is not achieved through ongoing negotiations, including the option of a democratic unitary state rejecting racism, hegemony and occupation. The development of struggle against Israeli apartheid and racism, return to the idea of declaring the state on the 1967 borders are examples of these strategic alternatives.
   - Continuing the struggle to release the prisoners and detainees, ending the external siege, lifting internal checkpoints...are important tasks in the coming period.
   - Calling on the UN and the Security Council to shoulder their responsibilities in resolving the conflict and ending the occupation; and continuing the drive to issue supporting resolutions by the Security Council based on Chapter VII of the Charter which makes them legally binding and enforceable.
   - Restoring our direct and strong relations with the Israeli peace camp and revitalizing our joint action for a just peace, without

mingling it with normalization with Israel. This is rejected while the occupation continues.

...

The Palestinians are a genuine people with a clear identity and clear affiliation to their homeland. They maintained their attachment to this identity and to their homeland through their national struggle for almost a century, aiming to liberate their land from occupation and settlement. The Palestinian Arab people constitute one political unit whether at home, in the West Bank and its heart Jerusalem, in the Gaza Strip, behind the Green Line or in the diaspora.

...

Our Movement pays special attention to the United Nations and it works to re-activate the UN's role in the Palestinian cause.... Fatah realizes the risks of the current unipolar international system which led to bloody wars focused on our region, destroying Iraq and Afghanistan, spreading sectarian and ethnic contradictions, and using brute force at the expense of the rule of law. However, this system was subjected to military failures and finally to economic defeats. This development heralds a multipolar world system which should bring back equilibrium into international relations and provides us with a greater opportunity to regain international legal support and action in favor of our rights.

Fatah adopts democracy and tolerance, rejecting extremism and terrorism in all its forms, especially state terrorism, and it deals in moderation with political realism.... Moderation does not mean cowardice and evading, but the rejection of extremism, and the attempt by some to ... cover failure through exaggeration and imprudence. Democracy does not mean bowing to American matrices or yielding to wrong or misleading concepts, but by the constant return to the public, broadening the base of its participation in decision-making, refusing dictatorship and the rule of autocracy. We will be mistaken if we ever agree to the course of a one man rule....

Fatah adopted these commitments because it is a movement of the entire Palestinian people, and not an elitist party.... That is why Fatah proposed a progressive vision of the future to the Israelis and rejected extremism and terrorism. However, distinction must be made between terrorism, which targets civilians for aggressive political objectives, such as state terrorism practiced by Israel against our people, and the legitimate resistance against foreign occupation and peoples' struggle for their freedom, independence and self-determination against racism

and all forms of foreign domination and hegemony, within the confines of international law....
Our duty to confront the Israeli siege of Gaza requires our performance of the following actions:

strengthen the steadfastness of Gaza in the face of the siege; give it a priority in providing national support through budgetary finance and international grants, and solving the pressing problems of Gaza people living abroad, particularly students and patients

launching an international humanitarian campaign against the siege and starvation, and informing the world about the crimes against humanity committed by Israel against the people of Gaza, and to link resuming negotiations with Israel with lifting the siege

separating the Palestinian economy gradually from the Israeli market, especially in electricity, fuel, gas and basic foodstuffs, replacing it by the Egyptian, Jordanian and Arab markets

working to implement the International Convention for the Rafah Crossing, trying to develop it by denying Israel the opportunity to control the opening and closing of this vital crossing

...

Jerusalem is the capital of Palestine and its heart, the first *qibla* and third holiest shrine of Islam, the city of peace and the symbol of divine religions. No peace can be installed without the return of Jerusalem as the eternal capital of the State of Palestine. Fatah considers all the decisions of Israel's annexation of Jerusalem, its settlement, displacement of people and changes of its features as null and void and their consequences must be abolished, in implementation of international resolutions that condemned all attempts to Judaise Jerusalem. Jerusalem is an integral part of the land of Palestine occupied in 1967. Fatah commits to the following tasks regarding Jerusalem:

embodying of Jerusalem as an eternal political capital of Palestine and a spiritual capital for the Arab nation, Islamic and Christian world

upholding absolute commitment to the resolutions of international legitimacy and the International Court of Justice advisory opinion on Jerusalem, which confirms the invalidity of Israel's decisions of annexation, and building the apartheid wall

providing means of support related to preservation of Jerusalem and resist its Judaisation

...

- providing all the facilities that the Movement can provide, and those provided by the National Authority to support the steadfastness and perseverance of our people in Jerusalem and to support projects that provide essential services to the residents of Jerusalem to strengthen their steadfastness and preserve their national and cultural identity
- supporting Jerusalemite institutions and maintain their continuity in serving the steadfastness of Jerusalemites, to build new institutions, to maintain the Arab character of Jerusalem, and work to reopen the institutions shut down by Israel
- activating Fatah channels, and those of the National Authority, with the Islamic and friendly countries for the implementation of special Arab projects to preserve the identity of Jerusalem and its Arab character and face the settlement and Judaisation attacks
- establishing a special fund for Jerusalem to receive local, regional and international donations and to unify them in order to consolidate the steadfastness of the people of Jerusalem
- strengthening the role of research centers to publish information, historical and cultural studies, organize conferences and seminars about the city of Jerusalem and to publish their proceedings in the media to raise the issue of Jerusalem at the global level
- activating Fatah Jerusalem Commission as a Fatah reference for Jerusalem Affairs."

Fatah Constitution (1964):

"Article (1) Palestine is part of the Arab World, and the Palestinian people are part of the Arab Nation, and their struggle is part of its struggle.
Article (2) The Palestinian people have an independent identity. They are the sole authority that decides their own destiny, and they have complete sovereignty on all their lands.
Article (3) The Palestinian Revolution plays a leading role in liberating Palestine.
Article (4) The Palestinian struggle is part and parcel of the world-wide struggle against Zionism, colonialism and international imperialism.
Article (5) Liberating Palestine is a national obligation which necessities the materialistic and human support of the Arab Nation.
Article (6) UN projects, accords and resolutions, or those of any individual which undermine the Palestinian people's right in their homeland are illegal and rejected.

Article (7) The Zionist Movement is racial, colonial and aggressive in ideology, goals, organization and method.
Article (8) The Israeli existence in Palestine is a Zionist invasion with a colonial expansive base, and it is a natural ally to colonialism and international imperialism.
Article (9) Liberating Palestine and protecting its holy places is an Arab, religious and human obligation.

...

Article (12) Complete liberation of Palestine, and eradication of Zionist economic, political, military and cultural existence.

...

Article (17) Armed public revolution is the inevitable method to liberating Palestine.

...

Article (19) Armed struggle is a strategy and not a tactic, and the Palestinian Arab People's armed revolution is a decisive factor in the liberation fight and in uprooting the Zionist existence, and this struggle will not cease unless the Zionist state is demolished and Palestine is completely liberated.

...

Article (22) Opposing any political solution offered as an alternative to demolishing the Zionist occupation in Palestine, as well as any project intended to liquidate the Palestinian case or impose any international mandate on its people.
Article (23) Maintaining relations with Arab countries with the objective of developing the positive aspects in their attitudes with the proviso that the armed struggle is not negatively affected.
Article (24) Maintaining relations with all liberal forces supporting our just struggle in order to resist together Zionism and imperialism.
Article (25) Convincing concerned countries in the world to prevent Jewish immigration to Palestine as a method of solving the problem."

Economic Development

Political Platform of Fatah (2009):
"Fatah aims at a gradual separation of the Palestinian economy from the Israeli market, especially in electricity, fuel, gas and basic foodstuffs, replacing it by the Egyptian, Jordanian and Arab markets.... Fatah supports the demands of our people for equality, restoring their rights to achieve economic, social and educational development for themselves, their regions, towns and villages.

...

The following points are a summary of these tasks, although detailing them is the task of the 'National Construction Program' submitted to the sixth Conference separately:

- focusing on private sector support by creating an encouraging investment environment, granting facilities to investors and establishing a sound market mechanism to maintain legitimate and effective competition, restricting monopoly and achieving protection for the consumer. Encouraging economic production capable of competition
- respecting the right of every Palestinian to work and continue the efforts to provide employment opportunities, to comply with minimum wage; activate and support labor frameworks and trade unions
- encouraging the Palestinian Investment Fund and the private sector to invest in the housing sector, especially in the outskirts of cities threatened by settlement..."

State's Role vis-a-vis Religion

Political Platform of Fatah (2009):
"Islam and Divine Religions in the Strategy of Fatah: Palestine is the holy land of monotheistic divine religions, and Islam as the religion of the majority of the Palestinian people... is the official religion of the Authority and the state. Christianity enjoys the same holiness and respect. Fatah does not allow any discrimination between the Palestinians on the basis of religion, ideology or the strength of their belief.

We respect the freedom of worship for all, including Jews. Since its inception, our Movement called for a democratic non-sectarian state for Muslims, Christians and Jews. The Movement is inspired by Islam and other divine religions from which it derives its spiritual and religious values. It belongs intellectually to the Arab Islamic culture. It is the Movement of a people which maintains spiritual and moral values and the belief in God, His Prophets and the sacred Books. Fatah Movement does not accept sectarianism, rejects fanaticism and extremism, and believes that the divine religions promote fraternity, tolerance and coexistence among nations.

Fatah rejects the call to recognize Israel as a 'Jewish State', and adopts the demands of our Palestinian people in the territory of '48 to be recognized by Israel as full citizens with full rights."

Vision of State and Society

Political Platform of Fatah (2009):
"The Palestinian National Authority (PNA) was established in 1994 by a decision of the Palestine Liberation Organization. Fatah assumed most of its leading and administrative responsibilities. Yet, the PNA belongs to the Palestinian people and is governed through democratic elections. It is also an independent body. Fatah has the ability to influence the PNA especially when it assumes its leadership.

The Movement should form a clear vision of the Authority, including the future tasks Fatah is committed to implement through the PNA, once Fatah assumes its leadership through democratic legitimacy. Fatah should also select the tasks that it will call on the PNA to implement when it is outside the leadership of the Authority. The following points are a summary of these tasks, although detailing them is the task of the 'National Construction Program' submitted to the sixth Conference separately:

- emphasizing the principles of democracy, pluralism and peaceful transfer of power, consolidating those principles and protecting the freedom of individuals and their rights as the basis of state-building
- achieving security, safety and respect of the law, and re-building the security apparatus on national and professional foundations
- continuing building and rebuilding state institutions, preserving the constitution and the laws regulating political, economic and social life

- developing values and concepts based on the principles of our Arab and Islamic culture and international standards with regard to women, children, family and youth, political and civil rights and public freedoms
- strengthening the role of women by eliminating all forms of discrimination against them, protecting them against family and social violence, working to enable them to enjoy their civil, political, economic, social... and cultural rights...
- continuing to provide all kinds of support for the wounded and prisoners; develop specialized programs for the rehabilitation of ex-detainees and develop programs to take care of their families
- fighting corruption and conducting radical reform in the performance of the Authority and judiciary, protecting and enforcing its provisions and independence, respecting the law, developing mechanisms of governance based on the separation of powers and activating the principle of accountability
- strengthening the presence and participation of civil society...
- ensuring the right to participate in cultural life in all its dimensions...

One of Fatah's organizational tasks is to develop the role of women and to prepare a cadre of educationally, culturally and politically qualified women, broadening and strengthening the role of women in the Movement, encouraging their presence in leading positions.

...

While emphasizing the role of the Palestine Liberation Organization as the highest authority, embodying the national unity of the Palestinian people, the development of the concept of national unity into political partnership has become an urgent necessity in the coming stage. This should be based on clear terms of reference such as:

- respecting pluralism and the right to form political parties and factions in accordance with the law
- promoting the concepts of democracy and peaceful transfer of power at local and national levels
- resorting to the ballot box in the formation of local councils, trade unions, legislative bodies and other frameworks
- broadening popular participation in determining national public policies

- amending laws, especially those related to elections to give the emerging powers and parties a better chance to participate in the elections
- establishing a supreme constitutional court to resolve disputes related to the Constitution and other laws
- consolidating Palestinian political gains by insisting on the commitment to obligations and agreements is a decisive prerequisite for participation in Palestinian political life
- motivating the grass-roots bases to protect national unity and political partnership
- disseminating the culture of partnership, prioritizing the national public interest over the narrow selfish interests of the forces, factions and parties."

Fatah Constitution (1964):

"[Fatah's goal is]: Protecting the citizens' legal and equal rights without any racial or religious discriminatiSon.... Setting up a progressive society that warrants people's rights and their public freedom.... Active participation in achieving the Arab Nation's goals in liberation and building an independent, progressive and united Arab society.... Backing up all oppressed people in their struggle for liberation and self-determination in order to build a just, international peace.

In its determination to achieve liberation and bring about historical social changes, the Movement attempts to launch the revolutionary moral values which are on a bar with our struggle, and to create the feeling of human dignity. To this effect, the Movement tries to liberate the individual from all social ills, especially the discrimination women face, the thing that hinders their potential and effective contributions at all disciplinary levels."

CHAPTER FOUR

PFLP: *Arab Anti-Imperialists*

The Popular Front for the Liberation of Palestine and Its Ambiguous Stance on the Two-State Solution

Palestinian supporters praise the PFLP as a leading resistance movement of the 1960s and 1970s. For many Israelis, the party represents one of the most ruthless terrorist organizations in modern history. Following the end of the Cold War and the Israeli–Palestinian rapprochement of the Oslo Accords, the Marxist PFLP had considerable difficulty identifying its place within a transforming political landscape. However, to this day, the PFLP maintains significant support on the ground and remains the most influential PLO faction next to Fatah (table 4.1).

The Popular Front for the Liberation of Palestine (PFLP) was founded as a revolutionary movement following the Israeli occupation of the West Bank, the Gaza Strip, and East Jerusalem in 1967. The PFLP grew out of the secular, socialist Arab Nationalist Movement (ANM) and a number of other militant organizations including the Palestine Liberation Army. Many of its leaders graduated from the American University of Beirut. Despite inherent paradoxes, the movement adopted an ideology that combined strong notions of Arab nationalism with radical, Marxist–Leninist anti-Imperialism.

PFLP founder George Habash viewed Israel ("the Zionist enemy" in party statements of the 1960s) as a neocolonialist project of Western imperialism. The PFLP ruled out accepting an Israeli state anywhere between the Jordan River and the Mediterranean Sea and rallied for

Table 4.1 The PFLP at a glance

Official name	: PFLP / Popular Front for the Liberation of Palestine (al-Jabha al-Shabiya li-Tahrir al-Filastin)
Year founded	: 1967
PLO membership since	: 1968 / 70
PLC members 1996	: 0 (boycotted) 2 seats won by PFLP-affiliated individual candidates
PLC members 2006	: 3
Ideological orientation	: Marxist Arab Nationalism
Leadership base	: Damascus, Ramallah, Gaza

a "people's war" that should be based on "agitating and organizing the masses." For the PFLP, the struggle for Palestinian ambitions was "first of all a class struggle," as its 1969 platform stipulated.[1] The revolutionary struggle would bring about a One-State Solution that would liberate Palestinians from internal and external oppressors and would grant minority rights only to Palestine's original Jewish inhabitants.

Unlike Fatah, the PFLP openly rejected neighboring Arab regimes, which it perceived as reactionary, and advocated for overthrowing the "Arab bourgeoisie" along with Israel through the mobilization of masses in a pan-Arab revolution.

Given these revolutionary objectives, the PFLP adopted armed struggle as its raison d'être. Within one year of its founding, the organization backed by Iraqi financial assistance commanded up to one thousand guerilla fighters and had gained considerable popularity. When it joined the Palestine Liberation Organization (PLO) in 1968 (according to some sources in 1970), the PFLP became the organization's second largest PLO faction. Though its relations with the PLO have been severely strained at times (notably as the PLO took its first steps toward embracing a Two-State Solution) the PFLP has consistently maintained its stature in the organization, thanks in part to the fact that attempts to renew the mandate of the PLO's parliament (the Palestinian National Council, PNC) have been repeatedly postponed. The PFLP has lobbied for a "democratization" of the PLO "on the base [sic] of proportional representation," as indicated in a 2006 statement.[2] In view of significant backing not only in the Palestinian Territories but also in the Diaspora, such calls have been put forward with the clear objective to counter Fatah's near-total control over the organization.

In its early years, debate within the PFLP concerning the most effective means of resistance led to the establishment of several splinter groups, including the Palestinian Popular Struggle Front (PPSR), Ahmad Jibril's PFLP-General Command, and the Democratic Front for the Liberation of Palestine (DFLP). With the exception of the DFLP, none of these breakaway organizations was able to garner a comparable level of influence.

From the start, the PFLP relied heavily on foreign logistical and financial support, most notably from Iraq and Syria, where the PFLP established its headquarters to protect its leadership from Israeli reprisals. The PFLP also reached out to the Soviet Union and China for aid and international recognition as the leading Palestinian Marxist–Leninist party.

The PFLP's military wing (later named the Abu Ali Mustafa Brigades) was one of the forerunners of Palestinian global terrorist activities. In the late 1960s, it engaged in terrorist operations, which included bombings, that caused the death of dozens of Israeli civilians and a series of dramatic plane hijackings. Also, the movement relentlessly targeted perceived Palestinian collaborators, for instance, Palestinians employed in the Israeli-run administration.

Terrorist operations abroad were frequently carried out in cooperation with international leftist terror groups such as Japan's Red Army and the German Baader-Meinhof group. One of these operations, the 1970 Dawson's Field hijackings in Jordan, is widely thought to have triggering the Black September clashes between the Jordanian army and the PLO, in the course of which the PFLP and other groups were forced to flee to Lebanon. For the PFLP, the defeat in Jordan was especially difficult to accept, given its exclusive focus on military operations at the time. One of the PFLP's bloodiest operations took place in May 1972, when members of the group killed 28 passengers at Ben Gurion International Airport in Tel Aviv.

In 1974, after the Arab defeat in the Yom Kippur / October War, the PLO adopted the Ten Point Program (brought forward by the DFLP), which authorized the organization to establish an "independent combatant national authority for the people over every part of Palestinian territory that is liberated."[3]

The program was widely interpreted to signal the PLO's willingness to sacrifice, at least temporarily, its goal of liberating all of historical Palestine. In response, the PFLP boycotted PLO Executive Committee meetings where the faction held (and continues to hold) two seats and formed the Front of the Palestinian Forces Rejecting Solutions of Surrender backed by Iraq and Libya. PFLP leader George Habash rejected the Ten Point Program as a first step toward a two-state proposal and vehemently condemned the PLO's change in course. The ensuing boycott of the PLO resulted in considerable loss of influence for the PFLP. The party only decided to rejoin the PLO's Executive Committee in 1981.

In 1978, the PFLP shifted strategies, deciding to refrain from "external operations" and purging the organization from at least some dissidents who refused to comply with this decision. This meant restricting armed attacks to Israeli targets inside Israel, the West Bank, and Gaza. Entangled in the Lebanese civil war, the organization's militant operations became less frequent. The collapse of the Soviet Union resulted in ideological uncertainty among PFLP cadres. In terms of programmatic stances, the end of the Cold War also caused a noticeable change in rhetoric. While the PFLP had been notorious for wholeheartedly embracing fiery Marxist–Leninist jargon since its inception, the reduced vibrancy of Marxism caused a moderation in public statements. The end of the Cold War, however, not only questioned the persuasiveness of long-held ideological beliefs but also caused a decrease in material and financial support for the PFLP.

Confronted with the rise of Hamas in the late 1980s, the PFLP gradually lost ground. Although it continued to adamantly call for the complete "liberation of Palestine," in 1988, the PFLP's secretary general, George Habash, approved the Palestinian Declaration of Independence in Algiers, which was interpreted as a first step toward the PFLP accepting an interim Two-State Solution as a tactical concession. While this was interpreted as a step toward moderation, in 1991, the PFLP vehemently rejected the United States-led military operation against Iraq and thus renewed a more confrontational anti-Western stance. In line with this, the party also rejected the 1993 Oslo Accords, emphasizing the disadvantages and perceived injustice of the Oslo Process. Together with Hamas and eight other Palestinian factions, the PFLP again formed a rejectionist front based in Damascus. However, unlike Hamas, the PFLP largely refrained at first from obstructing the implementation of Oslo through violent means.

The PFLP's rejectionist stance led to the boycott of the Palestinian National Authority's (PNA) general elections in 1996, a decision that resulted in the group's loss of influence in the Palestinian Territories. Although the PFLP remained a popular movement in parts of the diaspora, most notably in the refugee camps of Lebanon and Syria, managing its power base in the West Bank and Gaza proved challenging, and its ability to conduct "armed resistance" was curbed significantly by Israeli forces and the newly established security apparatus of the PNA.

In the years following the signing of the Oslo Accords, the PFLP began to gradually come to terms with political realities. While continuing to reject Oslo and endorse armed struggle against Israel, the PFLP reversed its complete rejection of the PNA and began an important partial transformation into an opposition movement that could be integrated de facto into the political system. To compensate for their loss of political influence due to their decision to boycott elections, PFLP leaders sought to establish a network of party-affiliated civil-society organizations in the West Bank and Gaza.

At the movement's general congress in 2000, George Habash announced that the party would participate in future local and general elections. This was an important indicator that the PFLP was indeed beginning to slowly embrace a dual role: political opposition party in the PNA and, essentially, a rejectionist resistance movement in diaspora. Given the PFLP's relatively strong support outside of the Palestinian Territories, a possible transformation toward a political party focusing exclusively on political processes in the PNA proved much more difficult for the PFLP than for other Palestinian factions.

During the previous year, an agreement was reached with the PLO leadership that implied PFLP's tacit acceptance of negotiations with Israel and of a temporary Two-State Solution (the agreement called for the implementation of UN Security Council resolutions, including the endorsement of a Palestinian State within the pre-1967 borders), though the organization continued to reiterate its preference for a One-State Solution.

The outbreak of the second *intifada* in 2000 put the PFLP's gradual and ambiguous shift toward moderation on hold. On August 27, 2001 PFLP general secretary Abu Ali Mustafa (Mustafa Zabri) was killed in an Israeli helicopter attack on his office in Ramallah. He was the most prominent Palestinian official to be assassinated since the second *intifada* broke out almost a year earlier. Tens of thousands of Palestinians took to the streets in mourning during an emotional funeral procession. In response, the PFLP ordered the assassination of Israeli minister of tourism Rehavam Ze'evi in October of that same year.

Under heavy US pressure, the PNA banned the PFLP's military wing on October 21, 2001 and arrested Ahmad Sa'adat, the PFLP's newly elected secretary general, and other PFLP leaders for "breaches of public security and damaging Palestinian national interests," a move that soured relations between the PNA and the PFLP for years to come. In protest against Sa'dat's detention, the PFLP again briefly suspended its participation in the PLO Executive Committee. In 2003, a PFLP-led group gained notoriety when it stole 100,000 USD from the local branch of al-Quds Bank in Beit Jala, near Bethlehem, with the alleged intention of distributing the money to needy refugees. The perpetrators were later arrested by PNA police. Later that year, the continuing *intifada* brought further PFLP attacks against Israeli targets, including a December 24, 2003 suicide bombing near Petah Tikva.

In the following years, the PFLP remained a thorn in the side of the PNA, repeatedly questioning its authority and legitimacy. In September 2003, during a telephone interview from his Jericho detention facility, General Secretary Sa'adat called for a break with the Oslo-based Palestinian institution, accusing the PNA of "not representing the Palestinian people because it operates within the framework of the Oslo Accords."[4] In 2006, Israeli forces stormed the Palestinian prison that held Sa'adat and transferred him to an Israeli detention facility, where he remains today.

After the end of the second *intifada*, the PFLP attempted to challenge the dominance of Fatah and Hamas by forging alliances with other Palestinian leftist movements in advance of the 2005 presidential election and the 2006 parliamentary elections, with mixed results. Although initially determined to boycott the 2005 presidential election, the PFLP decided at the last minute to back the Palestinian National Initiative's (PNI) Mustafa Barghouthi, who went on to win 19 percent of the vote. In the 2006 parliamentary elections, however, the PFLP's Martyr Abu Ali Mustafa List only performed well in the party's established strongholds of Ramallah, Bethlehem, and the Gaza Strip. The party secured 4.25 percent of the total vote, allotting the movement three seats in the PLC, filled by Khalida Jarrar, Jamil Majdalawi, and Ahmad Sa'dat.

While the PFLP thus fared better than any other non-Fatah PLO faction, the results fell short of the impressive performance in the 2005 presidential elections. The failure of the PFLP to mobilize larger parts of the electorate has often been attributed to the PFLP's ambiguous stance among theoretical rejection, practical accommodation, and radical socialism, which alienated not only the political establishment within the PNA but also the voters who felt that the PFLP's rhetoric of class struggle failed to address and was not in tune with the pressing issues of their daily lives.

With Sa'adat sitting in an Israeli jail, PLO Executive Committee member Abdal Rahim Malouh emerged as the PFLP's strongman in the West Bank. He gained the support of Fatah leader Mahmoud Abbas, who, when Malouh was imprisoned by Israel in 2007, appealed personally to Israeli prime minister Ehud Olmert on Malouh's behalf. Malouh has since openly sided with Abbas on several issues, most importantly the rift between Hamas and Fatah.

In its capacity as an opposition party, the PFLP has remained, however, a staunch critic of the PNA, rejecting the legitimacy of governments in both Gaza and the West Bank. In 2011, the PFLP repeatedly voiced criticism of Palestinian prime minister Salam Fayyad's policy of state-building. The PFLP has also denounced the PNA's economic policies, which, according to a 2012 statement, "are helping to spark inflation and skyrocketing food, water and electricity prices and rapidly deteriorating economic conditions for the vast majority of the Palestinian people."[5] In its capacity as a resistance movement, the PFLP has repeatedly rejected the PNA president's call to disarm its military wing in an open act of defiance against Mahmoud Abbas.

Such actions have strained PFLP relations with the PNA and have made it difficult for the PFLP to sustain formalized political procedures. While a complex organizational structure remains in place (see chart 4.1), Israeli (and occasionally PNA) interferences have long hampered formalized decision-making processes. Thus, the PFLP's last National Congress was held in 2000.

At the same time, the PFLP's oppositional stances have earned the movement a significant and loyal support base largely but not exclusively outside of the Palestinian Territories. In December 2009, on the movement's forty-second anniversary, the faction mobilized thousands of supporters in Gaza, Ramallah, Nablus, Algiers, and Beirut. The movement's red flag remains a familiar and persistent sight in Palestinian towns and refugee camps in and outside of the Palestinian Territories. In recent years, the PFLP's position on the Israeli–Palestinian conflict has come to resemble Hamas's policy of "phased liberation": The PFLP strives to achieve the "interim goal of a sovereign, independent, Palestinian state on 1967-occupied land, with Jerusalem as its capital, and the return of all Palestinian refugees and their descendants to the homes and land from which they were displaced." At the same time, the PFLP's "strategic goal," however, remains the "establishment of a democratic nation in all of historic Palestine," as noted in a 2006 party statement.[6]

This stance essentially enabled the PFLP to bridge the dualism between its role as an oppositional party in the PNA and its wider agenda to overcome the existing status quo as a revolutionary movement. The PFLP has long maintained an adamant position toward rejecting bilateral negotiations to finding a solution to the Israli–Palestinian conflict. Instead, the organization has promoted the continuation "of all forms of resistance,

104   Political Parties in Palestine

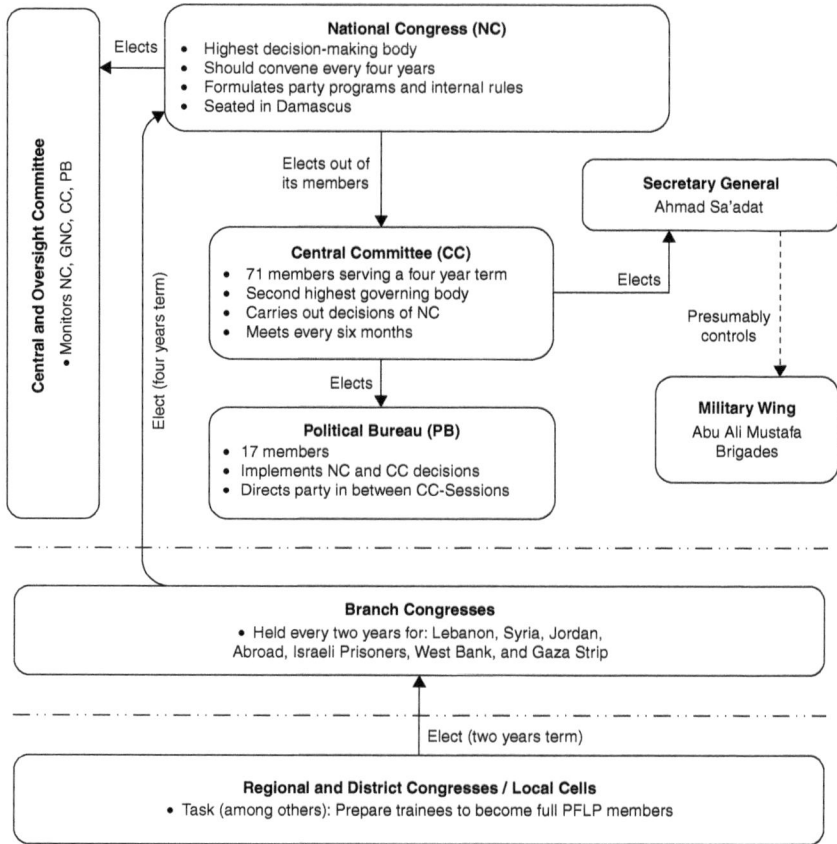

Chart 4.1 Organizational structure of the PFLP.

including military resistance until the occupation is ended," as the PFLP outlined in a statement on the thirty-ninth anniversary of the founding of the PFLP in 2006.[7] Furthermore, the PFLP continues to call for an internationalization of diplomatic initiatives within the framework of the United Nations. In line with this, PFLP general secretary Ahmad Sa'adat called for an end to negotiations with Israel in May 2010.

The PFLP's use of violence has resulted in the group's designation as a terrorist organization by the United States and the European Union. Following the Lebanon War of 2006, PFLP statements hailed the "resistance" of Hezbollah, which "demonstrated that victory over our Zionist enemy has become an achievable reality" and praised the "patriotic people of Iraq," who engaged in "resistance against the invasion and occupation forces" of the United States.[8] In October 2011 and in January 2012, the PFLP's military wing in Gaza claimed responsibility for heavy rocket and mortar fire on Israel, illustrating that, for the PFLP, "resistance" remains indeed a core element of the organization's ideology. In the general Palestinian public, acts of violence have generally lost support in recent years, although certainly the principle of armed resistance continues to resonate with a substantial part of the PFLP's support base. Despite the fact that the traditional role of the PFLP as Fatah's prime challenger has long been taken over by Hamas, the party remains a solid hallmark and important organization within the Palestinian political spectrum.[9]

George Habash

George Habash, known as "the conscience of the Palestinian Revolution," is considered by many Palestinians to be one of their most prominent early leaders. Habash's firm belief that the realization of Palestinian ambitions could be attained only through armed struggle earned him an additional moniker: "godfather of Middle East terrorism" (*TIME Magazine*).

Born into a Christian family in Lydda (Lod) in 1926, George Habash left Palestine in the 1940s to study medicine at the liberal American University of Beirut. He returned during the Arab–Israeli War of 1948 to serve as a medical orderly in his hometown captured by Israeli forces in July 1948. He witnessed the expulsion of Palestinians and would later explain to a Western journalist that it was this personal experience that prompted him to abandon his Christian faith: "Thousands of human beings expelled from their homes, running, crying, shouting in terror. After seeing such a thing, you cannot but become a revolutionary."[10]

Habash engaged in student politics following his return to Beirut and, shortly after graduating in 1951 with a degree in pediatrics, he co-founded the Arab Nationalist Movement (ANM). On the basis of revolutionary socialist thinking, the Palestinian-dominated movement called for Arab unity in order to struggle effectively against "Western Imperialism" and the State of Israel. The ANM acted underground in several Arab countries including Jordan, where Habash eventually settled. With his comrade and future PFLP second in command Wadie Haddad, Habash opened a clinic and school for Palestinian refugees. He also pursued "revolutionary" activities against Israel. In 1957, Habash participated in an ideological anti-monarch-based attempted coup against the Jordanian king and was forced to relocate to Syria, from where he was expelled to Lebanon in 1963.

An ardent supporter of Gamal Abdel Nasser's brand of Arab nationalism, Habash initially opposed independent Palestinian groups engaged in guerilla warfare and instead called for conventional warfare of Arab states. After the devastating defeat of the Arab armies in the Six Day War, however, he reversed his position. Habash transformed the ANM by merging it with several militant groups, creating the PFLP. Habash became the PFLP's first general secretary in 1967.

Gaining notoriety as the alleged mastermind of several spectacular airplane hijackings, Habash headed the second largest faction in the PLO and was known throughout the 1960s and 1970s both as one of the most influential Palestinians and as Yasir Arafat's chief political rival. His uncompromising stance on "the liberation of every millimeter of Palestine," as Habash reiterated on many occasions,[11] prompted him to leave the PLO's Executive Committee in 1974, resulting in a decline in his political influence. One of the most wanted Palestinian militants, Israeli forces repeatedly attempted to capture Habash, most famously in 1973 by intercepting an international airliner in which he was believed to be a passenger and forcing it to land in Israel.

In Damascus in 1980, Habash suffered a stroke from which he never fully recovered. His public appearances became less and less frequent. Nevertheless, in 1993 he launched an attack on Yasir Arafat, accusing him of betraying the Palestinian cause by signing the Oslo Accords. Years later he would reiterate that "there is no chance of justice for Palestinians through a 'Peace Process'. There's no hope for diplomacy to work with the Israelis."[12]

Habash's health deteriorated in the 1990s. He resigned as general secretary of the PFLP in 2000, after 33 years in that position. In 2008, at the age of 82, Habash died of a heart attack in Amman. His influence is remembered to this date as commemorated on the fourth anniversary of his death, in January 2012, the Ramallah-based *al-Hayat al-Jadida* praised Habash as a "tremendous leader of the revolution."

Ahmad Sa'adat

Ahmad Sa'adat, the current General Secretary of the PFLP is part of the post-Habash generation of PFLP leaders and has spent the past decade in Israeli and Palestinian prisons. His incarceration has not prevented him from frequently issuing calls for national unity and lashing out against the Oslo Accords.

Ahmad Sa'adat was born in al-Bireh in the central West Bank in 1953. The son of Palestinian refugees, Sa'adat became an activist in the Palestine Student Union at the age of 14, following the Six Day War. Attracted to the PFLP's Marxist ideology and to its strong Arab Nationalist stance, he joined the organization two years later. In 1969, he was arrested by Israeli authorities and detained for three months on charges of illegal activity. Numerous prison terms were to follow. He spent over half of the 1970s in detention.

Sa'adat has said these experiences deepened his understanding of Marxism, which in turn strengthened his commitment to the PFLP. Trained as a mathematics teacher in Ramallah, Sa'adat was elected to the PFLP's Central Committee in 1981 and to the political bureau in 1993 while serving a term in administrative detention. A year later, he was made the PFLP's leader in the West Bank.

Sa'adat has been imprisoned briefly by the PNA several times. During his detention following a 1996 PFLP attack on Israeli settlers, he began a hunger strike. It was an effective tactic; the PNA freed him, but following his release he fell into coma and was hospitalized in Ramallah.

Sa'adat's repeated prison terms have earned him a reputation as a loyal party activist, one who, rather than going into exile, has remained in the Palestinian Territories, despite the constant threat of imprisonment. When PFLP general secretary Abu Ali Mustafa was assassinated by Israeli forces in 2001, Sa'adat was elected as his successor. The choice of Sa'adat, known for his strong roots in local Palestinian society, was widely seen as the PFLP's attempt to strengthen its presence in the Palestinian Territories. It heralded a noticeable departure from the political leanings of his immediate predecessor. Recalling the original positions of George Habash, Sa'adat announced at his inaugural press conference that the "right of return," an independent Palestinian state with Jerusalem as its capital, and retaliation for Abu Ali Mustafa's assassination were the key objectives of his term.

Two weeks later, the Israeli minister of tourism was assassinated by the PFLP. The operation was condemned by the PNA, which outlawed the PFLP's military wing. In January 2002, the PNA took Sa'dat into custody. The arrest sparked protests throughout the West Bank, and the PFLP political bureau suspended its participation in the PLO's Executive Committee. Sa'adat was at the time the most prominent-political figure ever detained by the PNA.

While held in Yasir Arafat's Ramallah governing complex, Sa'adat witnessed the siege laid by Israeli forces and was later transferred to

Jericho prison where he was monitored by the US and British guards as part of a US-brokered deal between the PNA and Israel. Although the Palestinian High Court of Justice ruled in June 2002 that Sa'adat's detention was illegal, Palestinian authorities ignored the ruling and Sa'adat remained incarcerated until 2006. Throughout this time, he continued to be politically active, speaking out against the Road Map for Peace and affirming his objection to the Two-State Solution on the grounds that "the solution of two states coexisting peacefully and in security would not end the historical conflict between our nation and the Zionists of Palestine."[13] He also announced his intention to run in the Palestinian legislative elections in 2006, pressuring the PNA to agree to his release.

When the US and British observers were removed from the Jericho prison in March 2006, Israeli forces attempted to transfer Sa'adat to an Israeli detention facility. After hours of clashes that resulted in the deaths of two Palestinian security guards, Sa'adat and his fellow inmates surrendered. In December 2008, an Israeli military court convicted Sa'adat of heading a "terrorist organization," holding him responsible for actions carried out by the PFLP, and sentenced him to 30 years in prison. He has since been held in solitary confinement for extended periods of time, which has provoked a wave of international left-wing activism calling for his release.

In June 2010, Sa'adat smuggled a message addressing a meeting of US activists in Detroit from his "prison of the occupation" that called on "oppressed peoples to organize and stand together against racism, colonialism, oppression and imperialism."[14] Despite calls for his release, he was not among the 1,027 prisoners swapped for captured Israeli soldier Gilad Shalit in October of 2011.

In 2012, Sa'dat participated in a hunger strike of Palestinian prisoners in Israeli detentions, protesting against solitary confinement. On April 17, 2012 he was transferred to Ramla prison hospital after suffering a deterioration of his health. Posters calling for his immediate release continue to be widespread throughout the Palestinian Territories, illustrating his enduring relevance as one of the more prominent current Palestinian leaders.

★ ★ ★

Interviews with PFLP Decision Makers

The following interviews were conducted with PFLP representatives from Gaza and Ramallah. Khalida Jarrar is one of three PFLP members currently representing the party in the PLC. She was previously the PFLP's candidate for the post of mayor of Ramallah and is considered to represent the party's ideological mainstream. Kayed al-Ghoul is head of the Gaza branch of PFLP and member of the Central Committee. He is perceived as one of the PFLP's leading strategists and is believed to represent the conservative wing within the movement.

Interview with Khalida Jarrar, Member of the Palestinian Legislative Council

In what ways is the PFLP unique within the Palestinian party system?

The PFLP is a truly leftist party. We believe in Marxism and its analysis of class struggle. Therefore we have a comprehensive political, social, and economic view on the current state of occupation and its effects on Palestinians.

We oppose the Oslo agreement. Since the revelations of the Palestine Papers [confidential information on Israeli–Palestinian negotiations leaked by *al-Jazeera*] it has become evident that these negotiations will leave Palestinians with far less than what the nation demands. Palestine will just be squeezed more and more. Instead of direct negotiations between Israelis and Palestinians under the guidance of the United States, we want the UN to implement the internationally recognized resolutions of the Security Council to end the occupation and to establish a Palestinian state based on the pre-1967 borders. Furthermore, the full right of return for refugees must be guaranteed.

With respect to the economy, we are against a free market policy, in which the rich only become richer and the poor stay poor. Instead, social justice is a central issue the PFLP advocates.

Concerning our view on society, we believe in the full equality of men and women and therefore demand an end to all gender discrimination. Frankly speaking, even within our party, achieving this aim is a constant struggle that has only resulted in slow progress.

Does the PFLP's demand for the implementation of UN Security Council resolutions mean it supports a Two-State Solution?

As a tactical step, yes. Eventually, we are aiming to form one secular democratic state in which all people can live: Jews, Christians, Muslims, and others. But, first, true democracy needs to be achieved and elections have to be held. With respect to the Palestinian context, the PLO needs to be reformed.

The PFLP is currently the second largest party in the PLO; elections would probably diminish your share.
So what? This is not about the party's welfare. This is about the needs of the nation. There has to be democracy. This is the reason we were part of the united opposition against the postponement of the local elections in 2011. Eventually, we went to court and we won. Hopefully, elections will take place in the near future.

What about democratic procedures in the PFLP? The last national congress was held in 2000.
Internal democracy is crucial for the PFLP. But as a party that is persecuted and under occupation, there are certain limitations. We face organizational obstacles since our activists are located partly in the West Bank, partly in Gaza, partly in exile, and partly in Israeli prisons. Moreover, leading cadres like former general secretary Abu Ali Mustafa have been assassinated. Others, like current general secretary Ahmad Sa'adat, have been arrested by the PNA and after that by Israel.

The PFLP favors "all forms of resistance" and is believed to have assassinated an Israeli government minister. What is the PFLP's current stance on this?
In all our history, the PFLP has never attacked civilians. We engage in all forms of struggle according to international law. This includes attacks against militants but not against civilians. To overcome the occupation, the PFLP believes in all forms of resistance offered under international law to a people under occupation.

What about airplane hijackings in the 1960s and 1970s? Were the victims not civilians?
That was a strategy to draw the attention of the international community toward the situation of the Palestinian people and their suffering under occupation. I do not think anything like this would be a possible or necessary strategy today. Today, the international awareness for the Palestinian cause has increased. Especially on the civil society level, there is strong international support for Palestinians while popular resistance has become the main means to stand up against the occupation. That is the reason why we have adopted measures such as engaging in the boycott campaign against Israel and making use of legal means against repressive policies.

Your party is still on the terror list of many states.
That is correct. Yet the real terrorists are the Americans and the Israelis. Nevertheless, we should struggle to be removed from these lists. With

the help of our international friends we are on a good path in this respect.

How active is the PFLP in Gaza?

We are very active. In fact, the situation in Gaza does not differ from the situation in the West Bank. In both places, the PFLP faces severe repression and arrests on a regular basis. We have authoritarian rule both in Gaza and in the West Bank. Take, for example, what happened when the Palestinian people showed solidarity with anti-Mubarak protesters in Egypt. They were prevented from going to the streets by both Hamas and the PNA. Women demonstrating in Gaza have been threatened by the police. In Ramallah, the police beat up young people protesting in solidarity with the Egyptians. Both governments are afraid of democratic developments as we currently witness in Egypt.

The Palestinian left is fragmented. Are there efforts to unite leftist parties?

We are trying hard, regularly holding talks with the PPP, al-Mubadara [PNI], and independent intellectuals about the issue of a common leftist list for the upcoming elections. Sometimes, the leftist parties along with independent intellectuals organize common demonstrations such as the solidarity campaign for the Tunisian revolution. But we face major obstacles. For example, it is unacceptable for us that some leftist parties such as the DFLP are currently part of a government under occupation. If we were offered independence, that would be a different matter.

The last elections were very disappointing for the left. If elections were to take place now, the left could receive up to 30 percent. This, however, is only possible through unity. Otherwise, there is just a choice between two right-wing parties: Hamas, the religious right-wing and Fatah, the secular right-wing. Palestine should not be a two-party system. We see the devastating results of this. All opinions have to be represented. That is why we need to form a real alternative.

Is there any cooperation between you and the Israeli left?

Not officially. The Israeli and Palestinian regimes work against a unity of the left parties. Nevertheless, channels of communication do exist.

What is your position on the state-building activities of the PNA?

Socially and economically we differ from Salam Fayyad because we do not support his free market policy of raising taxes and prices while reducing state subsidies. To stand firm against these neoliberal tendencies, we cooperate closely with trade unions, social movements, and civil society organizations.

Interview with Kayed al-Ghoul, Head of the PFLP Gaza Politburo

How far has the PFLP changed since its founding?
The PFLP was established in 1967 as a nationalist Arab party rooted in Marxist–Leninist theory. The Palestinian people's right to self-determination was the basic consensus. Back then, our aim was a One-State Solution, a democratic secular state in all of historic Palestine for people of all religions to live in. Unfortunately, Israel and the international community did not accept this. We at the PFLP predicted that the Oslo Accords would lead to nothing for the Palestinian people. The fundamental problem is that the areas occupied by Israel in 1967 were treated as disputed area and not as areas to be handed back. There were negotiations about them instead of the drafting of a plan for redeployment. In the end, it resulted in severe limitations on the free movement of Palestinians. We opposed negotiations from the very beginning. It was only later that others understood that we were right all along. It is our firm conviction that negotiations will not lead to an end of the conflict.

In recent years, all Palestinian factions have committed themselves to the Peace Process. However, Israeli society has turned its back on us and shifted to the right. Israel is not ready for peace. The failure of the Peace Process also led to a fortification of Hamas and splinter groups. This is part of the reason it gets harder and harder for moderate forces to conclude a peace treaty. Ninety percent of Palestinians no longer believe in successful peace negotiations. We as the PFLP believe that there has to be pressure from the international community, for example, by means of an international conference as an alternative to the negotiations revoking UN resolutions.

What is the alternative strategy proposed by the PFLP?
We are convinced that all forms of resistance are permissible and have the backing of international law. The respective mode depends upon the circumstances on the ground and the state of the conflict. Palestinians have been pursuing the road of negotiations since 1993, but what are the results? According to international law, we are entitled to use all

forms of resistance. Of course, civilians must not be harmed in armed struggle, only military targets.

Yet in the past the PFLP has repeatedly carried out terrorist operations against civilians. Has there been any critical examination of these actions within the party?

At that time, these actions took place in order to shed a spotlight on the situation of Palestinians. Meanwhile, such acts have been completely stopped. Such acts simply did not serve the purpose. PFLP members who have not yielded to this understanding have been expelled from the party.

The PFLP has not held a Party Congress since 2000. What does that say about internal democracy?

The congress has not taken place because of the national split between Fatah and Hamas. But that should not serve as an excuse. We are now preparing for another Congress.

The PFLP is considered a terrorist movement by the European Union and the United States. What does this mean for your party?

This classification is severely unjust. We are in compliance with international resolutions, even though this means diminishing historical Palestine. The Israeli parties who do not accept international law are not listed as terrorists. The international community is embracing double standards.

How does your role as an opposition party differ in Gaza and the West Bank?

In the early years, we were fighting for liberation. Since the establishment of the PNA we have been fighting for liberation and democracy. Since the [2007 Fatah–Hamas] split, we have had to act in many ways. In Gaza, there is the problem of increasing Islamization, the problem of the blockade followed by rising prices and monopolization. We have been campaigning against a tax increase and for an improvement of education and health care. The split and the blockade are the roots of all these problems. And furthermore Hamas now has a firm grip on Gaza. There have been numerous arrests. The West Bank also has established a large security apparatus and supporters of opposition parties have been arrested on grounds of presenting an alleged security risk. Many nongovernmental organizations that were run by Hamas have been closed down. We are afraid that we are building up two Palestinian societies moving in different directions. This is why the split has to end.

★ ★ ★

Excerpts from PFLP Party Documents

The following excerpts are taken from the Statement on the Thirty-nineth Anniversary of the founding of the PFLP from 2006,[15] and the election platform of PFLP from the same year.[16] Further excerpts are taken from the Platform of the PFLP from 1969.[17]

View on Israeli–Palestinian Conflict

Statement on the Thirty-nineth Anniversary of the Founding of the PFLP (2006):
"Since the establishment of the PFLP, which emerged from the Pan-Arab Movement, we have been loyal, for decades, to the struggles and sacrifices of our people, and have continuously persevered to achieve the goals and aspirations of the liberation of Palestine and the establishment of a democratic nation, in all of historic Palestine, as a strategic goal—without diminishing the importance of achieving our interim goal of a sovereign, independent, Palestinian state on 1967-occupied land, with Jerusalem as its capital, and the return of all Palestinian refugees and their descendants to the homes and land from which they were displaced. We consider the right of return the most essential of our interim goals and the main path to our strategic goal.

The Palestinian cause has entered a complex stage, as the Zionist enemy and the influential forces in what is called the 'international community' continue to deny our people's rights, and endeavor to revoke or reduce these rights—in an attempt to force our people to submit and surrender.

At the same time, the Zionist enemy continues its brutal aggression against our people—murder, destruction, assassination, house demolition, the uprooting of trees, land expropriation, settlement expansion, the continued construction of the Apartheid Wall, a suffocating political and economic siege, torture, and massive oppression.

[We assert] the importance of continuing all forms of resistance, including military resistance, until the occupation is ended; and do NOT accept that negotiation with the enemy is the only strategic method to confront the occupation. We demand that the file of the Palestinian 'issue' be transferred back to the supervision of the UN through an international conference—this will be an essential and welcome shift from the previous, ineffective means of negotiation: bi-lateral talks with the enemy, the Road Map proposed by the Quartet (US, European Union, Russia, and UN), and the enemy's attempts to impose unilateral solutions. We call upon all Palestinian forces to unequivocally and especially reject the latter.

The grave situation in the Gaza Strip: Despite the fact that the five main Palestinian factions in the Gaza Strip agreed to stop rocket attacks against Israel, in exchange for the enemy's cessation of attacks against our people, Israel continues its attack against Palestinians in the West Bank. The PFLP states that:

- We will continue to support the halting of rocket attacks in return for Zionist withdrawal from the areas it re-invaded in Gaza and the West Bank, as well as its commitment to halting all incursions and attacks—whether assassinations, home demolitions, attacking and arresting activists, ground invasions, or air raids. If the enemy violates any of this, we consider ourselves no longer obliged by the agreement.
- We do not consider this agreement on halting rocket attacks to include halting other forms of military and armed resistance.
- We do not consider the halting of rocket attacks to be a general 'ceasefire.' Any future discussion of this will require a Palestinian internal dialogue—to reach an agreement on what we will require from the enemy in return for a ceasefire."

PFLP Election Platform (2006):
"According to international resolutions, Palestinians have the right to establish their own independent state that has full sovereignty over all the territories occupied in 1967 with Jerusalem as its capital. Moreover, international resolutions preserve the right of return for the Palestinian refugees to their homeland.

PFLP calls for the exercise of all forms of struggle and resistance in order to achieve the national goals of the Palestinian people.... The *intifada* and resistance—within the framework of a national strategy-are given priority by PFLP....

PFLP underscores the fact that any discussion of UN resolutions should look into means and mechanisms for their implementation—not amendment or change.

PFLP upholds that any line of attack to resolve the Palestinian cause should be based on the complete implementation of international resolutions and not through fragmented projects like the Oslo Accords or the Road Map since these are mere attempts to contain and abort the Palestinian national struggle and resistance.... PFLP calls for the convention of an international conference whereby the Palestinian people can be provided with international protection, and Israel can be compelled to respect international law....

For the purpose of dismantling the Apartheid Wall, Israeli settlements, military checkpoints and all forms of racial oppression created by the Israeli military occupation forces, PFLP urges the Palestinian people never to cease their resistance and struggle.... PFLP calls for the enactment of a Palestinian law abrogating all legislations that have facilitated settlement activities and land confiscation by the Israelis, including the Ottoman law and Israeli military laws."

PFLP Platform (1969):

"The war of June 1967 disproved the bourgeois theory of conventional war. The best strategy for Israel is to strike rapidly. The enemy is not able to mobilize its armies for a long period of time because this would intensify its economic crisis. It gets complete support from US imperialism and for these reasons it needs quick wars. Therefore for our poor people the best strategy in the long run is a people's war. Our people must overcome their weaknesses and exploit the weaknesses of the enemy by mobilizing the Palestinian and Arab peoples. The weakening of imperialism and Zionism in the Arab world demands revolutionary war....

The Palestinian struggle is a part of the whole Arab liberation movement and of the world liberation movement. The Arab bourgeoisie and world imperialism are trying to impose a peaceful solution on the Palestinian problem but this suggestion merely promotes the interests of imperialism and Zionism, doubt in the efficacy of people's war as a means of liberation, and the preservation of the relations of the Arab bourgeoisie with the imperialist world market. The Arab bourgeoisie is afraid of being isolated from this market and of losing its role as a mediator of world capitalism....

Therefore, the struggle of the Palestinian people must be supported by the workers and peasants, who will fight against any form of domination by imperialism, Zionism or the Arab bourgeoisie.... It is a great mistake to start by saying that the Zionist challenge demands national unity for this shows that one does not understand the real class structure of Zionism. The struggle against Israel is first of all a class struggle. Therefore the oppressed class is the only class which is able to face a confrontation with Zionism.... The decisive battle must be in Palestine.

The armed people's struggle to Palestine can help itself with the simplest weapons in order to ruin the economies and the war machinery of their Zionist enemy. The moving of the peoples struggles into Palestine depends upon agitating and organizing the masses, more than depending upon border actions in the Jordan valley, although these actions are of importance for the struggle in Palestine.

When guerrilla organizations began their actions in the occupied areas, they were faced with a brutal military repression by the armed forces of Zionism. Because these organizations had no revolutionary ideology and so no program, they gave in to demands of self-preservation and retreated into eastern Jordan. All their activity turned into border actions. This presence of the guerrilla organizations in Jordan enables the Jordanian bourgeoisie and their secret agents to crush these organizations when they are no longer useful as pressure for a peaceful solution.... We must not neglect the struggle in east Jordan for this land is connected with Palestine more than with the other Arab countries. The problem of the revolution in Palestine is dialectically connected with the problem of the revolution in Jordan. A chain of plots between the Jordanian monarchy, imperialism and Zionism have proved this connection.... The harmony of the struggle in the two regions must be realized through co-coordinating organs whose tasks will be to guarantee reserves inside Palestine and to mobilize the peasants and soldiers in the border-territories. This is the only way in which Amman can become an Arab Hanoi: A base for the revolutionaries' fighting inside Palestine."

Economic Development

PFLP Election Platform (2006):
"The main principle governing our economic program is the utilization of available economic resources to build up the steadfastness of our people, provide them with their basic needs, and achieve social justice in terms of equal distribution.

We call for:

- Free the Palestinian economy from Israel and the cancelation of the Paris Protocol that gives room for Israeli hegemony over the Palestinian economy and paralyzes all efforts to build a developed Palestinian economy.
- Reinforce resistance against military checkpoints and barriers to allow for free movement and access for goods and people.

- Combat poverty and unemployment, and reorganize resources and create work opportunities especially for the poor and oppressed and for victims of the Israeli military occupation.
- Develop the role of the public sector and widen production base.
- Enact a tax law that does justice to the poor and contributes to social justice."

<u>State's Role vis-a-vis Religion</u>

PFLP Election Platform (2006):
"PFLP aims to establish a state where all people have equal rights irrespective of religion."

<u>Vision of State and Society</u>

Statement on the Thirty-nineth Anniversary of the Founding of the PFLP (2006):
"We call upon all, including our own comrades, to work on building and supporting national unity, and we believe that the essence of this unity will be based on the following factors:

- The reactivation and re-establishment of the Palestine Liberation Organization (PLO) as the sole, legitimate representative of the Palestinian people. This includes the rebuilding of the Palestine National Council via elections, on the basis of proportional representation, as agreed upon in the Cairo Dialogue of [2009–2010]; the PLO's Central Council and Executive Committee, respectively; and the PLO's popular institutions, in an effort to bring democratization to the PLO in a way that would protect our national rights and restore respect for the Palestinian National Charter.
- The importance of forming an actual, national unity government based on the political program of the Palestinian National Consensus Document. We also stress our rejection of any attempt to defuse this document, whether through amendments or by basing its implementation on other documents that may annul it. The PFLP has been at the forefront of those demanding the formation of this government ever since the election of the Palestinian Legislative Council (PLC) in Palestine.

And since a national unity government is one of the main demands of our people as well, we call upon all Palestinian resistance—and popular forces to participate in the current dialogue on the formation of this government, and insist that none of these forces attempt to isolate others from participating."

PFLP Election Platform (2006):

"PFLP looks forward to establishing a state where all people have equal rights irrespective of religion, race, color or sex. PFLP aims to represent and defend the interests of laborers and the poor.

PFLP works for building a Palestinian society founded on the principles of democracy, equality and social justice.

PFLP affirms the position and role played by laborers in the Palestinian society whether on the level of resistance of occupation or the building of society."

PFLP Platform (1969):

"Arab militarism has become an apparatus for oppressing revolutionary socialist movements within the Arab states, while at the same time it claims to be staunchly anti-imperialist. Under the guise of the national question, the bourgeoisie has used its armies to strengthen its bureaucratic power over the masses, and to prevent the workers and peasants from acquiring political power.

So far it has demanded the help of the workers and peasants without organizing them or without developing a proletarian ideology. The national bourgeoisie usually comes to power through military coups and without any activity on the part of the masses, as soon as it has captured power it reinforces its bureaucratic position. Through widespread application of terror it is able to talk about revolution while at the same time it suppresses all the revolutionary movements and arrests everyone who tries to advocate revolutionary action.

The Arab bourgeoisie has used the question of Palestine to divert the Arab masses from realizing their own interests and their own domestic problems. The bourgeoisie always concentrated hopes on a victory outside the state's boundaries, in Palestine, and in this way they were able to preserve their class interests and their bureaucratic positions."

CHAPTER FIVE

PNI: A History of Nonviolence

The Palestinian National Initiative's Quest for an Alternative Approach

National unity, nonviolent resistance, good governance, and social justice are the Palestinian National Initiative's (PNI) key concerns. The party was founded in 2002 and purports to offer an alternative to Palestinians who do not identify with Fatah or Hamas. The PNI is led by a popular leader, Mustafa Barghouthi, although this has so far not translated into a broader public support base in parliamentary elections (table 5.1).

The PNI was founded by Mustafa Barghouthi, Ibrahim Dakkak, Edward Said, and Haider Abdel Shafi in 2002, at the height of the second *intifada*. A group of prominent Palestinians with leftist backgrounds came together to advocate for "Palestinian liberation" through popular struggle and the democratization of political institutions. The fundamental ideology of nonviolence distinguished the group from the militant approach represented by Hamas and the Popular Front for the Liberation of Palestine (PFLP), and from the approach of certain more militant wings of Fatah, which at that time similarly employed military and terror operations.

The secular intellectuals who formed the PNI called for an "independent, democratic, and sovereign Palestinian state with East Jerusalem as its capital on all of the Palestinian land occupied since 1967," as stipulated

Table 5.1 The PNI at a glance

Official name	: PNI / Palestinian National Intitiative (*al-Mubadara al-Wataniya al-Filistiniya*)
Year founded	: 2002
PLO membership since	: – (application pending)
PLC members 1996	: –
PLC members 2006	: 2 (Independent Palestine list, one without party membership)
Ideological orientation	: Leftist, consultative member of Socialist International (SI)
Leadership base	: Ramallah

in the PNI's founding document.[1] At the same time, they were highly critical of what they perceived as the nepotistic and authoritarian structures of the Fatah-dominated Palestinian National Authority (PNA). This focus on internal proceedings of the PNA was explained by the PNI's conviction that "ending occupation and achieving independence is contingent upon the empowerment of the Palestinian people and the institution of democratic practices," as was outlined in the 2002 founding document.[2]

The PNI's leaders originally aspired to supplant leftist parties such as the Palestinian People's Party (PPP) and the Democratic Front for the Liberation of Palestine (DFLP) with a broad left-wing social movement that would essentially act as an umbrella coalition of different leftist factions. However, institutional self-preservation of leftist factions soon made clear that this ideal of uniting the fragmented Palestinian left proved unrealistic. While the PNI has repeatedly joined with other leftist groups to put forth electoral lists, the factions failed to unite and the left remained fragmented. Thus, despite the PNI's aims for a single strengthened left, the movement has simply emerged as one among the many leftist factions.

Unlike the more established left-leaning factions with membership in the Palestine Liberation Organization (PLO), however, the PNI focused strictly on seeking pragmatic solutions and avoided abstract ideological deliberations frequently associated with other leftist factions.

After its founding, the PNI established a network of local branches in municipalities and affiliated youth and women's organizations in the West Bank and Gaza, but not in the Palestinian Diaspora. The party benefited from significant personal connections to nongovernmental and grassroots organizations, especially medical relief institutions, where influential figures of the party continue to hold senior positions to this day. While this strong institutional engagement in the civil society has proven advantageous, the PNI has struggled at times to distinguish between political party activism and civil society movement. This dualism between party and movement has not been rooted in the desire to protect strong connections with the Palestinian Diaspora, as has been the case with other leftist factions. Rather, the PNI maintains a character that they hope will further appeal to activists from the established leftist factions.

This blurring of roles between movement and party has been exacerbated by bureaucratic informality of the PNI's institutions. PNI branches are actively engaged throughout the West Bank and Gaza Strip, operating in local and district councils, and regularly holding elections for their local, district, youth, and women's leaders. However, the PNI has not held a national party congress since its founding, in contravention of its self-declared objectives of democratizing Palestinian society (see chart 5.1).

The PNI attributes this deficiency to the split between Gaza and the West Bank, which prevents the free movement of delegates and candidates. In addition, the organization's leadership has repeatedly opted to postpone comprehensive internal elections on the ground fearing that holding a national party conference will oblige the PNI to disclose the identities of its leadership, exposing them to political retaliation by Israel and the PNA.

From the outset, the PNI has distinguished itself through an unconditional focus on nonviolence, a stance only shared to a similar extent by the PPP. Together, both movements are the only PLC factions that have never established a military wing. After the end of the second *intifada*, leading figures from the PNI, including its secretary general Mustafa Barghouthi, and its co-founder, Edward Said, were among the first public figures to embrace popular resistance activities, most notably the Anti-Apartheid Wall Campaign against the Israeli separation barrier, built largely on Palestinian territory.

The PNI, however, did not attract broad attention until the PNA presidential elections in 2005. The international boycott of Hamas catapulted the PNI's candidate for presidency, Mustafa Barghouthi, into the position of Mahmoud Abbas's prime competitor. The endorsement of Barghouthi by the Popular Front for the Liberation of Palestine (PFLP), whose attempts to support a common candidate with the Democratic Front for the Liberation of Palestine (DFLP) and the Palestinian People's Party (PPP) had failed, gave Barghouthi's campaign a significant boost. Cashing in on widespread disillusionment with Fatah, Barghouthi presented himself as a force of reform, campaigning that "people are fed up

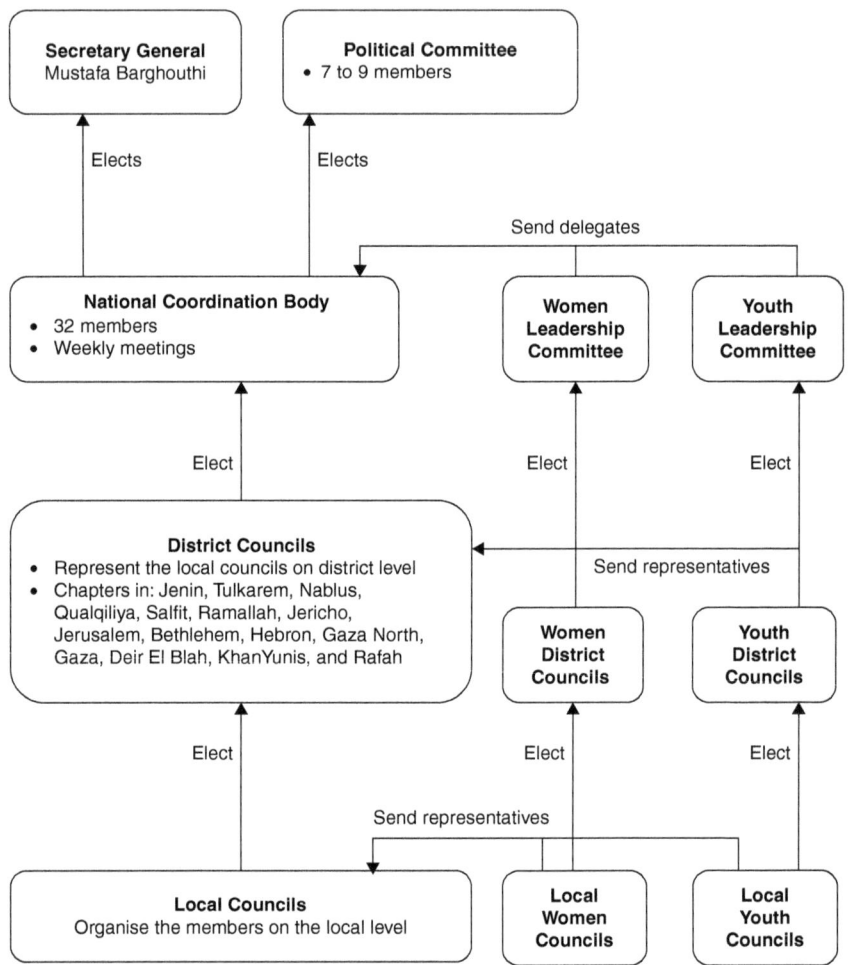

Chart 5.1 Organizational structure of the PNI.

with the system, they are fed up with corruption, they are fed up with favoritism. People want change."[3]

Despite the PNI's lack of experience in election campaigns and its inadequate party administration comprising mostly of volunteers, Barghouthi secured a respectable 19 percent of votes. According to exit polls conducted by the Palestinian Centre for Policy and Survey Research, the PNI attracted mainly young, educated voters who were not as attached to the hierarchies of the PNA as were supporters of

Mahmoud Abbas. Though the PNI failed to repeat this initial success in the municipal elections held in September of the same year (the PNI candidates and its coalition partners gained seats in 16 out of 104 municipalities), hopes were high when the PNI participated in the Palestinian Legislative Council (PLC) elections of 2006.

Along with a number of independent civil society candidates, the PNI formed the Independent Palestine list. As the PFLP, which had supported the PNI in the previous year, now participated in the elections as a competing faction, the PNI was forced to compete on its own. The Independent Palestine list was, in its own words, "a truly democratic and independent alternative [for] the large majority of silent and unrepresented Palestinian voters, who favor neither the autocracy and corruption of the governing Fatah party nor the fundamentalism of Hamas."[4]

For the PNI, results were disappointing: in an atmosphere of political polarization between Hamas and Fatah, the Independent Palestine list received 2.7 percent of the vote. Two representatives, Mustafa Barghouthi and Rawya al-Shawa (who does not hold party membership), gained seats in the PLC. The outcome demonstrated that Barghouthi's personal charisma and popularity did not automatically translate into a wide voter support base for the PNI in PLC elections.

With only two seats in the PLC, the party could not realistically challenge the two dominant movements, Hamas and Fatah. The results from the 2006 elections also prevented the party from providing a public platform for its younger activists, who had hoped to use PLC seats to strengthen the PNI by establishing a second rank of party leaders.

Despite these challenges, the PNI and its leader remained visible players in Palestinian politics. Mustafa Barghouthi's efforts to mediate between Hamas and Fatah gained widespread recognition and praise and he was subsequently appointed as minister of information in the National Unity Government of 2007. Since this time, the PNI has struggled to widen its support base mainly through grassroots activism in universities, through nonviolent resistance, and in public media campaigns including initiatives to boycott Israeli products. Underlying these efforts are attempts to merge a popular social and political agenda into wider support for the PNI as a political party.

As a consultative member of the Socialist International (the worldwide organization of social democratic, socialist, and labor parties), the PNI has drawn on the experience of its social democratic and socialist sister parties, and enjoys political backing from many European parliamentarians. The PNI's international appeal is facilitated by the movement's clear and unequivocal rejection of violence. The recent adoption of nonviolent forms of struggle by several Palestinian parties such as Fatah and, to a lesser extent, elements within Hamas, is often attributed to the PNI's role in promoting peaceful popular resistance as an alternative to open-ended negotiations with Israel.

According to the PNI, the Oslo Accords and the US-backed Road Map for Peace (2003) gave rise to an "endless 'interim' stage that Israel can use to deepen its grip on occupied land," as articulated in the PNI's political platform from 2007.[5] For the PNI, the status quo merely facilitates what Mustafa Barghouthi has denounced as Israeli apartheid: "Apartheid is here. There is one set of Israeli laws applied to Palestinians in the West Bank and another set applied to Jews in the West Bank. Israeli settlers live illegally in beautiful subsidized housing on stolen Palestinian land while we are relegated to smaller and smaller *bantustans*."[6] Faced with the prospect of continued bilateral negotiations between Israel and the Palestine Liberation Organization (PLO), the PNI in 2011 staunchly advocated for the unilateral declaration of a Palestinian state and called for a united stance from Hamas and Fatah.

Unsurprisingly, the success of nonviolent activism in the revolutions of the Arab Spring in 2011 was perceived with enthusiasm by many in the PNI, who felt that their preferred method of struggle in the confrontation with Israel had now proven its merits and would boost the PNI's public appeal.

Thus, when the PNA postponed municipal elections in 2011, the PNI and other leftist movements vehemently objected, organizing demonstrations and accusing the PNA of antidemocratic practices. Barghouthi claimed the continued postponement of elections made "a mockery of the interests of the Palestinian people" and was causing the "slow death of Palestinian democracy."[7]

Despite the publicity that such campaigns generated for the PNI, the party's ambitious aim to fill the void between Hamas and Fatah and to emerge as the third major force in Palestinian politics has clearly not been realized. At least in part, this is due to the fact that other political players have also come forward to offer voters alternatives, including current prime minister Salam Fayyad's Third Way list, which gained two seats in the PLC in 2006. The limited success of the PNI in elections has also often been attributed to a leadership that was singularly brought together by the secretary general and is, as a result, perceived to be elitist. Observers have also noted that the secular stance of the PNI is largely incompatible with the Palestinian mainstream where party politics and religious affiliation continue to remain firmly intertwined.

Political aims of the PNI have also been hindered by efforts of established political forces to block the emergence of a viable alternative. Tensions between the PNI and Palestinian security forces in the West Bank, by and large under Fatah control, were reported during preparations for the 2010 and 2011 municipal elections. PNI activists were repeatedly harassed and arrested by PNA forces, an indication that the PNI was perceived by the political establishment to be a greater threat than the 2.7 percent results in the PLC elections might suggest. The PNI has also been prevented from joining the PLO. An application for membership in 2004 was met by heavy resistance from existing members, particularly Fatah, and resulted in continued exclusion and thus limited relevance of the PNI in Palestinian politics. Only in December 2011 was the PNI admitted into the "interim leadership" of the PLO in anticipation of comprehensive reform to the PLO following the Fatah–Hamas reconciliation agreements signed at the time.

Relations between Hamas and the PNI are often less tense. Although the two factions are positioned at opposing ends of the ideological spectrum, the PNI's policy of uncompromising, nonviolent resistance has made possible its continued low-key presence in Gaza. In addition, Mustafa Barghouthi's high-profile activism, including his participation in the first flotilla to breach the blockade of Gaza, has earned respect from within the Hamas leadership.

Recent student elections in the West Bank demonstrate that among the younger generation of Palestinians, the PNI remains a relevant player. In November 2010, the PNI list won 7.4 percent of the vote in the student council elections at al-Najah National University in Nablus. Should this success translate in the coming years into national electoral success, the PNI may become increasingly relevant if they are indeed able to mobilize student support. As observers have frequently pointed out, this, however, is contingent on a more inclusive approach to selecting leadership positions. In addition, there is the risk that the party might fall victim to its own programmatic success as the PNI's unique stance of nonviolent activism becomes increasingly diluted as other Palestinian factions adopt similar policies. Whether the PNI will be able to generate broader-based electoral appeal beyond the label of nonviolent resistance and address concerns of intellectual elitism will very likely determine the long-term course of the party.[8]

Mustafa Barghouthi

Mustafa Barghouthi is a leading proponent of nonviolent resistance, an outspoken member of the PLC, and a former presidential candidate. Committed to advocating for the Palestinian cause to the international community, he has also gained a positive reputation for his mediation efforts between Hamas and Fatah.

Born in Jerusalem in 1954, Mustafa Barghouthi studied medicine in Moscow and returned to the Palestinian Territories in 1978. He practiced in hospitals in East Jerusalem and Ramallah before attending Stanford University, where he completed a graduate degree in management. While working at East Jerusalem's Muqasem Hospital, Barghouthi began to engage in political and social activism. In 1983 he co-founded and was later elected director of the Palestinian Medical Relief Society (PMRS), and co-founded the Health, Development Information and Policy Institute (HDIP), an organization that offers educational programs, political analysis, and assistance with health issues.

Barghouthi participated in the 1991 Madrid Peace Conference and unsuccessfully ran for the PLC on a PPP ballot in the 1996 elections. He also represented the PPP in the PNC and served as one of its general secretaries. Increasingly frustrated with both political stagnation and the stance of the PPP, Barghouthi co-founded the PNI in 2002 and has served as its secretary general since this time. Barghouthi sought to present a political alternative to Palestinian voters, one which steers clear of the religious outlook of Hamas and the internal deficiencies in the democratic process often associated with Fatah. As one of seven competitors for the Palestinian presidency in 2005, Barghouthi gained 19 percent of the vote.

Frequently travelling between Ramallah, Gaza, and Damascus, Barghouthi co-mediated a compromise between Fatah and Hamas that led to the National Unity Government of 2007, in which he served as minister of information. When President Abbas dissolved the National Unity Government in June of that year, Barghouthi refused to serve in the interim government headed by Salam Fayyad, criticizing lack of legitimacy. Despite this, in recent years, Barghouthi has been repeatedly mentioned as a candidate for different government positions, including the post of prime minister.

Barghouthi has been one of the most outspoken Palestinian leaders of nonviolent resistance and has accused Israel of implementing an "apartheid system."[9] He participated in the first Gaza Flotilla and regularly attends rallies and demonstrations against house demolitions, expropriations, and the separation barrier. Barghouthi was part of the Palestinian delegation to the International Court of Justice in The Hague in 2004, which resulted in the court's advisory opinion on the illegality of the barrier. In response to the continuation of settlement construction in the Palestinian Territories, Barghouthi has become an ardent advocate of boycotting Israeli products. In 2012, he argued that "it is crucial that we substitute Israeli products with Palestinian and alternative products in both Palestinian markets and homes. If we reduce our consumption of Israeli goods by 10 percent it will create 100,000 job opportunities for Palestinian graduates, reduce unemployment and strengthen our steadfastness."[10]

His decade of political activism has resulted in repeated arrests by Israeli authorities. In January 2002, following a press conference in East Jerusalem, Israeli forces arrested Barghouthi and reportedly broke his knees with rifle butts, claims that the Israeli military has denied. In March 2012, Barghouthi was injured in demonstrations held at Qalandia check-point when hit by a tear gas canister fired by Israeli security forces and in an ensuing brawl with violent Fatah activists who challenged Barghouthi's leading role in the rally.

In the years since the end of the second *intifada*, Barghouthi has become a celebrity of the international media, including leading Arabic news channels and *The Daily Show* in the United States. In 2011 the influential US publication *Foreign Policy* included Mustafa Barghouthi in its list of the "Top 100 Global Thinkers" and applauded his determination to "pioneer an alternative path that emphasizes nonviolent tactics to delegitimize the Israeli occupation and demands that the Palestinian national movement live up to its ideals."[11] In March 2012 he was invited to address the annual conference of the US-based Jewish lobby group J-Street.

Barghouthi's international reputation and intellectual outlook have, however, prompted criticism that the PNI is essentially an elitist organization focused on the role of its secretary general. Others, including moderate forces within Hamas, have expressed an appreciation for his political positions and efforts to overcome the split between Hamas and Fatah. In June 2011 and again in June 2012, Hamas's leadership proposed Barghouthi as Palestinian foreign minister in a still to-be-formed transitional government.

Edward Said

It is an often overlooked fact that prominent Palestinian academic Edward Said was involved in establishing the PNI. The renowned author of the now classic study *Orientalism* co-founded the party in 2002.

Edward Said was born into a Christian family from Jerusalem in 1935. The circumstances of his early childhood have been somewhat controversial. While he often stated to have spent parts of his formative years in Jerusalem, critics have questioned this account, claiming that he spent his childhood in Cairo, where his father, a US citizen, had established himself. After attending English schools in Cairo and Alexandria, Said migrated to the United States in the early 1950s, earning his BA in English literature from Princeton University (1957) before continuing his studies at Harvard University, where he received his MA and eventually his PhD (1964).

A tenured, full professor of the English Department at Columbia University, Said lectured at universities in North America, Europe, and the Middle East. Considered one of the founders of postcolonial criticism, Said received countless awards (among them Harvard University's Bowdoin Prize and the Lannan Literary Award for Lifetime Achievement) as well as more than a dozen honorary doctorates. In his most famous academic publication *Orientalism*, Said described the nature of Western studies of Islamic Civilization and deconstructed what he described as racist and imperialist tendencies.

Aside from these academic pursuits, Said was committed to advocating on behalf of Palestinian national aspirations. Between 1977 and 1991, he served as an independent member of the Palestinian National Council (PNC), the legislative body of the PLO. He played a leading role in American Professors for Peace in the Middle East, acted as a consultant to the UN for the International Conference on the Question of Palestine, and assisted in drafting a Palestinian constitution.

In the course of carrying out these political activities, Said became increasingly critical of the PLO leadership, eventually resigning from the PNC in 1991. A long-standing supporter of Yasir Arafat, he vehemently rejected the 1993 Oslo Accords, famously dubbing them "an instrument of Palestinian surrender, a Palestinian Versailles," since—as he put it—the PLO "ended the *intifada*, which embodied not terrorism or violence but the Palestinian right to resist, even though Israel remains in occupation of the West Bank and Gaza."[12]

His rejection of Oslo was in part based on his conviction that the fate of Palestinian refugees and Palestinians living in Israel was largely ignored and that the signing of the accords did not curb Israeli settlement expansion in the Palestinian Territories. These condemnations resulted in both praise and strong criticism, including from the PNA, which temporarily banned the sale of his books. Following the failed

Camp David negotiations, Said publicly praised Arafat's rejection of Ehud Barak's offer, which resulted in a warming of his relations with the PNA leadership.

In July 2000, Said caused controversy during a visit to Lebanon, where he met with Hezbollah leader Hassan Nasrallah shortly before hurling a rock at Israeli border installations. Said later described the act as an expression of joy over the Israeli withdrawal from South Lebanon and regretted that "the comic quality of the situation did not come out."[13]

In 2002, Said co-founded the PNI. In an op-ed published in the Egyptian weekly *al-Ahram*, Said argued that "a new secular nationalist current" was necessary, because "negotiating an improvement in the occupation is tantamount to prolonging it. Peace can only come after the occupation ends."[14] One year later he passed away from leukemia at the age of 67.

★ ★ ★

Interviews with PNI Decision Makers

The following interviews were conducted with Mustafa Barghouthi (see biography) in Ramallah and Ayed Yaghi in Gaza City. Mustafa Barghouthi has acted as secretary general of the PNI since the party's founding and represents the PNI in the PLC. Barghouthi also briefly served as minister of information in 2007. Ayed Yaghi is a medical doctor and civil society activist from Gaza. Like many PNI leaders, he is a former member of the PPP, and defected from the party to establish the PNI. He currently serves as the PNI's chairman in the Gaza Strip.

Interview with Mustafa Barghouthi, Secretary General, Member of the PLC
What is the PNI's unique contribution to Palestinian politics?
First of all, al-Mubadara represents not only a political but also a social movement. Our party strikes a balance between the three major issues that we focus on: first, we focus on liberating the Palestinian people from occupation in its struggle for self-determination; second, we focus on social rights for Palestinians; and third, we focus on democracy. We are not willing to compromise on any of these issues.

Furthermore, al-Mubadara is a truly independent party vis-a-vis the two dominant movements Fatah and Hamas. We substantially differ from both–partly politically and partly socially—and in this respect, more and more people regard us as a viable alternative to the bipolarization existing between Fatah and Hamas.

Essentially, al-Mubadara is unique because it is a progressive and new movement. When I say progressive, I mean this in the sense that al-Mubadara is probably the only Palestinian party that has a real women's organization and genuine female leadership as well as strong youth organizations, which are not dominated by the older generation.

When the PNI was founded, the Palestinian left was already fragmented. Why was forming a new party necessary?
Haidar Abdel Shafi, Edward Said, and I had been thinking about a third way party since 1994 or 1995, particularly after the signing of the Oslo Accords, with which we did not agree. And by the way, time has shown that we were absolutely right in our rejection.

But more importantly, in the course of the Oslo Process, the PNA was established, creating for the first time an internal separation of social issues from the issue of the occupation. These factors required a new approach. In my opinion, the established parties simply did not adapt to the fact that a new phase of transition had begun.

In the beginning, we thought that there was no need for a full-fledged new party and that a coalition of parties independent from Hamas and Fatah could succeed to represent a third way. That is why from 1996 we were regularly meeting and discussing how to form such a front. Even when we started al-Mubadara, we did not regard it as new party. Instead, we thought that it would become a coalition of members from different parties. For a number of years we were trying to convince other parties to become part of this initiative. This included the PPP of which I was still a member at that time. Gradually, we realized that those parties were too inflexible and incapable of such a development. So, we decided to move into the direction of founding a full-fledged party.

Our biggest learning experience was the presidential elections in 2005. It was then that we realized that we really have a convincing vision, a sound program, and a good leadership. The remaining challenge was the organization itself, which was not very sophisticated. And at one point, the PPP gave me an ultimatum—to stop or to leave the party. I chose al-Mubadara and it was the right decision.

How does the PNI view the prospects of a Two-State Solution?
Chances for a Two-State Solution are definitely shrinking. We warned against this development already back in 1998. We spoke about the

very high risk that the whole concept of a Two-State Solution could vanish in discontent. Now, this risk is real. If things do not change, you might soon see many people giving up on the idea of a Two-State Solution.

The PNI formally calls for two states. Is the scenario of a One-State Solution also discussed in earnest?

The One-State Solution is not our preference, but of course, it is an option. Our focus is simply the struggle against a system of discrimination and apartheid against Palestinians. If these problems can be addressed by a One-State Solution that offers equal rights to all its citizens, we are ready for that.

Nonviolent resistance has been a cornerstone of the PNI's activities and message from the beginning. Why did the party focus on this approach?

Al-Mubadara was probably the first party to speak about nonviolent resistance and it certainly was the first party to actually practice it. We adopted it immediately after Israel started building the wall. Over the course of the last eight years, we have been criticized by almost every other Palestinian party for this concept. Again and again we were told we were not militant enough.

For me, this is another unique feature of al-Mubadara: we say what we do and we do what we say. We do not claim that we are not part of the government while some of our members are actually serving in the cabinet. You might be able to cheat yourself but you cannot cheat your people. We do what we think and our popular nonviolent approach is the best example.

Of course, we have had difficult times: I remember a meeting with a Hamas leader who mocked our nonviolent approach with sexist remarks like "So how is your women's struggle going?" But this has changed. I remember very well when I arrived on a humanitarian ship to Gaza—it was the beginning of the Flotilla Movement. People were full of respect and even asked me to address their leaders about the value and importance of nonviolent resistance. I believe today that all parties practice nonviolent resistance or they do not practice any resistance at all. Effectively, there is currently no other form of resistance. Hamas wants a cease-fire. Although Fatah members keep talking about armed struggle, we know very well that they are opposed to it. I think our nonviolent approach is succeeding and has become the main form of struggle in Palestine today.

Unlike the PNA, the PNI calls not only for a boycott of settlement products but also for a comprehensive boycott of Israel. Why?

Yes, our boycott includes all Israeli goods. Boycotting the occupier, after all, is precisely what Gandhi did in India. In general, a boycott of settlement products would certainly be more focused. However, the practice of Israeli companies in the occupied territories makes it impossible to differentiate between goods produced in the settlements and goods produced in Israel proper.

Are you not concerned that a boycott of Israeli goods will alienate the Israeli peace camp?

I do not think so. I just returned from a conference organized by the Jewish-American group J-Street. And I spoke very frankly also about the question of boycotts. To be honest, I took a risk. I was expecting to be met with harsh criticism but chose to be frank anyways. And then the opposite happened. Instead of criticism there were standing ovations.

The PNI is sometimes criticized as being a "one man show." Is this criticism justified?

Any institution in the Middle East has similar structures focusing on leading personalities. By criticizing us as a one man show, in fact, our opponents try to transform one of our advantages into a weakness. This is not a one-person party. A successful political party needs to be based on a combination of different elements: A decisive leader, a convincing program, and a strong and broad internal organization. To accuse us of being successful on these levels does not make a lot of sense.

Also, such critics tend to neglect the fact that al-Mubadara was founded as a coalition of several well-known personalities such as Haider Abdel Shafi. Abdel Shafi or Edward Said, one of the most famous Arab intellectuals in the world were much better known at that time than me.

But this is also about perceptions: When we built up party structures, a solid leadership was also established. But these personalities have not always been willing to engage in media work to the same extent that I am. This sometimes creates the wrong impression. We actually have several popular leaders like Raja Shehadeh, who was the founder of the first human rights organization in Palestine, al-Haq, and a well-known author. His publications are well respected and read throughout the world. And of course there is Salah Khawaja, a very popular and well-known activist and leader. Also, many of our leaders are still rather young. But this will change.

How does the PNI justify the fact that it has not yet held a general party conference to elect its leadership when the party purports to represent a force for democratic change?

It is correct that the PNI has not yet held a general conference. But this does not mean that we have not had elections. As a matter of fact, every position in the party has been legitimized by an electoral process. Elections have regularly taken place on the local, the district, and the national level. Central party leadership positions such as the position of secretary general were elected in 2003 and 2007. The big issue for the holding of a general conference on the national level is the difficulty of ensuring that our members from Gaza and abroad will be actually able to participate.

How does the PNI view the current work of the PNA under Prime Minister Salam Fayyad?

We appreciate many things that Salam Fayyad has done, especially in the area of reforming institutions. Nobody can argue that his creation of a central accounting system in the West Bank is a bad idea. Also, when he interacts with the grassroot level, he acts as a role model.

Nevertheless, we do not agree with many of the economic policies that Fayyad applies, and we are concerned that these policies are basically unabated neoliberalism. Furthermore, we do not agree with the way he allocated the PNA budget. The fact that 34 percent of the budget is spent on security matters and only 1 percent on agriculture for example is unacceptable. This has to change. For example, we have exerted pressure on the PNA to establish a student loan fund as one of several reforms we would like to see.

We very often disagree on how to deal with the poorer sectors of the community. We would never accept and we struggle against the health insurance law that the PNA passed since it does not take into consideration the needs of poor people. Moreover, we oppose the new planned taxing system that will tax people without pension. So, in the field of economy there are several issues on which we differ. We are also cautious about Fayyad's so-called state-building project prior to having a state. We are extremely worried—and Fayyad should be worried as well—that Israel will squeeze us into 40 percent of the land and tell us "this is Palestine."

One more important issue is the issue of democracy and the issues of arbitrary and political arrests, which we think are completely unacceptable. We need elections to be held and we need a fixed date!

How do the PNI and Fatah cooperate as fellow members of the SI?
Inside the Socialist International, we are cooperating in an excellent way. But outside the SI we have had problems. Why is Fatah, which controls the PLO, preventing us from joining the organization? We applied several years ago and have not been accepted. At the same time, small groups that received merely 0.5 percent of the vote in recent elections are part of the PLO and receive funding from the body. We are excluded and discriminated against in the same way that Hamas is.

Another important issue is the way the security apparatus deals with us—they keep interrogating party activists, they keep intimidating party activists, and this is unacceptable in terms of fair competition between the parties. Despite these obstacles, we see our relationship in the future as one of partners in a national unity framework.

How can the lingering crisis between Hamas and Fatah be overcome?
The most important thing for us is to get democracy back on track. We do need a unified leadership. But this leadership must be formed on the basis of democracy and must be legitimized by elections. The respective parties must be represented proportionally in a national unity government according to the votes of the people. It does not make sense that someone who is supported by 1,000 people receives the same share as a person supported by 400,000. So our idea is unity on the basis of democracy.

Interview with Ayed Yaghi, PNI Chairman in the Gaza Strip

What would you say have been the PNI's most significant milestones since it was established in 2002?
The presidential elections in 2005 were crucial. Previously most people did not know about al-Mubadara, even though they were familiar with our founders, Haider Abdel Shafi, Edward Said, and Mustafa Barghouthi. It was not until Barghouthi's impressive election campaign that people started to learn about our party.

Hopes were high when al-Mubadara formed a list with other social actors like independent personalities, water committees, and workers' movements for the PLC elections in 2006. The result was alright but not up to our expectations. We had hoped to receive at least five percent of the vote. On the other hand, we were happy to enter the PLC despite the polarization between Hamas and Fatah.

After the elections, Palestine witnessed a dangerous period of internal clashes. During this time, al-Mubadara was an influential actor in mediating between Hamas and Fatah, which gave us credibility in both movements. Although it was difficult to agree on a common agenda, we managed after a long dialogue with Hamas and other factions to form a National Unity Government in which Mustafa Barghouthi became minister of information.

How does the PNI's situation in Gaza and the West Bank differ?
Since the Hamas takeover in Gaza we are facing more and more obstacles. This happens both in Gaza and in the West Bank. Of course, restrictions that we face are not as severe as those that Hamas faces in the West Bank or Fatah faces in Gaza, but it has become more difficult to remain independent. Hamas wants us to support their agenda in Gaza while in the West Bank Fatah and others try to pressure us as well. In early 2011, Salam Fayyad asked us to become part of a new government but we refused because we do not want to be instrumentalized by any group.

In Gaza, Hamas does not consider us a supportive party. Although they generally respect us, we are not permitted to stage popular resistance activities, we cannot put our logo anywhere and even a few of our activists have been detained for some time.

While in the West Bank, al-Mubadara is popular because of its nonviolent resistance and social activities as well as because of its efforts to introduce student loans, support for the party in Gaza is based on other features. Here, al-Mubadara enjoys support primarily because of Mustafa Barghouthi's popularity and the party's mediation efforts between Hamas and Fatah.

The main dividing line runs between the PLO factions and Hamas. Even though we occasionally participate in meetings with PLO members—after the Hamas takeover we jointly established a national work committee—we are excluded and do not benefit from the cooperation. When the last International Conference on Palestinian Prisoners took place, both the PLO and Hamas sent a delegation while we were ignored.

How would you describe the PNI's relations to Hamas in Gaza?
At the end of December 2010, Hamas invited us to join the government in Gaza. In fact, they put severe pressure on al-Mubadara, PFLP, Islamic Jihad, and others to accept. We rejected this demand and our negative answer caused problems. The internal security forces were putting pressure on us and some of our members were asked to work for the security services and to report on our activities.

In the West Bank, the PNI focused on nonviolent resistance. Is this possible in Gaza?

In cooperation with the national work committee we tried to start popular, nonviolent resistance against the siege in 2008. For example, we were demonstrating at the Beit Hanoun Checkpoint. Usually Hamas prevents us from entering the buffer zone because they want to keep the borders quiet. We often prepared official requests to hold demonstrations but these were mostly rejected. We are also encouraging Hamas members to participate in popular actions, since they have a huge following. Our attempts have not been very successful so far.

The PNI is often labeled a "one man show." Does this pose a problem?

To the contrary, Mustafa Barghouthi's popularity is very helpful. People are seeking charismatic personalities. The only problem with respect to Gaza is that Dr. Mustafa cannot access the Gaza Strip easily. Many people would like to speak directly with him.

His reputation in Gaza is outstanding. He was the first important politician to come after Ariel Sharon's Gaza disengagement in 2005 and to talk with ordinary people. When Gaza was bombed in 2008 and 2009 by the Israeli army, he was also the first to visit the people whose houses were destroyed. Certainly, his involvement in the flotilla events helped to boost his popularity.

Founded by intellectuals, is the PNI an intellectualist party?

No, we reach out to all strata of society and our supporters come from different backgrounds. Our election list consists of members from all regional parts and professions, from urban people to Bedouins. We are not at all a "party of doctors" as some say. Honestly speaking, I sometimes wish we had not less but more intellectuals among our ranks. One other striking feature of al-Mubadara is that 80 percent of its members are either women or below the age of around 27. So it is a young movement.

Is forming a joint leftist list the key to restrengthening the left?

I hope this will be achieved but I do not see real progress. Interests are differing between the parties, and personal animosities prevent reaching an acceptable agenda for all. What is most important is that ordinary people just do not respect the traditional leftist parties anymore.

* * *

Excerpts of PNI's Programmatic Documents

The following excerpts are drawn from the PNI's 2007 Political Platform.[15] Further excerpts are taken from the PNI's foundational document from 2002, titled The Palestinian National Initiative: Leading the Palestinian People toward Freedom, Independence, Justice, Democracy, and a Life of Dignity.[16]

The Israeli–Palestinian Conflict

Political Platform (2007):

"The PNI advocates for an independent, sovereign, viable and contiguous Palestinian state on all Palestinian Territories occupied in 1967. The PNI seeks a just and lasting peace with Israel, based on a final settlement of all core issues: settlements, borders, the removal of the Apartheid Wall, Jerusalem, refugees and water. It does not support a return to an Oslo-type process with an endless 'interim' stage that Israel can exploit to deepen its grip on occupied land.

Any agreement that tries to improve conditions under Israeli military rule rather than ending it outright is tantamount to prolonging the occupation. The PNI calls for a genuine international peace conference between united Palestinians and Israel to solve the core issues for a just peace. The PNI maintains that Palestinians have the right to resist occupation, but that this resistance should be nonviolent, and directed by a united leadership.

The PNI strongly believes that Israel will not end the occupation by itself, but only under pressure from the kind of international solidarity activity and sanctions that forced an end to the Apartheid Regime in South Africa. Freedom and independence will only be achieved through democracy, as only a government with a popular mandate can legitimately negotiate on behalf of the Palestinian people."

The Palestinian National Initiative (2002):

"The Palestinian people have proven their ability to resist and withstand occupation while continuing their struggle for freedom and self-determination. Our people have sacrificed unconditionally by creating the Palestinian struggle, initiating the first and second popular uprisings against oppression and occupation, and affirming our determination to gain freedom and a just peace based on peaceful coexistence. The countless killed and wounded in these struggles and the sacrifices of their families must not be in vain. These heroic struggles must be honored and transformed into tangible results for our just cause.

It is now time to empower and organize our people to achieve our goal of a just peace by ending the occupation and securing the removal of all settlements; by establishing an independent, democratic, and sovereign Palestinian state with East Jerusalem as its capital on all of the Palestinian land occupied since 1967; by safeguarding the right of Palestinian refugees to return to their homes; by implementing the relevant United Nations resolutions; and by thwarting any attempts to annex occupied land or to isolate and racially oppress the Palestinian people....

We also present [this vision] as a framework for the building of nationhood, to work for positive change, to celebrate national non-violent resistance against occupation, and to present an opportunity to all Palestinians who have the interest of their homeland at heart to participate productively in national and social service....

[The PNI is] working to free all political prisoners: The freedom of those imprisoned by the occupiers represents the first condition for progress towards a just peace."

Economic Development

Political Platform (2007):
"Clear laws and mechanisms must be introduced to protect investment projects and other economic activities against undue interference or pressure from government officials. Unemployment must be fought and work as well as training for the unemployed must be provided. New graduates must be incorporated into the workforce. This is the best place to which financial support can be directed.

The PNI promotes social justice to guarantee the right of all Palestinians to a life of dignity and pride. It aims to secure access to health, education and housing service and to employment on the basis of need and merit, and not political patronage, for all, particularly women, youth, the elderly, the poor, and people with disabilities."

The Palestinian National Initiative (2002):
"Providing work for the unemployed, as well as training and incorporating new graduates into the work force, is one of the most important elements of our social and economic future.... We must work on:

- developing infrastructure projects with the aim of creating jobs
- developing support programs for training and employing new graduates in national institutions and in the private sector
- supporting Palestinian farmers and their noble stance against the cancerous spread of settlements
- directing foreign aid towards creating job opportunities and effective investment for the tens of thousands of unemployed Palestinians and towards bolstering the national economy
- dismantling all economic monopolies, reviewing government investment accounts, and safeguarding the freedom of investment in a fair and egalitarian manner for all Palestinians in accordance with the law
- supporting activities of economic growth that achieve the best possibility of social justice for those deprived, especially the displaced, refugees, villagers, young workers, and the poor
- supporting the production sector, protecting it from monopolies, and outlawing the use of political and security positions to gain economic advantages
- imposing detailed monitoring of the procedures of employment, especially in the government, to prevent abuses of power, nepotism, and favoritism
- developing programs and activities that upgrade individual and institutional abilities

[The PNI will work towards] securing Health, Education, Social Welfare, and the Rights of Women. We propose:

- a comprehensive plan for healthcare and health insurance that provides quality treatment for all citizens, offers the appropriate treatment for cancer and for terminal illnesses, improves childcare and maternal care, and establishes developed rural centers capable of providing proper primary care...
- a fundamental solution to the crisis of higher education by establishing transparent national loan programs available to all students, thereby realizing the dream of Palestinian families to provide education for their children
- honoring education in all its stages, supporting kindergarten children and schools, and improving education to more modern levels
- providing a dignified living for teachers by making their salaries regular, and establishing an incentive program to encourage talented teachers to remain at the local universities

- creating laws for social welfare and social security that guarantee dignified retirement in cases of old age, disability, and injury. This also applies to those who participated in the struggle, including veterans of the Palestinian struggle, families of those killed and wounded, the imprisoned, and new retirees, in accordance with the rules of civil service
- responding to the needs and protecting the rights of the disabled and injured
- supporting the role of mothers, families, and teachers of the kindergarten and elementary stages in shaping proper morals and values in the Palestinian citizens
- investing in Palestinian youth in all areas of health, education, and culture, because they are the future of the Palestinian people."

State's Role vis-a-vis Religion

No Reference.

Vision of State and Society

Political Platform (2007):

"Our starting point is our deep belief in the abilities of the Palestinian people to struggle, to be successful in their efforts to build an independent Palestinian state, and to work for the rights of Palestinian refugees.... Our challenge is to create the right systems, structures, and circumstances to empower the people and involve Palestinians in the national struggle by electing trusted and respected leaders to the right positions in our civil governance structure.

The work of NGOs and civic organizations has a major role in instilling and nurturing democratic principles in our society. A sustainable and high-quality system of higher education must be promoted to meet the developmental needs of Palestinian society. The role of the Palestinian woman for her great contribution should be honored by acknowledging her rights and meeting her needs on an equal basis with men."

The Palestinian National Initiative (2002):

"We present this national initiative in response to the demands for greater national unity that have been made for many years. It is an effort to join all Palestinian men and women in a common cause to achieve their freedom and build their future and the future of their children....

Our starting point is our deep belief in the abilities of the Palestinian people to struggle, to be successful in their efforts to build an independent Palestinian state, and to work for the rights of Palestinian refugees. Our people have a deep-rooted history of struggle, and we have human resources that vie with those of developed countries in education level and expertise. Our challenge is to create the right systems, structures, and circumstances to empower the people and involve Palestinians in the national struggle by electing trusted and respected leaders to the right positions in our civil governance structure.

This belief reflects our confidence that we can affect what happens to us; that it is possible to improve our performance; that progress, real reform, and the support of nation-building is continuous work; and that the demand for positive change is a duty for every citizen.

We must emphasize that the internal process and reform of Palestinian nation-building are matters that concern the Palestinian people and institutions. Its implementation must be accomplished through dialogue with the Palestinian people rather than through the influence of external pressure. There must be absolute defiance of the attempts of the Israeli Occupation Forces to interfere in our internal affairs, for they seek to keep our people weak, hostage to racial enslavement, and handicapped in our struggle for justice....

Our main goal is the realization of the Palestinian dream of building an independent homeland through the practice of real citizenship, with complete rights and duties. Only in this way will the Palestinian people feel that are their own masters, their will is independent, they have complete freedom over their land, and they are able to build their future within a framework of security, freedom of speech, and sovereignty of law.

The realization of the hopes and ambitions of the Palestinian people is contingent upon ending the occupation. Likewise, ending occupation and achieving independence is contingent upon the empowerment of the Palestinian people and the institution of democratic practices. We must strive to suppress any activities that compromise our struggle and do away with double-speak in political discourse so that we may have confidence in our collective power and be clear in our collective goals....

The building and nurturing of our resistance demands flexibility as well as clarity of vision in order to bring about the failure of destructive

Israeli tactics. We must make occupation fail as well as benefit from previous experience in order to build the foundation for the future Palestinian state, so that it can be a state of institutions, equality, law, active participation, and merit. The task of building must be directed toward serving the interests and needs of the Palestinian citizens, especially those who are underprivileged and marginalized.

Thus it will be necessary to:

- create an interim unified national leadership that can produce a strategic plan and put forth collective national goals to which everyone is committed on the basis of complete decision-sharing. The greater interest of the homeland must take precedence over factional and personal interests
- honor and activate the institutions of the Palestine Liberation Organization through a democratic process, including elections for our national parliament
- conduct regular free and democratic elections for all national institutions, including the presidency, the parliament, and the local councils and municipalities, on the condition that they take place with an international presence that can ensure transparency, fairness, and the absence of Israeli intervention. Democratic elections are an essential part of establishing a Palestinian state, which is to include all the occupied lands, most prominently the city of Jerusalem. We must treat elections as a vital issue of nonviolent resistance and Palestinian national self-determination
- institute a separation of powers and checks and balances, respecting the independence of judiciary systems in the application of law
- create a unified and organized treasury, a fair distribution system that meets the needs of the people, and sound organizations with transparent financial expenditure
- establish ministries and governmental institutions with clear structures that specify the various interests, positions, and roles, and are able to place the appropriate person in the appropriate position without favoritism or discrimination. These institutions, which are in great need of administrative reforms, must meet the needs of their workers and provide them with the elements of a dignified life
- instill the principle of serving the public as the main goal of public and civic institutions

- implement the rule of law immediately, putting into effect all laws passed by the legislative council, with laws pertaining to civil service being foremost
- specify in detail the interests, responsibilities, and commitments of all official and popular institutions, with a proper balance between fulfilling one's duties and achieving one's rights
- honor the role of the municipalities and local councils in the towns and villages through elections that take place as soon as possible; ensure that the citizen is the basis for the work of the local councils; provide independent funds for their needs according to laws that are clear and fair, that end the bad distribution of funds, and that meet the needs of the areas that are poorer and less developed, especially areas threatened by settlements
- prevent any structural flaws that may lead to corruption, misuse of public money, or misuse of position for personal gain by instilling values of accountability and competency in the work place
- reform security apparatuses
  - by doing away with the current system of hierarchy
  - by preventing its leaders from intervening in political and media matters. This can be done by constraining them with specific resolutions passed by the elected legislative body
  - by distancing them completely from economic activities and investment
  - by assigning a clear and official treasury for this apparatus
  - by submitting them to the rule of law and to an independent legal system
  - by instilling in them the interest and will to protect Palestinian national security, the rule of law, and the safety of our citizens....

All Palestinian citizens must be treated equally before the law. They should have recourse to a just legal system if their rights are violated or if their properties are attacked. The role of laws and courts is to protect the weak and guarantee the rights of all citizens. This calls for:

- the construction of a judiciary system that is independent and effective, providing the necessary resources to appoint and train judges and determine the structure of their work so as to preclude any external interference or political pressure
- the elimination of the courts of the state security apparatus

- the reinforcement of the role of the higher courts to form a complete legal resource
- the provision of clear laws and mechanisms to protect investment projects and other economic activities against undue interference or pressure from government officials...
- the honor of the role of the Palestinian woman for her great contribution by acknowledging her rights and meeting her needs on an equal basis with men."

CHAPTER SIX

PPP: *The PNA's Loyal Opposition*

The Palestinian People's Party's Balancing Act

A successor to the Palestine Communist Party, the Palestinian People's Party (PPP) remains a strongly socialist organization to this day. Unlike most Palestinian parties, the PPP adopted non-violence and supported a Two-State Solution since its inception. The party has long been closely affiliated with the PNA, which has made it difficult for the PPP to present itself as an independent political force (table 6.1).

The Palestinian People's Party (PPP) traces its roots to 1919 when Jews and Palestinians founded the anti-Zionist Palestine Communist Party (PCP). In 1924, the party joined the Communist International. Following a 1943 split from its Jewish members, the party's Palestinians established the National Liberation League (NLL), which supported the Soviet Union in backing the 1947 UN Partition Plan. The NLL was the only Palestinian party to support partition at the time.

After the creation of Israel in 1948, the NLL dissolved: in the Gaza Strip it was disbanded by the administering Egyptian authorities while in the West Bank its members joined Jordan's Communist Party (JCP). In Israel NLL members merged with the Communist Party of Israel. The JCP had a relevant base among Palestinian refugees and established close relations with Palestinian trade unions. Following Israel's occupation of the West Bank in 1967 the JCP split into separate Jordanian and West Bank branches. The West Bank branch, which enjoyed autonomy from the mother party, initially remained loyal to Jordan and for a

Table 6.1 The PPP at a glance

Official name	: PPP / Palestinian People's Party (Hizb al-Shab al-Filastini)
Year founded	: 1982 as Palestine Communist Party (PCP)
PLO membership since	: 1987 as Palestine Communist Party (PCP)
PLC members 1996	: 0 (boycotted)
PLC members 2006	: 2 (in alliance with DFLP)
Ideological orientation	: Socialist
Leadership Base	: Ramallah

time rejected the concept of an independent Palestinian state in the West Bank and Gaza. In 1973, however, the West Bank branch began to advocate for Palestinian statehood on the basis of Security Council Resolution 242. In 1982, it gained full independence from the JCP and soon thereafter reestablished itself as the Palestine Communist Party (PCP), a movement that strictly adhered to Marxism and Leninist principles such as democratic centralism.

The party earned some support of students and trade unionists, thanks in part to an effective media campaign, although radical left-wing positioning continued to alienate the majority of socially conservative Palestinians. In 1987, the PCP joined the PLO, becoming the only member not engaged in "armed resistance" against Israel. The party program adopted in 1983 only contained a passing reference to militant operations as an abstract possibility. The party was given one representative on the 18-seat PLO Executive Committee. Currently, the PCP successor party PPP is represented in the PLO Executive Committee by Hanna Amirah, who is responsible for the Social Welfare department.

During the first *intifada*, the PCP played an influential role in organizing popular protests against the Israeli occupation of the West Bank and Gaza. The PCP's secretary general Bashir Barghouthi is credited with creating one of the first "popular committees" that steered the uprising's course. The PCP's grassroots activism made it an integral part of the United National Leadership of the Uprising (UNLU), which also comprised activists from Fatah, the Popular Front for the Liberation of Palestine (PFLP), and the Democratic Front for the Liberation of Palestine (DFLP).

As was seen with other leftist PLO factions, the collapse of the Soviet Union in the early 1990s brought ideological disorientation to the PCP. Confronted with the failure of Eastern European regimes, the PCP eschewed its strict Marxist views, deleted any reference to Leninism from party platforms and renamed itself the Palestinian People's Party

(PPP) in 1991. Bashir Barghouthi was elected secretary general of the PPP and remained in this position until his death in 2000.

The newly founded PPP argued that Marxist notions of class struggle should be put on hold in favor of uniting all Palestinians in the quest for national liberation. The party called for nonviolent resistance and for the founding of a Palestinian state alongside Israel's pre-1967 borders. In terms of economic policies, the PPP's strictly Marxist agenda was replaced by an approach that allowed for entrepreneurship and a free market economy.

Bashir Barghouthi played an important role in the negotiations leading to the 1993 Oslo Accords, which the PPP wholeheartedly endorsed, at first. Barghouthi was made minister of industry in the 1996 Palestinian cabinet and the party has been represented in several subsequent PNA governments since this time. PPP participation was either realized through a formal joining in government or (when the PPP was formally in the opposition) through individual party members who served in government positions. Until August 2012, PPP member Ghassan al-Khatib served as the PNA spokesperson in Ramallah, while PPP member Ismail Dweik served as minister of agriculture from 2009 to 2012, when he was suspended on charges of corruption.

While the integration of party leaders into the PNA apparatus proved beneficial for the PPP in some respects, it also proved problematic. Since the signing of the Oslo Accords, the PPP has lost some of its modest support base and has been largely marginalized within the PLO. The PPP (like the DFLP) was not permitted to participate in the closed-door negotiations at the Camp David Summit of 2000. Additionally, the PPP was in no position to use the institutions of the PNA to generate public support in the way Fatah did in the early years of the PNA.

In addition, critics argue that the PPP is partly to blame for its diminished support as activism was increasingly replaced by empty rhetoric. One leading PPP member claimed that, at one point, party activities consisted of "85 percent internal discussion and 15 percent external action."[1] Mustafa Barghouthi, who left the PPP, justified this decision by arguing that "sadly, the PPP seemed to have turned into a group of commentators on events, rather than participants."[2]

Contrary to other Palestinian factions, the PPP did however manage to maintain administrative checks and balances by electing its leadership at regular intervals (see chart 6.1). In October 1998, at the party's third General Congress held in Ramallah and Gaza, Hanna Amirah, Mustafa Barghouthi, and Abdel Majid Hamdan were elected to a three-

150   *Political Parties in Palestine*

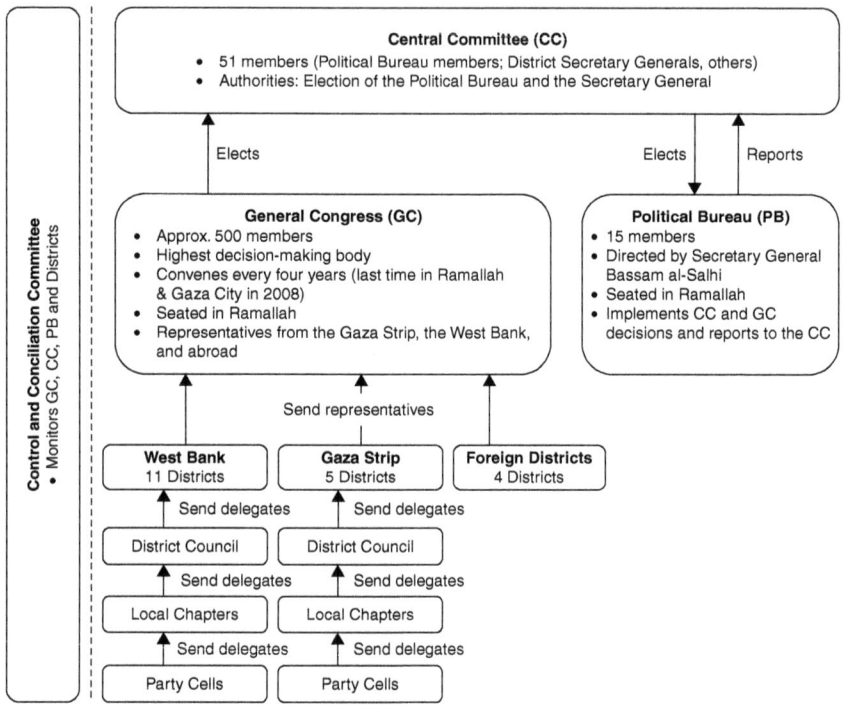

Chart 6.1 Organizational structure of the PPP.

member general secretariat, illustrating the PPP's inability at the time to agree on one single general secretary.

Internal struggles over the PPP's relations with the PNA and Israel, however, caused Mustafa Barghouthi to leave the party in 2002. A considerable number of PPP supporters and affiliated nongovernmental organizations followed Barghouthi to form the Palestinian National Initiative (PNI). These losses were felt in the 2005 presidential elections, in which the party's secretary general Bassam Salhi received 2.67 percent of the vote. During the campaign, tensions flared between the PPP and other left-wing parties, and unidentified gunmen fired shots at Salhi's headquarters in Ramallah in December 2005. In the PLC elections the following year, the party joined the DFLP and Yasir Abed Rabbo's FIDA to form the al-Badil list (The Alternative), but its impact remained modest with a minimal 2.8 percent of the vote, earning the appointment of two delegates, one for PPP and the other for DFLP.

In April 2008, the PPP held its fourth General Congress in Ramallah and Gaza City. 405 delegates from the West Bank and 160 delegates from the Gaza Strip came together to elect a new Central Committee (51 members) and a political bureau (15 members). Ten members of the Central Committee and three members of the political bureau were women. Bassam Salhi was reelected as secretary general by the Central Committee. The congress discussed the PPP's political program and accepted an updated program focusing on a wide array of social and economic issues and on nonviolent resistance as the "most appropriate form of struggle," as the program phrased it.[3] Notably, in the conference's closing statement the delegates declared unambiguously that the militarization of the second *intifada* had "a negative impact on the Palestinian cause and people."[4] At the same time, however, the updated party program underlined the previous stance taken in the 1980s that "the right to struggle against the occupation in all forms is guaranteed by International Law." With respect to a solution to the Israeli–Palestinian conflict, the new party program remained committed to the long-held party view of establishing an "independent socialist state of Palestine" on "the entire Palestinian Territories occupied in 1967 ... with complete sovereignty over this territory with its capital in East Jerusalem."[5]

Despite the party's limited role within the PNA and PLO, the PPP has maintained a noticeable local influence mostly due to its grassroots activities and involvement with affiliated nongovernmental organizations. Their political input also continues to influence state policy decisions. A recent campaign in coalition with other factions focused on the PNA prime minister Salam Fayyad's policy of raising taxes. While this constitutes a meaningful departure for a party closely affiliated with the PNA leadership, the campaign stopped short of criticizing the PNA presidency directly and focused exclusively on the policies of the politically independent Prime Minister Fayyad. As a result of this public campaign (which included several independent groups), Fayyad made substantial changes to previous cabinet decisions.

The PPP has historically played a politically progressive role in embracing the Two-State Solution and exclusively promoting means of nonviolence. However, its avant-garde stance and at times ambiguous entanglement with the PNA have prevented the party from gaining wider approval. Nevertheless, the PPP's political weight should not be dismissed entirely. In May 2012, the organization mobilized 10,000 supporters to the streets of Ramallah to commemorate the thirtieth anniversary of the party's founding, a turnout that is indicative of at least some political relevance.[6]

Bassam Salhi

Bassam Salhi has served as the secretary general of the PPP since 2003 and has come to represent a party that adheres to ideological principles but has shifted beyond a strict Marxist perspective. Salhi represents the PPP in the PLC and has been the party's presidential candidate since 2005, gaining 2.6 percent of the vote.

Bassam Salhi was born in al-Amari refugee camp in Ramallah in 1960. In the late 1970s Salhi became an activist at the Birzeit University, where he obtained a Master's degree in International Studies. He served as chairman of Birzeit's Student Council from 1979 to 1981 and later represented the student movement at the National Guidance Committee (NGC), a group of leftist organizations founded during the first *intifada*. Salhi was put under house arrest by the Israeli authorities several times. Such arrests continued after he was appointed leader of the Palestinian People's Party (PPP) in the Gaza Strip in the mid-1980s. His activism in Gaza was severely restricted by Israeli forces and he was eventually forced into hiding.

In March 1988, Salhi returned to the West Bank but remained underground. He was active in the United National Leadership of the Uprising (UNLU) during the first *intifada* and imprisoned between 1990 and 1993. In detention, Salhi was one of the leaders of a famous 1992 hunger strike and was elected to the PPP's political bureau *in absentia*. He was initially a supporter of the Oslo Accords.

Salhi was elected Secretary General of the PPP in 2003. Under Salhi's leadership, the party distanced itself somewhat from its Marxist origins. He was also a member of the 2004 Palestinian delegation to the International Court of Justice in The Hague that protested against the establishment of the Israeli separation barrier. Unlike most Palestinian political leaders, he has repeatedly participated in nonviolent demonstrations and rallies against the Israeli-built barrier. Salhi is a co-founder of the Palestinian Campaign for Freedom and Peace and is a vocal advocate for the Palestinian cause abroad.

Salhi has held several public offices. He represents the PPP in the PLC, held observer status in the PLO's Executive Committee, and ran in the PNA presidential elections in 2005. Salhi was briefly arrested in December 2004 when he attempted to campaign in East Jerusalem. He gained 2.67 percent of the vote and served as minister of culture in the short-lived 2007 National Unity Government. Salhi has since been frequently mentioned as a candidate for other cabinet positions.

While Salhi supported the Palestinian bid for membership at the United Nations in September 2011, he has become increasingly critical of PNA policies. When the PNA leadership, under heavy pressure from Fatah, decided to postpone local elections, Salhi called the move a "huge mistake."[7] In February 2012, Salhi was vocal in the PPP campaign against the economic policies of Palestinian prime minister Salam Fayyad, arguing that "Fayyad's policy, aspiring to reduce foreign support, doesn't make sense, because it puts the burden of the occupation on the Palestinian people and reduces their ability to deal with the oppression."[8]

★ ★ ★

Interviews with PPP Decision Makers

The following interviews were conducted with PPP leaders in Ramallah and Gaza. Bassam Salhi is currently secretary general of the movement (see biography) and previously served as minister of culture in the PNA government. Salhi also represents the PPP in the current PLC. When the interview was conducted, Ghassan al-Khatib served as PNA spokesman in his capacity as director of the Palestine Government Media Center. Khatib previously served as PNA minister of labor (2002), minister of planning (2005 to 2006), and participated in several rounds of Israeli–Palestinian negotiations in Madrid (1991), and Washington DC (1991–1993). He has also served as vice president of Birzeit University and is widely perceived as a critically minded independent intellectual. He is a member of the PPP's political bureau. Taysir Muhaysen is a member of both the PPP Central Committee and the political bureau. He was educated in Moscow and is actively engaged in several nongovernmental organizations in Gaza.

Interview with Bassam Salhi, Secretary General of the PPP

What makes the PPP unique among Palestinian parties?

The PPP is unique with respect to two issues. First, I consider the PPP as the father of a Two-State Solution. While the other movements concentrated their efforts on liberating the Palestinian homeland militarily, our organization accepted the reality of the partition in 1948 and advocated a Two-State Solution even before 1967. Eventually, the PLO simply adopted our pragmatic stance.

Our central point is advocating a Two-State Solution. We want to achieve self-determination for the Palestinian people. Even though the Israeli state currently destroys the possibility of a viable Palestinian state due to settlement activities, we need to stick to this idea and keep on demanding a state in the pre-1967 borders based on the UN Security Resolutions. The Road Map for Peace and other initiatives by a few leading nations have failed.

The Communist Party demanded one unified democratic state in the 1940s. But today, we have separate nations. Currently, a One-State Solution is only an option if self-determination is guaranteed in a framework that not only implies civil but also national rights for the Palestinians. But this is not a realistic scenario since Israel continues to be an apartheid state.

Second, the PPP has always focused on social and cultural issues besides our political vision of a Two-State Solution, whereas others neglected these important fields through their focus on military activities. In terms of political thought, the PPP remains uncontested in the Palestinian party spectrum. Naturally, all these activities are still based on a framework of Marxist thought.

How would you describe the PPP's relations with Israeli parties?

We have excellent relations with the Israeli communist party Hadash and with other leftist groups that are not represented in the Knesset. We cooperate especially in East Jerusalem, protesting against house demolitions and other discriminatory measures.

How active is the PPP in Gaza?

The position of the PPP in Gaza is quite good. The party is very active, both in the cities and in the refugee camps. However, we are forced to operate under a militant one-party regime. This is the main difference from the situation in the West Bank, although we are facing similarly dangerous developments here. Also in the West Bank, there is no control of the executive powers, the government, and the security forces.

There has been criticism that the PPP is largely co-opted into the PNA government despite its Marxist heritage. Can you comment on this?

We are not part of the government. One minister is a PPP member, but he joined the government because of personal deliberations. PPP member Ghassan al-Khatib, who has become the spokesman of Prime Minister Salam Fayyad, also does this is in his personal capacity.

Can you comment on the current state-building program of the PNA?
We need to build institutions, but Fayyad's approach is not the right way. Self-determination even without institutions is the key. Furthermore, as long as the occupation continues, we are unable to pursue the sort of independent economic policy that the current prime minister suggests. Such an approach would just take the responsibility away from the occupier and strengthen the current stalemate. We are against Prime Minister Salam Fayyad's free market policy but instead are pushing for a social market economy. That is why, for example, we have held demonstrations calling for a lowering of the value added tax.

Is there a need to unite the fragmented Palestinian left?
This is our goal—there have been several initiatives and we are working on this question but it is not an easy task. One obstacle is the self-interest of many in the parties. But the main problem is the clientelist structure of the PLO. Parties such as the DFLP and PFLP that profit from the established quota in the PLO feel quite comfortable with this unsatisfying situation.

How do you see the role of the left?
We should not act as a mere mediator between Hamas and Fatah, rather we should cooperate with all factions on the basis of the Cairo Unity Paper in order to fight the division of the Palestinian people.

Interview with Ghassan al-Khatib, Director of Palestine Government Media Center

The PPP was one of the few Palestinian movements next to Fatah that wholeheartedly supported the Oslo Accords. Has the assessment of Oslo within the PPP changed during the past years?
The PPP participated in the Madrid Peace talks and in the bilateral negotiations in Washington, but was not part of the Oslo negotiations. When the Oslo Declaration of Principles was signed, the PPP voted in support. But when the PLO continued negotiations and reached the so-called Interim Agreement, also called Oslo II, to establish the Palestinian Authority, the PPP did not support that agreement.

Can you elaborate on the reasons?
We did not support Oslo II for three reasons. First, because its details restricted the possibilities of the PNA to establish a Palestinian state.

Second, because Oslo II failed to stop the Israeli expansion of settlements, and third, because many of the guarantees of Oslo I were restricted severely by Oslo II. I will give you an example. Oslo I stipulated that the PNA will have legislative powers. Oslo II, however, stipulated that the Palestinians have the right to issue legislations only pending Israeli approval in a joint committee. So, in effect, Israel was given a veto on the legislative powers. Thus, Oslo II was not about shifting responsibilities from Israel to the Palestinians but rather about shifting authority from Israel to joint committees. This is one of the reasons why we did not support Oslo II.

Originally, the PPP called for the mobilization of "revolutionary masses." At the same time, representatives of the movement have been in government almost without interruption since 1996. How do you explain this approach?

The party has not always been part of the Palestinian National Authority. We were sometimes in and sometimes out of government. In the first three years of the establishment of the Palestinian National Authority, the PPP was not part of the cabinet. Later, we participated in the government for a few years and after that we were out for another few years. After the death of Bashir Barghouti who was minister of industry, we were also out of government. We joined again when I served a minister of planning until the elections in 2006. Then we were out and only joined the National Unity Government for three months. So it is difficult to say that we were in government constantly.

But how do you explain the constant change from government to opposition?

We were in government whenever we felt that we could push the performance of the PNA into the right direction. And we were out of government whenever we feel that our presence in the PNA would not be useful for the cause or would serve as a cover-up for things we did not want to be part of.

Critics have argued that the PPP gave up its status as an oppositional group without gaining real power to influence the course of the PNA.

Yes, I admit that the party was from a public perspective too vague in this regard. From an outside perspective it would be difficult to see us either clearly in the PNA camp or in the opposition camp. One of the reasons is that the party was in most cases supportive of the general political line of the PNA. We had difficulties to be in the opposition because we were not against the Two-State Solution. But at the same time, the PPP was critical of the way the PNA and the way the negotiations were managed. That is why our position was complex. We were supportive of the Palestinian National Authority politically and we were opposing the PNA in practice.

Would you say the PPP is still a Marxist movement?

That depends on what is meant by "Marxist." Today, terms carry different meanings when compared to 20 or 30 years ago. The PPP is now in the process of discussing its ideological character. Between now and the congress, which is supposed to take place before the end of 2012, we should be able to arrive at a clear ideological definition. Today, the PPP is a leftist and a socialist party supporting the working class.

In the last conference of 2008, the PPP already adopted a new program and elected a new leadership. What was the significance of the conference?

There was little political significance in the sense that the new political program did not significantly differ from the previous one. The PPP has been steady in supporting the Two-State Solution and has been devoted to the struggle in order to end the occupation and to allow the establishment of the Palestinian state within the borders of 1967. However, that congress was significant because it helped maintain internal stability and allowed for the creation of a new generation of leadership. Before 2008, we were confronted with a generation gap in our leadership. Before 2008 and since the death of the party's long-standing leader Bashir Barghouti, we had to elect trilateral committees: instead of one secretary general we had three. In 2008, were able to elect one secretary general, a proper political bureau, and a Central Committee.

Speaking of the new generation of leadership, how would you assess the PPP's grassroots work? Are you able to attract new and younger generations of members?

We are able to attract to a certain extent new recruitments from grassroots, but mainly in rural areas. We still have a weakness in urban areas. During the preparations for the next conference, we are planning to put this as one of the focal points. For our next phase, we need to have more visibility and more strength and new generation recruitment, also in urban areas.

The PPP is one of the few Palestinian movements that have rejected violence from the start. Lately, other factions have adopted similar stances. Are they following the PPP's example?

The PPP's position was one of many factors that contributed to moving different Palestinian factions to nonviolence. I would not say that PPP stance was the reason for that positive development, but it was one of the factors. The PPP was a pioneer in two strategic visions: In the middle of the past century, the PPP was the first to adopt the position of "two states for two peoples" in historical Palestine. That is why the PPP (which was not yet called PPP at that time) was the only political group supportive of the Partition Plan. At that time, it was like swimming against the stream. It cost the party dearly, because that position was highly unpopular. It took the other Palestinian political movements until the mid-1970s to adopt the Two-State Solution.

The second pioneering accomplishment of the PPP is nonviolence. The PPP always thought that violence is not to the advantage of the weaker party, the Palestinians. It is in favor of the stronger party, Israel. That is why the Israelis can be expected to always try to push us into the field of violence.

What is the PPP's stance on Palestinian unity and the split between the West Bank and the Gaza Strip?

The split is highly detrimental to the vital interests of the Palestinian people and we hold both, Hamas and Fatah, responsible for that. We believe that the approach of solving this problem only by dialogue between these two factions would be the wrong approach. The right approach would be a collective effort of all factions to tackle this problem. There are regional parties and governments such as Iran that contribute to that split and use it to their advantage. Also, the behavior of the Israeli government is an important factor consolidating the split.

Interview with Taysir Muhaysen, Member of the PPP Central Committee and the Political Bureau, Gaza

How would you describe the PPP's current ideological outlook?

We are rooted in the heritage of European political thought, namely in Marxism, and we are still holding on to this Marxist set of beliefs. At the same time, we are deeply rooted in Palestinian society. As a matter of fact, the PPP represent a rich tradition of the Palestinian left, which dates back to more than a hundred years. This also proves that ideologies are not restricted in their appeal to specific nations or cultures.

We are committed to this Marxist heritage, but we have also more recently modified certain aspects of our approach. In view of the end of the Cold War, the fall of the Berlin wall, the first *intifada*, and the Gulf war, we have altered some of our positions but not the basis of our political beliefs. Speaking with Hegel, it would be adequate to say that we have been engaged in a dialectic process in which we have undertaken a critical reading of our earlier positions.

Today, we are more of a popular party rather than a strictly Marxist movement. Thus, we have broadened not only our organizational outlook and have moved away from centralism but we have also widened our outreach to not focus exclusively on specific groups such as the working class.

What does this mean in terms of concrete positions?

We believe in two states, in a peaceful solution to the conflict, and in popular resistance. Our party participated in the Madrid Conference 1991, and accepted Oslo as an interim framework. For us it was a chance to build bridges between nations. These convictions led us to join the PLC and several PNA governments. However, our participation was always based on two conditions: The implementation of Good Governance and on meaningful achievements in negotiations with Israel.

Since the split between Gaza and the West Bank in 2007, the situation has changed. Currently, these conditions are simply not being met. That is why we oppose joining the government in Ramallah and in Gaza. Our participation at this point in time would simply be useless.

At this stage, we have to focus on Palestinian unity, popular resistance, and on mobilization of the international community. In concrete terms, this also means that we oppose current policies in the West Bank and in Gaza. We oppose the curbing of civil liberties in both parts of Palestine, we oppose neoliberal policies of Prime Minister Fayyad, and we oppose the illegal government of Hamas in Gaza, its tunnel economy, and its social and economic policies.

Democracy and social rights are being violated in the West Bank and in Gaza. Corruption and poverty are growing and so is the income gap between Gaza and the West Bank, between cities and the countryside, and within society as a whole. These are the challenges we need to address.

How free is the PPP to work for this agenda in Gaza?
Hamas is attempting to establish what Gramsci would perhaps call a position of hegemonic dominance. Hamas tries to co-opt certain political parties and to generally limit freedom of action of civil society. Concerning Fatah, the situation is even worse, because the party is Hamas's main opponent. Here, the worst kind of oppression has been practiced.

In comparison, parties such as the PPP have been allowed more freedom. We can basically express our political positions, hold meetings, and organize public events and marches. However, the scope of our work and the questions that we are allowed to address are restricted. When we recently held a press conference against house demolitions that were ordered by the Hamas government, for instance, we had apparently crossed a red line and actually had to go underground for two weeks.

And what kind of political engagement is tolerated in Gaza?
In short: Empty activism. Any kind of political action that is taking place today in Gaza is both without clear objective and at the end of the day meaningless. The Gaza disengagement of Ariel Sharon has left us confronted with two main challenges: The questions of whether Palestinians can take over political responsibility and the question of whether we can overcome the split between the West Bank and Gaza. Both challenges have not been met.

The West Bank is effectively being governed by the World Bank, while Gaza is run by militants who fire rockets. The internal Palestinian split has only deepened. But as long as these two key challenges are not adequately addressed, anything else is meaningless. The key is national unity.

In any national unity government, the PPP would likely only play a marginal role. How do you explain the structural weakness of the Palestinian left?
Our long-term secretary general Bashir Barghouthi once said that anyone working for justice and equality cannot expect to be supported by everybody. I find this assessment very accurate. In Gaza, the composition of society clearly does not favor us. It is a highly conservative society. Also, of course, the global collapse of the political left with the disintegration of the Soviet Block weakened our political standing. In a second wave, the resurgence of political Islam has become a strategic challenge and so far we have not been able to react correspondingly.

How do you plan to address this challenge?
First, by increasing the role of young people in our party. I very much hope that the upcoming party convention at the end of 2012 will bring

more young people into a position of influence. We need to mobilize the younger generation and openly discuss their role within the organization. And, of course, at the horizon looms the question of finally uniting the fragmented left, the secular, and the democratic Palestinian movements. We will have to develop an updated program that calls for a welfare state, a mixed economy, and a combination of democracy and social justice. There is a lot of work to be done.

How would you characterize intraparty relations between Gaza and the West Bank?

The split between Gaza and the West Bank obviously is a grave challenge for the party. We simply do not have enough face-to-face meetings. Video conferences at our Central Committee sessions only go so far. Intraparty relations are also strained since the Gaza branch is being neglected.

This problem however goes deeper than just the current political and geographical split. The minor role of Gaza also has to do with problems of center and periphery. Historically, Gaza has always had strong social relations to the coastal strip, not so much to the West Bank. People in Gaza traditionally have turned toward Jaffa and Haifa and not to Ramallah and Bethlehem. Objectively, however, there is also no denying that our support base in the West Bank simply is much greater than it is here at Gaza. So, this has to be taken into consideration.

★ ★ ★

Excerpts of PPP Progammatic Documents

The following excerpts are taken from the PPP's Strategy to Establish the Independent Palestinian State from 2009;[9] from the PPP's Political Program as ratified in its fourth General Conference (2008);[10] from the program of the *al-Badil* list, which the PPP joined in the 2006 legislative elections;[11] and from the PPP's Election Program from 1995.[12]

View on Israeli–Palestinian Conflict

Strategy to Establish the Independent Palestinian State (2009):
"The Palestinian People's Party aims to achieve national independence and establish a sovereign independent state within the borders of June 4, 1967, as a democratic secular state with East Jerusalem as its capital, and to achieve a just solution for the refugees through implementing Resolution 194.

In light of the failure of the political process, the party requests the Palestinian National Council to declare unilaterally the borders of the independent Palestinian state on all territories occupied in 1967 with East Jerusalem as its capital and to work to seek Arab and international recognition of these borders.

Urgent tasks to be confronted in order to achieve statehood:

To expand, organize and unify popular resistance in the face of the occupation and settlements through committees that resist the wall, through boycotting goods and through other means.

To formulate a clear strategic role for the Gaza Strip and its status in protecting the national project and in reinforcing the steadfastness of its people. The Gaza Strip must not remain solely a military front that confronts the occupation because this transformed the Gaza Strip into a target of continuous Israeli strikes and [caused] the isolation of the Gaza Strip."

Political Program of PPP (2008):

"The Palestinian People's Party is the party of freedom and national independence. The PPP aims to guarantee the inalienable rights of our people and stands at the forefront of self-determination... Its objective is to end the occupation (military and through settlements) of the entire Palestinian Territories occupied in 1967 and to establish a democratic and independent Palestinian state with complete sovereignty over this territory with its capital in East Jerusalem.

...

The PPP believes in harmony between the nature of the Palestinian National Program and the forms and means of struggle. The *intifada* and the popular resistance are seen as the most appropriate form of struggle, yet, the right of our people to struggle against the occupation in all forms is guaranteed by International Law...

[The PPP believes that success can be achieved by] organizing and mobilizing the masses and directing their energies against the occupation and by strengthening steadfastness. The struggle against the occupation implies actions against policies that are based on racism, settlement expansions, conversions,... the siege of Jerusalem and its Judaization.

[It also implies actions against] the siege on the Gaza Strip, the disintegration of the West Bank, and against military barriers, bypass roads, settlements and the wall of annexation and racial segregation.

Cooperation and coordination with the Israeli peace forces that reject the occupation and support the Palestinian people's rights, particularly with the Communist Party of Israel, [are further objectives of the PPP].

[The party advocates] refusing normalization and works for expanding the campaign to boycott Israel. Israel bears the political and moral responsibility for the emergence of the Palestinian refugee issue and for the tragedy of homelessness, displacement and ethnic cleansing suffered by the Palestinian people... Any solution for the refugee issue must be based on UN Resolution 194 and on the recognition of Israel's political and moral responsibility for the creation of the Palestinian refugee problem. The settlements and land confiscations and the building of a wall of annexation and apartheid are direct manifestations of the Israeli occupation and are contrary to International Law.

...

The struggle against settlements and against the annexation wall of apartheid is a strategic struggle against the essence of the Zionist project which is based on the absorption of soil and on controlling water sources. A cessation of settlements is a condition for any serious negotiations for peace with Israel...

Palestinian prisoners are prisoners of war... They [must] be treated on the basis of international conventions, particularly the Geneva Conventions III and IV."

Program of al-Badil List (2006):

"[We demand] a complete stop of settlement activities, the dismantling of existing settlements, and the resumption of the work of Palestinian institutions in Jerusalem. [Furthermore, we reject] partial settlements and temporary ones including Sharon's plan for temporary borders for the Palestinian State and call for organizing an international conference in order to achieve a comprehensive solution that will respect international resolutions securing a full withdrawal of Israeli forces to the lines of 4th of June 1967, dismantle all settlements, establish the Palestinian State with Jerusalem as its capital, and resolve the question of the Palestinian refugees according to resolution 194, which offers them the right to return to their homes."

The PPP's Election Program (1995):

"The Palestinian Legislative Council will be charged with defining negotiations for the solution of the Palestinian question. The current focus produces unjust agreements and results in a fragmented national territory. It does not include adequate mechanism to lead to national independence.

[What is needed] is an alternative approach that corrects the course of negotiations and establishes a frame of references based on the withdrawal of Israel from the Palestinian Territories occupied since 1967 (including East Jerusalem) and focuses on an implementation of UN resolutions regarding the question of refugees. The Palestinian People's Party addresses its people to:

- correct the course of negotiations to defend freedom and unity of the Palestinian Territories
- end settlements
- protect the Arab character of Jerusalem
- safeguard a return of the refugees and migrants.

We accept the principle of negotiations in order to arrive at a just solution and at an end to the Israeli occupation and the traces of Israeli settlements in our territory. The next round of negotiations will prove decisive since it will focus on self-determination, Jerusalem, settlements, refugees, migrants, and borders.... We demand a change of the course of the current negotiations and call for:

- a broadening of national unity and the elaboration of a Charta of a Palestinian consensus that defines red lines concerning the negotiators' mandate to discuss the withdrawal of Israel from the 1967 territory and the case of Jerusalem
- Arab coordination with Israel on progress in negotiations
- a participation of the European Union in the negotiations
- a confirmation that the question of refugees shall be solved in line with UN resolutions."

Economic Development

Strategy to Establish the Independent Palestinian State (2009):
"[The PPP aims] to develop Palestinian social achievements in various economic sectors, both in the PNA and outside the PNA, mainly to apply the social security system and activate its fund and expand it to include all workers. To find legal solutions through direct commitments from the PNA to the issues of unemployment, retirement rights, and old age pension."

Political Program of the PPP (2008):
"Our party seeks to build a national economy that has the potential for internal growth, and ensures the gradual decrease of dependency on Israel and...foreign aid. To achieve this, our party is committed to the struggle for:

- boosting spending on infrastructure projects and public services for citizens
- redistributing income, benefitting the poor in need, and including investment in housing projects for these groups. The bulk of the budget should be dedicated to development and the fight against unemployment with the aim of raising the standard of living
- improving the investment climate for the private sector in the areas of production and export. This requires the cessation of the misuse of power that interferes with the concept of equal opportunities...
- rebuilding institutions and relevant ministries to help the process of development and reconstruction, and end conflict and chaos management through the establishment of a unified center with broad prerogatives to manage and implement this process
- adopting a policy of economic management aimed at attracting talented and experienced local Palestinians as well as expatriates
- ensuring transparency, accountability and effectiveness in a clear budget and financial system
- reducing the staff in the oversized administration and transferring supernumerary staff to development projects...
- developing mechanisms to ensure equal opportunities...and to stopping favoritism and nepotism and appointments based on partisanship
- granting agencies of local government, such as municipalities and local councils, greater powers in the performance of their affairs.

At the level of the national economy, [the PPP] strives to encourage national production and to give industry and agriculture greater attention, taking into account the interest of workers and employers, as well as of peasants and farmers through:

- developing and promoting investment in industry, agriculture and tourism, and establishing specialized banks to do so
- achieving terms of trade that are suitable for our national industries and ensure Palestinian products access to the overseas market...

- creating appropriate mechanisms to take advantage of foreign aid, allocating it to the private sector specifically in the area of finance in order to serve the national economy and to promote the participation of economic sectors in the formulation of economic policy
- putting an end to monopolies, which constitute a burden on the national economy and disrupt the possibility of building the foundations of an independent state liberated from dependency. Preventing the migration of capital and Palestinian industry abroad
- attracting investors and the capital of Palestinian expatriates...
- amending the tax system in line with the economic capacities of the Palestinian Territories in order to encourage investment
- working on Palestinian–Arab cooperation as a contribution to the development of a local export-oriented industry as a prelude to disengagement from the Israeli economy.

The result of the effective state of war since the intifada has been bankruptcy and the closure of hundreds of small and large factories, which caused enormous damage to the land and agriculture. The construction of the racist wall has deepened the destruction of infrastructure. Therefore, we strive for:

- the equal distribution of infrastructure projects, so as to include all regions, cities and villages, particularly roads and telecommunications networks, sewage and rain water drainage, and water and electricity networks
- Palestinian independence in the energy sector through building power plants, building the Palestinian electricity system, and controlling high-voltage lines including those linked to the network of the State of Israel, while maintaining the privilege of the Jerusalem Electricity Company
- the modernization of management of the electricity sector and improving its performance through intensive training, and raising the level of salaries and social status of workers in this sector
- the establishment of regional transmission lines to surrounding Arab countries, in order to facilitate future cooperation with them
- the independence of the transportation sector by improving the status of roads, the installation of traffic signals and by addressing the problems of pedestrians in the city centers.

Our party will work for:

- reducing the value-added tax significantly, which was imposed on the Palestinian side by Israel
- ensuring the free movement of goods and people between the Gaza Strip and Jerusalem and the West Bank
- developing a policy that does not abide by the level of prices in Israel...
- severing the national economy from dependence on the Israeli economy and abolishing the unfair economic agreements in place, which increase the dependency of our economy on Israel
- deepening economic integration with the economies of Arab countries...
- promoting joint Arab development funds
- subjecting regional economic normalization to Israel's willingness to resolve the conflict according to international resolutions on the questions of Jerusalem, settlements, refugees, and to its response to the principle of an independent Palestinian State on all the territories occupied since June 1967 with its capital in Jerusalem."

Program of al-Badil List (2006):
"[We plan to] wage a war against corruption and nepotism and dishonesty toward public funds, and demand equality among citizens, regardless of their political affiliations, in occupying public jobs and taking advantage of public services and governmental facilities.

[We intend to] reorganize the budgets in a way that will give priority to a program that will fight against unemployment and take care of the families of the martyrs, those with special needs and victims of Israeli aggression and support the steadfastness of Jerusalem and other areas subject to the Israeli racist wall, and to improve the infrastructure and educational, municipal and health services.

[We intend to] support the agricultural sector with development of the deprived rural areas and the provision of basic services."

The PPP's Election Program (1995):
"[The PPP calls for] a policy of development that supports and protects the national economy. The economic integration with Israel has to be ended. Professional opportunities for the unemployed have to be created. The standard of living of the masses has to be raised."

State's Role vis-a-vis Religion

Strategy to Establish the Independent Palestinian State (2009):

"[The PPP] struggles towards preserving a secular, pluralistic system based on a separation between religion and the state. In Jerusalem [the PPP will] struggle to ensure freedom of worship and free access to places of religious worship for various religions."

Political Program of PPP (2008):

"The Palestinian State as provided for in the Declaration of Independence [will guarantee all Palestinians the right] to develop their national identity and their cultural rights, and to enjoy full equality in rights, in religious and political beliefs under a democratic parliamentary system based on freedom of opinion and freedom to form political parties. The State will care for minority rights and guarantee respect for minority–majority decisions and social justice and nondiscrimination on the basis of race, religion, color, or sex. [The PPP] respects religious freedom and will maintain the holy places of all religions and will defend them. [The PPP believes in the] separation of church and state and will enact laws that guarantee freedom of belief."

Program of al-Badil List (2006):

"The Constitution ensures the rule of law and an independent judiciary on the basis of fulfilling the full Palestinian spiritual and cultural heritage of tolerance and coexistence of religions… We will struggle to resist trials by Israel to isolate and Judaize Jerusalem, and to establish a unified national reference for the citizens of the holy city acting on the basis of a plan to support the steadfastness of the citizens and protection of lands and estates in addition to defending the sacred sites of Moslems and Christians."

PPP Election Program (1995):

"Our party commits itself to care for religious and cultural monuments and guarantees freedom of religion and free access to holy places."

Vision of State and Society

Strategy to Establish the Independent Palestinian State (2009):

"The basic pillar of the Palestinian People's Party is to link national liberation tasks and democratic and social progress. The key to this is to achieve complete harmony between maintaining the Palestinian

People's Party as an open democratic party with a leftist identity and social content and maintaining its capacity to work seriously in defending the social and economic rights of the poor.

We need to exert efforts to build a progressive socio-political bloc from the leftist and social forces and independent forces in order to cause core changes in the national, social and democratic fields.

Moreover, the PPP must develop the struggle towards achieving equal rights and opportunities for Palestinian women. The party fights all forms of discrimination against women at home and in the workplace, [works] to attain women's social rights and develop social statute laws, and struggles to achieve equality between men and women in rights and duties."

Political Program of PPP (2008):

"The PPP struggles in order to accomplish a democratic Palestinian state, independent and fully sovereign, based on the separation of powers and on a peaceful transfer of power and political pluralism. Individual and public liberties and popular participation, legal equality without distinction between men and women and without discrimination on the basis of religion or ethnicity [has to be guaranteed]. ...

The long-term goal is an independent socialist State of Palestine with complete sovereignty based on equal rights and opportunities, social justice and participatory democracy. We strive to achieve this goal by democratic and peaceful means on the basis of respect for popular will."

Program of al-Badil List (2006):

"[We intend to] develop the education sector, and to secure its material and human needs in order to enlarge the field of educational services, especially at the university level, and reduce the costs of learning, and adopt a democratic-national orientation, and reject all foreign pressures to distort these curricula, and at the same time encourage cultural and artistic creativity, and respond to the legal demands of the workers in the educational sector.

[We intend to] secure sufficient funds to develop the health sector, in a way that enables it to provide citizens with necessary medicine within the framework of a general health insurance system [We call for]:

- striving toward full equality between males and females in all political, economic, and social fields, the full participation of women in decision-making and the enforcing of laws that abolish all kinds of prejudice, and defend women's social status

- reinforcing the role of youth, enabling them to participate in decision-making processes, securing their right of access to education and work, development of their athletic, cultural and artistic talents, and providing them with work opportunities
- protecting basic freedoms and dignity for all citizens, respecting human rights and the establishment of a democratic parliamentary system securing a separation of powers and a peaceful exchange of power through regular elections
- fostering the development of a Palestinian constitution in a way that defines the responsibility of the executive authority towards the legislative council
- encouraging the development of an election law in a way that guarantees just representation of all social strata and regions in the parliament, including the reduction of the age of nomination and securing a quota of representation for women not less than 30 percent of the council seats
- putting an end to anarchy and security disorder, reconstructing the security system, imposing the law and reinforcing the authority of the judicial system and its independence, enriching its human and technical resources. Offering the legislative council the right to appoint judges
- pardoning the prisoners in PA prisons, and putting an end to political imprisonment
- establishing a national unity government adopting this program, including all forces who will participate in decision-making processes
- reviving the PLO as the sole and legitimate representative of the Palestinian people and reconstructing its institutions on a democratic basis and as a reference for the Palestinian Authority. A legislative election in the West Bank, Gaza Strip and Jerusalem, paves the way to do the same among the Palestinian Refugees."

PPP Election Program (1995):

"Unquestionably, the establishment of a Palestinian Authority on Palestinian territory was an important historical achievement.... However, this should not be confused with the establishment of a Palestinian State. The PNA does neither enjoy sovereignty on the ground nor in terms of legislative procedures. As a matter of fact, the occupation has remained in place in terms of the political, military, and economic dimension. Thus, the PNA is not an institution of Palestinian independence but a transitional authority. For it to fulfill this role, far-reaching changes in policies and in terms of negotiations have to be implemented. In view of this, we reiterate the following:

- We reject the sidelining of the PLO and the freezing of its institutions.
- We call for steadfastness against any attacks on democracy, Human Rights and demand an end to phenomena of corruption that is spreading in some public sectors.
- We demand the elaboration of a Basic Law that defines the prerogatives of Ministers and prevents erratic decision-making.

In the educational sector, our party will struggle for a reform of curricula in order to deepen national and democratic elements that will widen the horizon of human knowledge.

...

In terms of culture, we will struggle to defend Palestinian culture against attempts of sabotage and trends to introduce a culture of consumerism that glorifies violence and egocentrism.

...

We will defend the rights of artists, writers, journalists, and intellectuals to express their views and convictions. Also, we will practice freedom of opinion and expression, respect for the opinions of others and foster a democratic environment and the right to access information.

...

Our party's candidates commit to fighting for equality of women in terms of rights and obligations and will abolish any form of financial discrimination in the job market. The allocation of PLC seats to women who because of the current situation, social restraints, and the current election law might otherwise not gain a PLC seat. [The PPP] will also work to establish legal frameworks to fight violence against women. Violence against women should be defined as a violation of Human Rights.

... ...

[The PPP] will work for:
an abolishment of military orders that limit public freedoms of citizens and nongovernmental organizations
equality of citizens in front of the law and a strict separation of powers
an independent judiciary."

CHAPTER SEVEN

DFLP: *Palestinian Marxists and their Coming of Age*

The Democratic Front for the Liberation of Palestine (DFLP)

The DFLP was originally established as a radical Marxist–Leninist organization engaged in acts of "armed resistance." However, in recent years, it has largely put its militant past behind and become a more pragmatic leftist faction. It seeks a Palestinian State on the pre-1967 borders as an "intermediate goal" but at the same time rejects the Oslo Accords. Despite this, in 2009, it joined the caretaker government of Prime Minister Salam Fayyad (table 7.1).

The Democratic Front for the Liberation of Palestine (DFLP, or PDFLP as it was called until 1974) was founded in February 1969 as a breakaway organization from the Popular Front for the Liberation of Palestine (PFLP). Soon the Palestinian Revolutionary Left League and the Palestine Popular Liberation Organization joined the newly established movement. The split from the PFLP was precipitated by ideological disagreements concerning pan-Arabism, the role of diplomacy, and the efficacy of the use of terror operations to confront the Israeli occupation following the Arab defeat in the 1967 war. The DFLP's dissidents argued for a parallel approach to "armed resistance," popular struggle, and diplomacy. The aim (as stated in more recent party documents) was "involving itself in the national armed resistance movement, while presenting a democratic, radical solution to the Palestinian question that included adopting a labor

Table 7.1 The DFLP at a glance

Official name	: DFLP / Democratic Front for the Liberation of Palestine *(al-Jabha al-Demuqratiya li-Tahrir al-Filastin)*
Year founded	: 1969
PLO membership since	: 1969
PLC members 1996	: 0 (boycotted)
PLC members 2006	: 2 seats on list in alliance with PPP, one seat for the DFLP
Ideological orientation	: Marxist Leftist
Leadership base	: Damascus, Gaza, Ramallah

class ideology."[1] The conflict between the two factions included serious harassment of DFLP members by their former comrades. It was only after mediation by Fatah that the DFLP secretary general Nayef Hawatmeh was able to formally withdraw from the PFLP.

The DFLP attracted secular and leftist supporters, primarily from the urban areas of the West Bank, such as Bethlehem, and from the large Palestinian Diaspora mainly in Lebanon and Syria. Originally the DFLP had numerous Maoist followers, but this changed as growing Soviet support during the 1970s led to a more pro-Soviet Marxist stance, which in terms of realpolitik was reflected in nearly unquestioned support by the DFLP for Moscow's foreign policy in Afghanistan and elsewhere. In terms of organizational outlooks, the DFLP firmly adopted the Leninist principle of democratic centralism, which in some cases had severe repercussions for dissidents deviating from the line taken by the Central Committee. Like its parent organization, the PFLP, the DFLP received at different stages in its history financial and logistical support from the Soviet Union, China, Libya, and up to today (to a limited extent) from Syria. On its founding, the DFLP joined the Palestine Liberation Organization (PLO) and immediately became its third-largest faction, a position it continues to hold to this day.

The great importance that the Palestinian Diaspora plays in the DFLP is reflected in the organizational structure of the movement, which allocates a fixed quota to "district committees" in Lebanon and Syria. Also, the DFLP's political bureau has and continues to be based in Damascus (see chart 7.1). Since its founding, leadership and ideological outlook of the DFLP have been determined in several General National Conferences (in 1970, 1971, 1981, 1991, 1994, 1998, 2000, and in 2007). A long overdue Sixth National Conference has remained in the preparatory stages for years.

The DFLP initially held that Palestinian liberation could only be achieved through popular revolution and called for one democratic

DFLP: Palestinian Marxists

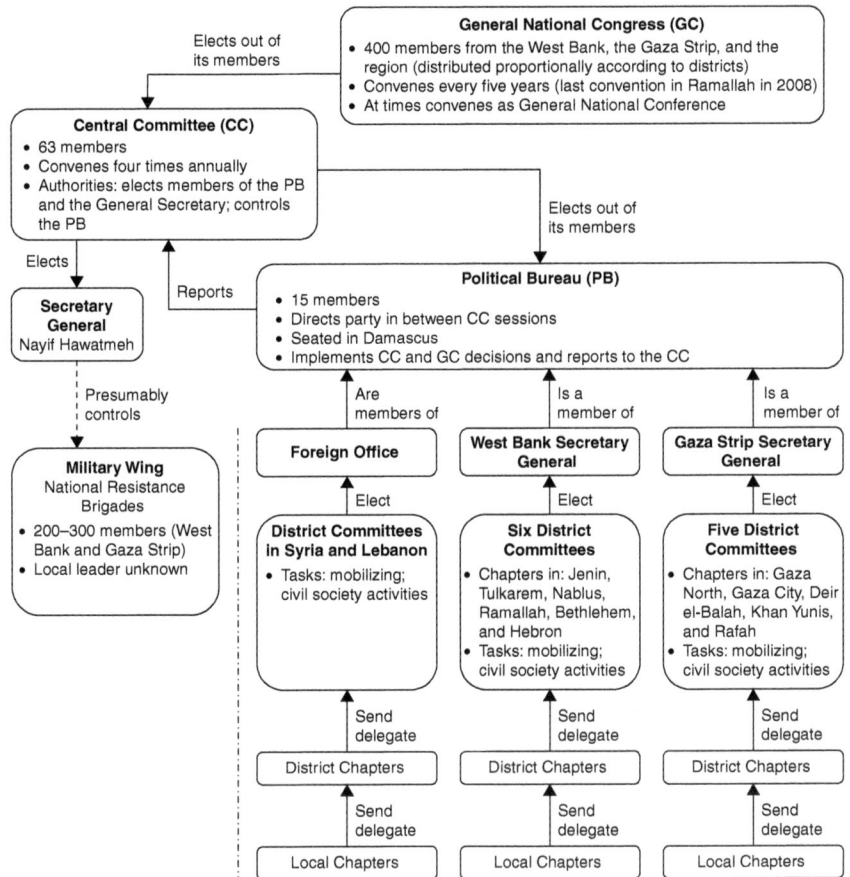

Chart 7.1 Organizational structure of the DFLP.

"classless" state for both Jews and Arabs, an objective that has more recently been replaced by the DFLP's embracing of the Two-State Paradigm as a temporary goal. This single state for Palestinians and Jews was to be achieved through revolution and "mass action," a process described in the organization's central organ *al-Hurriya* (Freedom), published and edited originally in Lebanon and later on in Syria.

Initially, the overthrow of Arab constitutional monarchies and other authoritarian regimes was central to DFLP ideology. Accordingly, the DFLP was one of the Palestinian groups to confront the Jordanian Monarchy, openly calling for the overthrow of the Hashemites at the

1970 congress in Amman, Jordan and attempting to organize workers and farmers in the north of Jordan into local Soviets. Targeted along with the PLO in the ensuing political crackdown known as Black September, the movement was forced to relocate to Lebanon and Syria. The crackdown in Jordan caused not only a geographical relocation of the DFLP but also a gradual process of ideological repositioning toward moderation. Confronted with the loss of its base in Jordan, DFLP institutions developed a Transitional Program that called for the establishment of Palestinian political structures in historical Palestine.

On the basis of this Transitional Program, in the June 1974 Palestinian National Council (PNC) session, the DFLP proposed a resolution calling for the establishment of an "independent combatant national authority for the people over every part of Palestinian territory that is liberated," effectively laying the groundwork for wider Palestinian acceptance of a Two-State Solution. However, the resolution clarified that this national authority was to be a first step toward "completing the liberation of all Palestinian territory."[2] At the PNC meeting three years later, the DFLP reiterated its support for the creation of a Palestinian authority on any territory "liberated" from Israel.

The DFLP's activities included not only dialogue with Jewish anti-Zionist groups but also attacks by its military wing, the National Resistance Brigades, against Israeli targets. The most ruthless of these was an assault on a school in the Galilee town of Ma'alot, where 25 Israeli children were killed in clashes between Israeli forces and a DFLP commando in 1974. The DFLP claimed at the time that "armed struggle" was a necessary strategy to force Israel to recognize Palestinian rights.

Like the PFLP, the Democratic Front over time distanced itself from Fatah's autocratic leadership of the PLO. Against the background of public attempts to once again merge PFLP and DFLP, the latter also briefly joined the camp opposing Yasir Arafat. As was the case with the PFLP, the influence of the DFLP declined in the 1980s and 1990s, when China and the Soviet Union reduced their support. The DFLP with its main support base outside of the Palestinian Territories also saw its standing diminish during and after the first *intifada*, in which political power shifted from those in exile to leaders in the Palestinian Territories. While the DFLP was a member of the United National Leadership of the Uprising (UNLU), it only played a marginal role in the *intifada*.

In 1991, the question of how to address the Madrid Peace Conference and the ensuing Peace Process caused a split in the DFLP. The majority, represented by Secretary General Hawatmeh, opposed Yasir Arafat's strategy and refused to back the talks held in Madrid. A smaller group, clustered around Yasir Abed Rabbo, backed the Peace Process and called for achieving autonomy in the West Bank and Gaza under the umbrella of a newly founded Palestine Democratic Union (FIDA). These ideological differences also caused a geographic division: the DFLP's branches in Lebanese and Syrian refugee camps remained mostly loyal to Hawatmeh, whereas FIDA was able to take over a considerable part of the organization in the Palestinian Territories.

Although the DFLP did not oppose a Two-State Solution as a welcome preliminary step, it rejected the Declaration of Principles (DoP) and Oslo Accords as surrendering Palestinian rights without receiving adequate political compensation. Yet, the DFLP's criticism was not merely based on disapproval of procedures, but on the perception that "applying the Oslo Agreements meant the continuation of occupation, settlement building and expansion, and the further repression and confiscation of Palestinian national rights," as described in a more recent party statement.[3]

Despite these objections, the DFLP ceased violent operations until the outbreak of the second *intifada* in 2000. Nevertheless, differences between the Palestinian National Authority (PNA) and the DFLP escalated and in 1994 PNA forces arrested 40 DFLP activists.

Along with the PFLP and Hamas, the DFLP boycotted the 1996 PNA elections based on the party's rejection of Oslo, a decision that resulted in further political marginalization in the Palestinian Territories. Their exclusion from the established forums of PNA politics led many DFLP supporters to turn to the nongovernmental sector to secure institutional influence. Although not a completely new strategy for the socialist Palestinian factions, it brought nongovernmental organizations (NGOs) to the center of the political struggle against Israel.

In 1999, the DFLP managed to heal its rift with Fatah when Arafat conceded to DFLP demands that the PLO would lead final-status negotiations and that a referendum be conducted before the ratification of a final agreement with Israel. Accordingly, the United States acknowledged the DFLP's factual and far-reaching cessation of "armed struggle" and the group was removed from the US list of Foreign Terrorist Organizations in the same year.

Nevertheless, the DFLP has continued to maintain National Resistance Brigades of approximately 300 militants, which over the past decade have carried out sporadic militant operations, including an attack in 2001 against Israeli forces in Gaza, the first DFLP attack since the Madrid Peace Conference. Such limited actions aside, the DFLP played only a marginal role in the second *intifada* given its limited support base on the ground and was in fact one of the first Palestinian groups to argue against the militarization of the uprising. On June 19, 2003, DFLP Secretary General Hawatmeh called for "continuing the *intifada* by popular and political means and an end to the armed uprising".[4]

When the Road Map for Peace was announced in June of the same year, however, the DFLP called it "unbalanced" and argued that it "would lead to the elimination of the uprising and national resistance before Israel stops the expansion of settlements".[5] In December 2003, the DFLP also opposed the Geneva Initiative (a proposed peace agreement drafted by Palestinian and Israeli members of civil society based on the Road Map for Peace, the Clinton Parameters and the Arab Peace Initiative), arguing that such track two negotiations would harm Palestinian national unity.

Since the end of the second *intifada*, the DFLP has been working to renew its organizational structures and relations with DFLP groups in exile. The DFLP participated in the 2005 presidential election, breaking with its previous stance of a comprehensive rejection of PNA institutions. Its candidate, Taysir Khaled, gained 3.35 percent of the vote. The party formed an alliance with FIDA and the Palestinian People's Party (PPP) in the 2006 general elections called al-Badil (The Alternative) which won two seats in the PLC (one for the DFLP), filled by Qais Abd al-Karim.

The DFLP's internal politics were reinvigorated during its fifth General Congress in 2007, which elected a new Central Committee of 63 members who later re-elected Hawatmeh as secretary general, as well as a 15-member political bureau.

In recent years, the DFLP has steered an ambiguous course on several topics, which has distorted formerly clear positions. On one hand, the DFLP in 2009 joined the West Bank caretaker government despite fierce criticism from other leftist parties who boycotted the cabinet as unconstitutional. While DFLP-member Majida al-Masri joined the PNA government as minister of social affairs in 2009 and continued to serve in the second Fayyad cabinet of 2012, the DFLP's Central Committee in 2012 argued against the "illusion of building a state under occupation", in what was effectively a direct challenge to the PNA state-building plan presented in 2009.[6]

As part of the government, the DFLP has been highly critical of the repeated postponement of elections and has remained a staunch opponent of negotiations with Israel prior to the cessation of settlement expansions. This criticism, however, has not prompted the party to withdraw from government. In March 2010, Secretary General Hawatmeh demanded that "both direct and indirect negotiations with Israel should be dependent on halting settlement activities" and criticized ongoing negotiations as "dangerous".[7] While the DFLP argued vehemently against militarizing the second *intifada*, its own military wing in Gaza has continued to carry out sporadic acts of "resistance". Thus, in April 2011, DFLP fighters launched two projectiles towards the Israeli town of Sderot from the Gaza Strip, proclaiming the attack a "response to Israel's lack of commitment to the truce [and its continued] shelling of unarmed people".[8]

While such acts have repeatedly generated publicity for the DFLP, they cannot conceal that the movement continues to suffer from a chronically weak support base in the Palestinian Territories. The limited role the party plays on the ground in the PNA, however, has at least been somewhat balanced by the significance the DFLP continues to have in the PLO. In this capacity, the faction has in its history initialized highly relevant intra-Palestinian discussions on the prospects of accepting the Two-State Solution and still enjoys relevant support in the Palestinian diaspora.[9]

Nayef Hawatmeh

Nayef Hawatmeh has acted as the DFLP's secretary general since 1969. Based in Damascus he has rejected the Oslo Accords but has been a long-time advocate of the Two-State Solution as a preceding step to the establishment of a singular democratic state for Palestinians and Israelis.

Nayef Hawatmeh was born into a Catholic Bedouin tribe in Salt, Jordan in 1938 and he joined the Arab Nationalist Movement (ANM) as a high-school student in Amman. After a brief stint as a medical student in Cairo, Hawatmeh returned to Jordan to work as a teacher, journalist, and writer. He would later earn a PhD from Moscow University.

When the pan-Arab ANM was banned in Jordan in 1959, Hawatmeh went underground. Sentenced to death *in absentia*, he fled to Iraq where he led the local ANM branch. There, Hawatmeh was imprisoned for 14 months on charges of participating in acts of resistance against the Iraqi prime minister Abd al-Karim Qasim. On his release in 1963, he left Iraq to fight the British occupation of Aden (Yemen), his memoirs of which are recounted in his book, *The Crisis of the South Yemen Revolution*.

Hawatmeh returned to Jordan in 1967, immediately after the Six Day War. Concerned that the war had dealt a near-fatal blow to pan-Arabism, he co-founded the PFLP, but split from that group to form the DFLP in 1969. As the elected secretary general, he also became a member of the PNC and the PLO's Executive Committee.

Still persona non grata in Jordan, he was again forced to leave in 1970. From his exile in Lebanon and Syria, Hawatmeh presented the historical National Transitional Program to the PLO in 1974, which discussed negotiations with Israel and a Two-State Scenario on the basis of UN resolutions. He was also one of the first Palestinian leaders to directly address the Israeli public, writing in the Israeli daily *Yedioth Ahronot* in April 1974. Though acknowledging his ultimate objective of a "democratic und unified state," Hawatmeh, in line with DFLP positions, maintained that the establishment of a Palestinian state in the West Bank and Gaza was a constructive step.

Hawatmeh's relationship with the PLO leadership headed by Yasir Arafat became increasingly rocky during the 1990s. He accused Arafat of autocratic tendencies and labeled the Fatah-backed Oslo Accords a complete "sell[ing]-out," and called Arafat "an American stooge."[10] Hawatmeh nevertheless formally reconciled with Arafat in 1999 as part of a closing of Palestinian ranks in anticipation of final-status negotiations with Israeli prime minister Ehud Barak. That year Hawatmeh also shared a historic handshake with Israeli president Ezer Weizmann at the funeral of Jordanian king Hussein, a gesture condemned by Palestinian Islamists and the PFLP. Hawatmeh has been based in Damascus for years and continues to lead the DFLP from exile to this day. Due to his absence from the Palestinian Territories, his post in the Executive Committee of the PLO has been filled by Taysir Khaled.

The DFLP's improved relations with Fatah and newly proclaimed commitment to negotiations with Israel caused the Israeli government to permit Hawatmeh (and others) to visit the West Bank in 1999. Shortly thereafter, however, Hawatmeh harshly criticized Israel in an interview, prompting Prime Minister Ehud Barak to personally withdraw the permission. In 2007 Israeli prime minister Ehud Olmert, at Mahmoud Abbas's request, agreed to grant Hawatmeh entry to Ramallah to participate in a session of the PLO Central Committee. The decision was intended to strengthen Abbas following Hamas's electoral victory, and was conditioned on Hawatmeh's willingness to disarm. Hawatmeh declined to travel to Ramallah under such conditions and to date remains in exile in Syria.

★ ★ ★

Interviews with DFLP Decision Makers

The following interviews were conducted with the current DFLP leadership in Ramallah and Gaza. Qais Abdul Karim (Abu Laila) is a former member of the PFLP and currently represents the DFLP in the PLC. Majida al-Masri is a member of DFLP's political bureau and in 2006 ran unsuccessfully for a seat in the PLC. Since 2009, al-Masri represents the DFLP in the PNA government of Salam Fayyad, serving as minister of social affairs. In March 2012, she was heavily criticized in Israel for allegedly calling for "the liberation of Palestine—all of Palestine" at a public rally. Only days later, she participated in demonstrations marking Land Day and received medical treatment after collapsing from tear gas inhalation. Al-Masri is considered one of the more successful PNA ministers, last but not least, because she has consistently protected the institutional independence of her ministry against Fatah.

Saleh Zedan is a member of both the DFLP Central Committee and the political bureau. He also serves as the party's secretary general in the Gaza Strip. Zedan is a former PNA minister of social affairs and represents the DFLP's political mainstream.

Interview with Qais Abdul Karim (Abu Laila), Member of the PLC and of the DFLP Political Bureau

How would you characterize the DFLP?

The DFLP is a Marxist organization with a pragmatic approach toward the Palestinian cause. The party has always been critical of both the Soviet and the Chinese version of Marxism, yet it refrained from any polemic against these dominating currents. From the beginning, the DFLP has been keen to elaborate a concrete analysis of the Palestinian situation advocating a revolutionary yet realistic way to challenge the state of occupation by taking into account the balance of forces on the ground.

At the beginning, the party had a short period of left-wing adventures, mainly in Jordan, but we ourselves criticized this phase, especially after the fatal events in Jordan in 1970 and 1971. Such a process of coming to terms with the past might be unique in the Palestinian political party spectrum.

As early as 1973, the DFLP was the first movement to start a debate on the necessity of a Transitional Program, that is a Two-State Solution and a reconciliation process with Israel—a step that was regarded by many Palestinians as treason.

What led to this decision?

The facts as they appeared on the ground. We insisted and still insist that material and national equality between Israelis and Palestinians can only be achieved in a Two-State scenario. Once this is achieved, then we can discuss the prospect of a secular democratic binational state.

What caused the split between the DFLP and the PFLP?

Unlike the PFLP, we were against terrorist attacks, hijackings, kidnappings, and so on. We therefore developed a different strategy. An approach that regarded armed struggle as leverage but not as the principal method of resistance. Furthermore, we maintained that armed struggle should focus on military targets and not on civilians. On the basis of these thoughts, the party developed a theory of a popular *intifada*, a concept that concentrated on mass demonstrations, civil disobedience, and other forms of nonviolent resistance that was adopted by the DFLP's General Congress in 1981.

Yet, the PFLP eventually also argued against targeting civilians. In how far do DFLP and PFLP positions actually differ?

Since its founding in February 1969, the DFLP has engaged in an intellectual struggle against some practices of radical terrorist nature used by the PFLP. From the DFLP's perspective, acts of terrorism such as the hijacking of airplanes harmed the Palestinian cause. The DFLP's position on violence has always been characterized by defining armed struggle as one supporting element in the general social resistance of the Palestinian masses. This was in contrast to the position of the PFLP, which held that armed struggle was the only path to liberation. The DFLP has, since the 1970s, embraced the concept of a popular mass uprising that should play the leading role in how to confront the occupation. Armed resistance takes place in the framework of this popular struggle and is seen as a reaction to the oppression of the occupation.

How does the DFLP today assess acts of terrorism such as the attack in Ma'alot?

The established institutions of the DFLP assessed such operations and came to the conclusion that our resistance had to be based on the principles of international law and had to refrain from targeting civilians. Also, it was decided to restrict our resistance to the territories occupied in 1967, which is exactly what the DFLP did during the second *intifada*.

Why does the party oppose the Oslo Accords?
We have been calling for a negotiated settlement for years. While calling for the implementation of UN resolutions related to the Palestinian cause, we also criticized the Oslo Accords because its parameters, in our eyes, could never lead to durable peace. Protesting against the accords, we left the PLO for some time. Obviously, the Oslo Accords have not led to independence. Being against Oslo is being for a Palestinian state.

The DFLP secretary general and many of its members are in the Diaspora. Where is your main power base?
The party not only is strongest in some of the Palestinian refugee camps in Lebanon but is also gaining influence in the West Bank. This was evident when our presidential candidate Taysir Khaled received 4.5 percent of the total vote in the West Bank. Of course, this is a small yet influential minority, notably with respect to mobilizing popular protests.

How does the DFLP function as part of the fragmented Palestinian left?
There is an agreement between the PFLP, the PPP, and our party to form a leftist front, but I am not sure if we will be able to unite. Progress has been very slow so far. Without an effective umbrella organization, we will not be able to overcome the rivalries between factions.

There are also significant political differences between the leftist parties, for example, on how to deal with the rift between Fatah and Hamas and on the issue of Mahmoud Abbas' presidency, whose term ended in 2009. We do not see the role of the left as mediators—we see ourselves as an alternative to the two dominating movements. In contrast, the PFLP in Gaza has repeatedly acted as a mediator and not as an independent actor.

How do you assess the internal dynamics of the DFLP?
As one of only a few Palestinian parties we have been holding party congresses on a regular basis over the past 15 years. This shows that there is contiguity and internal democracy.

Because women are underprivileged in our society, we try to offer equal opportunities within the party. Around 20 percent of our members are women, and 13 members of the Central Committee are female. Yet only 3 out of 15 members of the political bureau are women. I am not comfortable with these facts. While we do not impose a quota inside the party, we are calling for a quota in the PLC.

What is your stance on reforming the PLO?

To overcome the current fragmentation in the Palestinian political spectrum, groups like Hamas need to be included in the PLO. The body itself must be democratized on the basis of proportional representation.

How do you feel about the PNA and recent state-building efforts of Prime Minister Fayyad?

Even though we are part of the current government, we are critical of what has been labeled "Fayyadism." State building without a state is not a convincing strategy for independence. Prime Minister Salam Fayyad's concept draws on the illusionary experience of Oslo, which proved to be fruitless. During the second *intifada*, all these institutions were destroyed in the blink of an eye.

Interview with Majida al-Masri, Minister of Social Affairs and Member of the DFLP's Political Bureau

How would you describe the DFLP's ideological outlook? Is the term "Marxist" still adequate?

I would say it definitely is, yes. We are still a Marxist party. However, I would not consider us communist in the sense that communist parties often operated during the Cold War. Figuratively speaking, we do not feel the need to get out our umbrellas when it is raining in Moscow. However, the term Marxist is still adequate because our political focus still is very much on political and social classes and especially on the working classes. Yet, at the same time, in terms of ideology, I would describe the DFLP as pragmatist. We have our ideological strategy but we are committed to a national framework as stipulated by the PLO.

Yet, contrary to the major PLO faction Fatah, the DFLP rejected the Oslo Accords. What were the reasons for this position?

It is correct that we rejected the Oslo Accords at the time and we had ample reasons to do so. The current status quo illustrates the shortcomings of Oslo and proves our skepticism very justified. The Oslo Accords left the consensus of the PLO behind and pinned Palestinian hopes on

US goodwill. It split our territory into different zones of responsibility, and left the end result of a Palestinian state completely unclear.

We knew that the Oslo approach would not succeed, that the process would lead to a dead-end, and that it would not bring about a Palestinian state. That is why we conditioned our support for the process already starting with the Madrid negotiations on the condition that Israeli settlement expansions would stop, and that the UN would take a leading role. Notably, these positions are now adopted also by President Abbas.

Has the stance of DFLP on Oslo changed in the past years?
Certainly our position has progressed. We are still convinced that signing Oslo was wrong and a tragic mistake. Yet, we know that it cannot simply be undone. What is needed is a joint effort of all PLO factions to move beyond the Oslo framework and to rebuild a peace process in line with UN resolutions. When the interim period stipulated in the Oslo Accords ended, we assessed the situation and adapted our program accordingly. Our changing stance has also been illustrated by our approach toward the PNA. Initially, we boycotted elections in 1996. But in 2006 we participated in the elections and now also serve in the government.

What is the DFLP's vision for a solution of the conflict?
We differentiate between our long-term strategic vision and our intermediate goals. As Marxists, our strategic vision is to establish one democratic state for all people living in the land, be they Jewish, Muslims, or Christians.

Does this refer only to Jewish inhabitants who did not immigrate but have been rooted here for generations?
No, it refers to all people who are living in the land today. We of course know that, at present, this is an utterly unrealistic goal. We know that this will take a long, long time to become a reality.

For this to happen, the facts on the ground and the dominating mentality have to change fundamentally. Notably, not only among Israelis but also among Palestinians. But the day will come, when all people, Jews and Muslims will be able to enjoy their rights in one democratic state. Our intermediate objective is the establishment of a Palestinian state on the borders of 1967 with East Jerusalem as a capital and the right of refugees to return according to UN resolution 194.

Western states stopped considering the DFLP a terrorist organization in 1999. Yet, the movement still maintains a military wing. What role does "armed struggle" play for the DFLP today?

The position of DFLP has always been unique. For us, armed struggle has never been our only strategic choice. We were and we are convinced that the political circumstances should determine the best approach to reach our goals. So for us, armed resistance has always been only one option next to others such as public, political, and diplomatic struggle. We maintain that we have a right to resist the occupation.

That is also the reason why we have not deleted the notion of armed struggle from our program. But we are against targeting civilians and we have since the signing of Oslo refrained from any operations outside of the occupied territories. We were the only party that took this stance. Also, it is important to note that while we opposed Oslo, we refrained from engaging in operations to sabotage the process. We could have done so but we felt that this would have been counterproductive. For the present period, we are convinced that military operations will not serve our course. Violence is simply not a suitable strategy. Our clear focus is on popular nonviolent struggle.

Even though you originally opposed Oslo, the DFLP decided to join the government in 2009. Why did the party change its stance toward the PNA so fundamentally?

We changed our stance toward the PNA government because we feel that the role of the PNA has changed significantly since the signing of Oslo. We did not join the government to serve the interests of the Israelis to have a Peace Process without peace and a PNA that assists in maintaining the status quo. We joined because we want to serve the interest of the Palestinian people in terms of education, social development, and economic development. I know that some parties such as the PFLP still condemn the PNA for being a part of the Oslo framework but this misses the point. At this point, we need the PNA. The PNA under Abbas attempts to realize the aspirations and demands of the Palestinian people. That is the reason why we chose to embrace it despite our initial well-founded criticism.

But in 2012 the DFLP's Central Committee argued that it was an "illusion to build a state under occupation." Was this not a direct assault against the state-building policies of the government in which you serve as a minister?

I am serving in this position because the party asked me to do so. If the party changes its mind, I will leave my position. But I also believe that the concept of the PNA's state-building plan has changed. We completed the state-building plan of Prime Minister Fayyad last year [2011] and yet we still do not have a state. Today, also the prime minister agrees that being ready for statehood is only one part of a threefold strategy. The current strategy of the PNA also comprises political initiatives and public nonviolent struggle. And this stance is also a consensus within the DFLP.

What are the DFLP's natural allies in the political system? Will there be a new coalition with FIDA and the PPP in upcoming elections?

In my opinion this is an absolute must. The Arab Spring and the resurgence of Islamist parties pose a severe challenge for us. We have to find a way to form a strong coalition—not only prior to national elections but also at the universities and at the local level. A real unification of the left is certainly unrealistic at this point. It is always easy to split but very difficult to come together again. Yet, I truly believe in the necessity to join forces with other movements such as the PPP, FIDA, the PNI, and the PFLP.

How would you describe the position of DFLP in the West Bank since the breaking away of FIDA?

When Yasir Abed Rabbo left the party, this was a hard blow for us. He took with him a large part of our supporters. Yet, I would say that our standing in the West Bank has improved greatly. But, of course, it is in no way satisfactory. Especially not in view of the historical role that we as a party have played in paving the way for the acceptance of the Two-State Solution in the PLO. But of course, through our engagement with the PLO we have also suffered for the setbacks attributed to the organization.

How do you plan to expand your support base?

We need to work on vitalizing our party. Our last General Congress in 2007 already modified our political program. At present, we are in the process of preparing for our Sixth General Congress that will take place at the end of 2012. The elections of delegates is already underway in our local and district branches. In the Sixth General Congress, we will further update our political program. I am convinced that there will be significant changes.

The congress will focus on our lessons from the Arab Spring. As concerning elections, we need to tackle the election law so that it truly represents the will of the people. The present law with its focus on individual candidates distorts the results. We need an election law that treats Palestine as one electoral district with one set of political lists. In such a system, groups such as Hamas would fare much worse than in the previous elections.

The Arab Spring has had severe repercussions last but not least for Hamas, which effectively left Damascus. Why is the DFLP leadership still present in Syria?
We are still based in Syria because Palestinians are still based in Syria. We have hundreds of thousands of Palestinians living in refugee camps there. We cannot simply leave them alone. This is the reason why our secretary general is still based in Damascus. Yet, we are careful not to become involved in the ongoing conflict.

Interview with Saleh Zedan, Member of the Political Bureau of DFLP, Gaza

In the West Bank, the DFLP is part of the Fayyad government. What impact does this have on your position in Gaza under Hamas?
Actually, DFLP is not only part of the PNA government but also a central faction of the PLO. So we are part of two organizations that are opposed by Hamas. This does not exactly make things easier for us in Gaza. However, it would be inaccurate to consider us an uncritical member in government and the PLO. In the West Bank, we have opposed recent unjust policies and have openly presented alternatives to the neoliberal policies of Fayyad. I would even go so far to say that despite our serving in the government we are actually an opposition party in the West Bank. And the same is true regarding our position in the PLO, where we have had a distinct and critical voice opposing flawed positions on negotiating with Israel. Despite our critical stance in the West Bank and in the PLO, our current freedom of movement in Gaza is severely restricted and obviously much more limited than in the West Bank. In Gaza, we are quite simply in a position of comprehensive opposition to the ruling regime.

What does this mean in concrete terms?
The Hamas government here might allow political factions to express outrage over the treatment of political prisoners in Israeli jails or over the Palestinian right to return. Anything that goes beyond such positions is suppressed. Our main concern as DFLP is the living conditions of common people. In Gaza, the gap between the haves and the have-nots is constantly widening. We are talking about a general unemployment rate of 33 percent and about a new caste of more than

one thousand millionaires who benefit from the policies of siege and blockade. We find this utterly unacceptable.

Based on this concern, we are in fundamental opposition to a large part of Hamas's current social and economic policies in Gaza. However, to address such issues is basically impossible. For instance, some time ago, we wanted to protest against electricity cuts in different locations in the Gaza Strip. When we organized a protest in Nuseirat in the central Gaza Strip, however, the local and mostly young leaders of the protests were arrested and intimidated.

Does this mean that party activities are basically on hold in Gaza?
I would not go so far. Actually, we are allowed to hold meetings, and events that we organize can be attended by anybody who is interested. However, we are prevented from addressing the issues that we feel very passionately about. We are silenced on our main point of concern.

In the past, the DFLP played a decisive role in advancing positions of the PLO vis-a-vis Two-State Solution. Does this political heritage strengthen or weaken your position in Gaza?
It is true that via the Ten Points Program we have contributed greatly to Palestinian political thinking. And I believe that this is still a contribution that is being respected in Palestinian society also in Gaza. But obviously in a situation as in the present one, history is merely a background to the current pressing issues of social and economic inequality.

In a situation where your historical accomplishments are overshadowed and your freedom of movement is restricted, what can be done to gain political momentum?
Our starting point is that Hamas's popularity in Gaza is declining. People are tired of the ever-increasing focus on security. They want their social needs to be addressed. We need to mobilize the Palestinian people and work on overcoming the two lines that are dividing us as a people: the growing income disparity and the split between the West Bank and Gaza. In this process, there is no alternative to also confront the conservative forces of Hamas.

As concerning the bigger political picture and finding a solution with Israel, we need to base any new negotiations on a stop of settlement expansions and on international law. We need to focus not only on negotiations but also on increasing popular struggle activities for example against the so-called buffer zone along the wall that Israel built around the Gaza Strip. The wall has actually made a large proportion of our agricultural land a no-go zone. This policy must be confronted.

If the method of choice is nonviolent popular struggle, what role do the National Resistance Brigades, the military wing of DFLP, play?

Our military wing is a force to confront invasions. They are there to react, not to act. We have been removed from terror lists around the world, so our stance has been acknowledged. On a side note: our military capabilities are often repressed by Hamas, which attempts to present itself as the only faction that engages in resistance.

But even if you consider any military action of DFLP as a reaction to military incursions, does a military response not run contrary to the idea of nonviolent popular struggle?

Again, our military wing is a force that focuses on strategic defense. We, as a party, are against targeting civilians and we oppose any militant operation in Israel.

What impact does the split between West Bank and Gaza have on the cooperation between the two wings in both territories?

Obviously, Israel's policy of blockade makes it difficult for us. We cannot simply gather for formal meetings in Ramallah. I was personally prevented by Israel from attending PLO meetings. Our Central Committee and political bureau do convene regularly in Damascus. As concerning the presentation of DFLP activists in the party institutions, the situation could be worse. We currently have five members of the political bureau who are from Gaza. Of these, one recently moved to Ramallah, which brings the number down to four. We hope that the General Congress of DFLP at the end of 2012 will end with six Gazans in the political bureau.

Party Meetings are held in Damascus. The Hamas leadership recently left Syria in protest over Bashar al-Assad's crackdown on demonstrators. Why does the DFLP leadership remain in Syria?

Contrary to Hamas, we were able to position ourselves quite well in Syria. We want to see a peaceful solution to the conflict. We oppose the government's use of force and at the same time we are strictly opposed to an international intervention.

★ ★ ★

Excerpts from DFLP Party Documents

The following is excerpted from a January 29, 2012 statement released by the DFLP on the PNA's financial crisis[11] and from the Final Statement of Central Committee Session of the DFLP from December 2011.[12] Additional excerpts are taken from the DFLP 2007 Party Platform[13] and from the program of the al-Badil list, of which DFLP was a part in the 2006 PLC elections.[14] Furthermore, excerpts are taken from the DFLP's Transitional Program, adopted by the Central Committee in the fall of 1975.[15]

View on Israeli–Palestinian Conflict

Final Statement of Central Committee of DFLP (2011):
"We reaffirm that all forms of resistance for us, as a people under the occupation, are legitimate by international law, and we stress the importance of escalating popular resistance as being, together with mobilizing the international pressure, a main strategy to raise the cost of the occupation to force Israel to search for a political solution leading to the end of the occupation. The Central Committee calls on all Palestinian factions to do their best to promote popular resistance and widen its use to include all confrontation flashpoints.

The Central Committee stresses the importance of abiding by the Palestinian consensus, which rejects resumption of negotiations unless Israel pledges to adhere to international resolutions and completely halts the construction of settlements in Jerusalem and in all the Palestinian Territories.

The Central Committee renews the party's support for ... diplomatic efforts, which aim to obtain the recognition of Palestine on the borders of June 1967 with Jerusalem as its capital and Palestine's membership in all appropriate international institutions. The DFLP stresses the importance of pursuing this goal at the United Nations General Assembly in parallel with the efforts in the Security Council. It also calls for continuing the battle of joining international organizations after the latest step of joining UNESCO.

On the occasion of the sixty-fourth anniversary of the issuance of Resolution No. 181, the Central Committee welcomes the Palestinian refugees and their adherence to their right of return and the rejection of alternative solutions."

Program of al-Badil List (2006):
"[The list demands] a complete stop of settlement activities, the dismantling of existing settlements, and the resumption of the work of Palestinian institutions in Jerusalem. [Furthermore, the list rejects] partial settlements and temporary ones including Sharon's plan for

temporary borders for the Palestinian state and call for organizing an international conference in order to achieve a comprehensive solution that will respect international resolutions securing a full withdrawal of Israeli forces to the lines of June 4, 1967, dismantle all settlements, establish the Palestinian state with Jerusalem as its capital, and resolve the question of the Palestinian refugees according to resolution 194, which offers them the right to return to their homes."

Transitional Program (1975):

"[Our work is] based on the right of our people to return, to self-determination and to independence in a national state established on all Palestinian lands from which the Israeli occupation has been forced to withdraw.... The struggle to put an end to Israeli occupation in the occupied territories, to wrest the right of the Palestinian people to return to its homeland and to achieve self-determination within the framework of an independent national state—presently constitutes the central pivot of this Transitional Program. The occupation authorities are pursuing a settler-colonial policy that destroys the interests of all the national classes.

...

The Democratic Front struggles in the occupied territories to mobilize, organize, and lead the masses—using all available forms of mass, political, syndical, and armed struggle. Its aims are: To resist all measures taken by the occupation authorities for the seizure and purchase of land, to return confiscated land to their legitimate owners, and to evacuate Zionist settlements from these land... This right [to self-determination] is to be exercised in the framework of a fully independent national Palestinian state, under the leadership of the PLO in its quality of sole legitimate representatives of the Palestinian people, thus guaranteeing the establishment of a national authority in which all patriotic classes may be represented under a democratic system.

...

The immediate tasks faced by the Palestinian revolution in the Arab countries hosting large concentrations of Palestinians (Syria, Lebanon, Iraq, etc.) are, in general: Preserving and bringing out the independent national status of the Palestinian people by building professional, political, cultural, military (the militia), and mass organizations, which promote this status and help to defend it. Guaranteeing the Palestinian people's right to pursue its struggle against the Zionist enemy, through its freedom to enroll in the ranks of the resistance and its freedom to organize, to be armed, and to engage in political, propaganda and military activities.

...

In the territory occupied in 1948, the masses of the Palestinian people confront immediate tasks that can be summed up in the following: the preservation of their independent national identity, the defense of their direct democratic and national rights, the battle against Zionist attempts at dilution and absorption, and the struggle against the measures of eviction, uprooting, and land expropriation. These come in addition to the task of organized participation in the national movement of the Palestinian people and the task of resistance to all policies of Zionist occupation and expansion.

...

An immediate goal of the struggle of the Arab peoples, particularly in the countries confronting Israeli occupation, is to force a total and unconditional Israeli withdrawal from all the lands occupied in 1967, as well as to guarantee the rights of the Palestinian people to return and self-determination and to the establishment of an independent national state."

Economic Development

DFLP Statement on the PNA's Financial Crisis (2012):
"The measures mentioned are steps toward correcting the political and social policy of the government. And they must be followed by other brave steps addressing the issues of poverty and marginalization from which our people are suffering. Here we emphasize the following minimum steps:

- establishing a minimum wage tied to the rise in cost of living by immediately implementing Articles 86–89 of the Labor Law
- endorsing a comprehensive social security system and health insurance through an independent national fund supervised by a fair administration elected by the system's beneficiaries."

Final Statement of Central Committee of DFLP (2011):
"The Central Committee approved the proposals of the politburo of the Democratic Front to...plan for controlling government expenditures and reducing dependence on foreign aid in funding the state

budget, especially with regard to stopping unwarranted expenses, putting an end to the privileges of senior executives, reducing the cost of travel and external missions, reducing the consumption of state vehicles, telephones, and other operating costs, amending the income tax law and accrediting a progressive tax for high salaries and incomes in a way that participates in realizing equality between all social classes, and combating tax evasion which is facilitated by the occupation authority....

The Central Committee also called for continuing efforts with allied states to stop their investments in Israel and in the settlements, and called for crystallizing these proposals in a detailed tangible formula and mobilizing a mass campaign to urge the government to adopt them.

The Central Committee focused on the importance of correcting economic policies supporting the Gross National Product and protecting it from Israeli and foreign competition. It also called for reconsidering the government budget in favor of raising expenditures on education, health, social care, and municipal services, in addition to allocating a larger share of available resources to supporting the development budget of productive projects, especially small, medium and cooperative projects, as well as developing rural areas, in particular those which have been damaged by the racist annexation wall and settlements, in order to boost the steadfastness of their residents and develop infrastructure projects, public utilities, and the reconstruction of the Gaza Strip.

The Central Committee called for banning Palestinian investment in the settlements, whether directly or indirectly through hidden contracts. It also called for reinforcing the national boycott of settlement products, and for forming a National Control Agency with the aim of preventing them from entering national markets. On the other hand, the Central Committee called for creating alternative job opportunities for settlement employees.

The Central Committee studied the deteriorating economic and social situation in the Gaza Strip and the resulting suffering of its citizens and the frightful rise of poverty and unemployment rate. It stressed the necessity of escalating the exerted efforts at all levels to end the unfair Israeli blockade on the Gaza Strip, especially after the Shalit swap deal eliminated the false pretext of the Israeli government justifying its blockade."

Program of al-Badil List (2006):

"[We plan to] wage a war against corruption and nepotism and dishonesty toward public funds, and demand equality among citizens, regardless of their political affiliations, in occupying public jobs and taking advantage of public services and governmental facilities.

[We intend to] reorganize the budgets in a way that will give priority to a program that will fight against unemployment and take care of the families of the martyrs, those with special needs and victims of Israeli aggression and support the steadfastness of Jerusalem and other victimized arias by the Israeli racist wall, and to improve the infrastructure and educational, municipal, and health services.

[We intend to] support the agricultural sector with development of the deprived rural areas and the provision of basic services."

Transitional Program (1975):

"[The Democratic Front's aims are] to protect the national economy from steps taken to absorb and destroy it and from exorbitant taxation, and to preserve national economic projects, crafts, and agriculture. To organize the struggle of the working class against exploitation and discrimination and to guarantee its right to have independent syndical organizations.

. . .

The Organization of the Democratic Front in Jordan, which is the organizational framework for uniting the vanguards of the Palestinian and Jordanian laboring classes, works to mobilize all the patriotic classes to organize their struggle in order to: Put an end to imperialist influence, to achieve complete national liberation, to protect the country's independence from colonialist foreign 'aid', and to build an independent, rather than service-oriented, national economy.

This will correspond to the vital and immediate interests of the classes, chiefly the right of the working class to receive fair wages, to have comprehensive social security, and to fight unemployment and arbitrary dismissal. To achieve a radical agrarian reform; to free the peasantry from the despotism of big landlords, merchants, and usurers; to prohibit large landholdings; to distribute the land according to the principle 'the land to those who work it'; and to direct the agricultural policy of the state for the benefit of small and poor peasants, in terms of financing, irrigation, marketing, mechanization, and agricultural planning."

The State's Role vis-a-vis Religion

DFLP Party Platform (2007):

"The DFLP believes in a secular state with separation between religion and the state."

Program of al-Badil List (2006):
"We will struggle to resist trials by Israel to isolate and Judaize Jerusalem, and to establish a unified national reference for the citizens of the holy city acting on the basis of a plan to support the steadfastness of the citizens and protection of lands and estates in addition to defending the sacred sites of Moslems and Christians."

Vision of State and Society

Final Statement of Central Committee of DFLP (2011):
"The Central Committee calls for restructuring the Palestinian Authority and its role in rebuilding the administrations and the bodies of the Authority, free from the illusions of building a state under occupation. It must focus on supporting the steadfastness of the society, enabling it to bear the burdens of the long battle to end the occupation, and must face the challenges of putting an end to the unjust obligations signed with Israel, which contradict international law."

Program of al-Badil List (2006):
"[We intend to] develop the education sector, and to secure its material and human needs in order to enlarge the field of educational services, especially at the university level, and reduce the costs of learning, and adopt a democratic-national orientation, and reject of all foreign pressures to distort these curricula, and at the same time encourage cultural and artistic creativity, and respond to the legal demands of the workers in the educational sector.

[We intend to] secure sufficient funds to develop the health sector, in a way that enables it to provide citizens with necessary medicine within the frame of a general health insurance system.

[We call for]:

- Full equality between males and females in all political, economic, and social fields, the full participation of women in decision-making and the enforcing of laws that abolish all kinds of prejudice, and defend women's social status
- reinforcing the role of youth, enabling them to participate in decision-making processes, securing their right of access to education and work, development of their athletic, cultural and artistic talents, and providing them with work opportunities
- protecting basic freedoms and dignity for all citizens, respecting human rights and the establishment of a democratic parliamentary

system securing a separation of powers and a peaceful exchange of power through regular elections
- developing a Palestinian constitution in a way that defines the responsibility of the executive authority towards the legislative council
- developing of an election law in a way that guarantees just representation of all social strata and regions in the parliament, including the reduction of the age of nomination and securing a quota of representation for women not less than 30 percent of the council seats
- putting an end to anarchy and security disorder, reconstructing the security system, imposing the law and reinforcing the authority of the judicial system and its independence, enriching its human and technical resources. Offering the legislative council the right to appoint judges
- obtaining pardons for the prisoners in the PA prisons, and putting an end to political imprisonment
- establishing of a National Unity Government adopting this program, including all forces who will participate in decision-making processes
- reviving the PLO as the sole and legitimate representative of the Palestinian people and reconstructing its institutions on a democratic basis and as a reference for the Palestinian Authority. A legislative election in the West Bank, Gaza Strip, and Jerusalem, paves the way to do the same among the Palestinian Refugees."

Transitional Program (1975):

"[The Democratic Front's aims are:] to protect civil liberties, and to fight against policy of intimidation, detention, expulsion, and collective punishment. To guarantee the right of women, students, teachers, youth, and other groups in the population, to establish their own independent mass and professional organizations. To protect national culture and heritage, educational programs, and places of worship, from all Zionist policies of suppression, degradation and falsification.

...

The Democratic Front is struggling on all levels to consolidate the PLO as the sole legitimate representative of the Palestinian people and as the sole expression of its national consensus. The Democratic Front is also struggling to promote the unity of all the revolutionary and patriotic forces within the framework of the PLO; to democratically reform the political, military, and administrative institutions of the PLO; to strengthen the common front structure of the PLO on the basis of democracy, equality, and unity of the political program of national struggle; and to end unilateral actions, patronage, and domination from one group or another—all this in order that the PLO may become a genuine framework for a united front of national liberation."

TIMELINE OF POLITICAL EVENTS IN THE PALESTINIAN TERRITORIES

1948	Israeli War of Independence / Palestinian *nakba* (catastrophe). The founding of the State of Israel results in the exodus of approximately 700,000 Palestinians.
1959	Founding of Fatah in Kuwait.
1964	Founding of the Palestine Liberation Organization (PLO) during the 1964 Arab League summit in Cairo.
1967	Founding of the Popular Front for the Liberation of Palestine (PFLP).
1967	Six Day War results in the occupation of the West Bank, East Jerusalem, the Gaza Strip, and the Golan Heights by Israeli forces.
1968	Battle of Karameh: Jordanian military forces and Fatah militants stand their ground against Israeli forces. The battle results in increased popularity for Fatah.
1969	Split of the Democratic Front for the Liberation of Palestine (DFLP)—predecessor of PFLP.
September 1970	Black September: Heavy clashes between the Jordanian military and the PLO in Jordan result in the expulsion of PLO factions from Jordan.
October 1973	Yom Kippur War / October War:
1974	Release of the PLO's Ten Point Program, calling for the establishment of a Palestinian authority on "every part of the Palestinian territory that is liberated."
1975–1990	Lebanese civil war.

1982	Israeli invasion of Lebanon eradicates most PLO forces from southern Lebanon and Beirut. The PLO leadership relocates to Tunis.
1982	Founding of the Palestinian People's Party (PPP) as Palestine Communist Party (PCP).
1987–1993	The first *intifada:* Palestinians in the West Bank and Gaza engage in demonstrations, civil resistance, and low-intensity violence against the occupation of the West Bank and Gaza.
1987	Founding of Hamas in Gaza.
1988	The Palestinian Declaration of Independence is proclaimed by Yasir Arafat in Algiers.
December 1988	Yasir Arafat addresses the UN General Assembly and acknowledges "Israel's right to exist in peace and security."
1989	First militant operation conducted by Hamas: two Israeli soldiers are killed. The operation later leads to the arrest and conviction of Hamas founder Ahmad Yassin by Israeli forces.
1990/91	First Gulf War: Yasir Arafat's solidarity with Iraqi President Saddam Hussein leads to the expulsion of hundreds of thousands of Palestinians from the Gulf States.
October 1991	The Madrid Peace Conference signifies first formal negotiations between Israelis and Palestinians. Palestinians are represented by a joint Palestinian–Jordanian delegation; the PLO participates as an "advisory delegation."
1993	Letters of recognition exchanged between Israel and the PLO, signed by Israeli prime minister Yitzhak Rabin and PLO chairman Yasir Arafat.
1993/94	The signing of the Oslo Accords in September 1993 leads to the establishment of the Palestinian National Authority (PNA).
1996	The first elections for the Palestinian Legislative Council (PLC) in the West Bank, Gaza, and East Jerusalem result in a Fatah victory. The elections are boycotted by Hamas, PFLP, and others. Arafat is elected president of the PNA with 88 percent of the total vote.
1997	An Israeli assassination attempt against Hamas leader Khaled Mashal fails in Amman.
July 2000	The Camp David talks: US president Bill Clinton, Israeli prime minister Ehud Barak, and PLO chairman Yasir

	Arafat fail to achieve a "final status settlement" to the conflict.
September 2000	Visit of the Israeli opposition leader Ariel Sharon to the Temple Mount / *Haram al-Sharif* triggers the outbreak of the second *intifada*.
January 2001	Taba Summit negotiations fail to achieve a "final status settlement."
2002	Founding of the Palestinian National Initiative (PNI).
March 2003	Yasir Arafat, in response to US pressure, appoints Mahmoud Abbas as first prime minister of the PNA.
October 2003	Abbas resigns as prime minister, claiming lack of support from Israel and the United States and "internal incitement." He is succeeded by Ahmed Qurei as prime minister.
2003	The Middle East Quartet, composed of the United States, the EU, Russia, and the UN, proposes the Road Map for Peace, a framework for gradual progress toward a Two-State Solution.
March 2004	Hamas founder Ahmad Yassin is killed in an Israeli airstrike.
November 2004	Yasir Arafat dies in Paris.
2005	Municipal elections are held in the West Bank and Gaza: results highlight the strength of Hamas and the organizational weaknesses of Fatah.
2005	Israeli prime minister Ariel Sharon's disengagement from the Gaza Strip. The Israeli settler community is unilaterally evicted.
January 2005	Mahmoud Abbas is elected president of the PNA with 62 percent of the total vote. Hamas and others boycott the elections.
March 2005	An informal truce between Israel and 13 Palestinian factions marks the end of the second *intifada*.
2006	PLC elections result in a victory for Hamas's Change and Reform list. Subsequently, Israel and the Middle East Quartet impose a financial and diplomatic boycott on the PNA.
June 2006	Lebanon War between Israeli forces and Hizbullah fighters.
February 2007	The Saudi-brokered Mecca Agreement to overcome the split between Hamas and Fatah is signed by Mahmoud Abbas and Khaled Mashal. In March, the PLC establishes

	a National Unity Government, led by Prime Minister Ismail Haniya (Hamas).
June 2007	The National Unity Government fails to end frictions in Gaza, leading to full-scale conflicts. Hamas takes control of Gaza. Abbas dissolves the National Unity Government and appoints independent Salam Fayyad to head the emergency government and later the caretaker government in the West Bank. Israel and the Middle East Quartet resume full financial support for the PNA in the West Bank.
2007	Israel and Egypt establish a blockade of the Gaza Strip.
2009	Salam Fayyad is reappointed prime minister and he introduces his state building plan, *Ending the Occupation, Establishing the State*.
August 2009	Sixth General Congress of Fatah convenes in Bethlehem.
November 2009	Israeli prime minister Benyamin Netanyahu issues a ten-month "settlement freeze" in the West Bank. The policy does not apply to East Jerusalem.
May 2010	Gaza "Freedom Flotilla." Israel partly eases its blockade of the Gaza Strip. Exports from Gaza remain impossible.
January 2011	Palestine Papers are leaked by Qatari TV channel *al-Jazeera*.
May 2011	Cairo Reconciliation Agreement between Fatah and Hamas sets out a path for the creation of a transitional government and national reconciliation.
2011	Municipality elections are postponed in the West Bank and Gaza.
September 2011	PLO applies for full UN membership at the United Nations Security Council.
October 2011	In a prisoner exchange between Hamas and Israel, abducted Israeli soldier Gilad Shalit and 1,027 Palestinian prisoners are freed.
October 2011	The UNESCO General Conference admits Palestine as a full member. The United States reduces financial support for the PNA. Israel temporarily freezes the transfer of Palestinian taxes.
February 2012	The Doha Agreement between Hamas and Fatah reaffirms the implementation of the 2011 Cairo Agreement. The parties agree to hold elections in 2012 and to the establishment of an interim government led by Abbas.

May 2012	Internal Hamas elections in Gaza strengthen Ismail Haniya's position. PNA cabinet is reappointed in the West Bank: 13 Fatah members gain ministerial posts in the second Fayyad cabinet.
September 2012	Protests against unpopular policies of Prime Minister Salam Fayyad erupt throughout the West Bank.

NOTES

1 Political Factions in Palestine: Stagnation, Ambiguity, and Change

1. Nathan J. Brown, "Evaluating Palestinian Reform," *Carnegie Papers Middle East Series* no. 59 (May 2005).
2. Helga Baumgarten, "The Three Faces / Phases of Palestinian Nationalism 1948–2005," *Journal of Palestine Studies* 34, no. 4 (2005): 25.
3. As of 2012, the following political organizations are members of the Palestine Liberation Organization (PLO): the Palestinian National Liberation Movement (Fatah), the Popular Front for the Liberation of Palestine (PFLP), the Democratic Front for the Liberation of Palestine (DFLP), the Palestine Liberation Front (PLF), the Arab Liberation Front (ALF), As-Sa'iqa, the Palestinian People's Party (PPP), the Palestine Democratic Union (FIDA), the Palestinian Popular Struggle Front (PPSF), and the Palestinian Arab Front (PAF).
4. While these distinct phases of Palestinian factionalism are clearly distinguishable, alternative parallel forms of organization such as elements of traditional leadership have been permanent features of Palestinian politics for decades as well. See Abdelaziz A. Ayyad, *Arab Nationalism and the Palestinians 1850–1939* (Jerusalem: PASSIA, 1999). In this context, also the relevance of independent Palestinian grassroots activism has to be acknowledged. Here, the most prominent example is certainly the Palestinian *intifada* erupting in 1987. As political scientist Mary Elizabeth King puts it, ultimately the intifada was based on the initiative of activists, who "stopped waiting" for political movements to act and "became involved in the broad, popular mobilization" Mary Elizabeth King, *A Quiet Revolution: The First Palestinian Intifada and Nonviolent Resistance* (New York: Nation Books, 2007), 102. However, while the established Palestinian factions were clearly at first taken by surprise by this independent activism, they soon managed to regain the initiative and absorbed the unleashed political momentum.
5. In the text, "Palestinian Territories" is given preference to "Palestinian Territory" or "occupied Palestinian territories", as it is felt that this more adequately describes the areas currently under administrative control of the Palestinian National Authority (PNA), notably Areas A and B of the West Bank and the Gaza Strip as defined in the Oslo Accords.

6. Nathan J. Brown, *Palestinian Politics after the Oslo Accords. Resuming Arab Palestine* (Berkeley/Los Angeles, CA: University of California Press, 2003).
7. On the establishment of the PNA and the resulting characteristics of the emerging political system, see Nigel Parsons, *The Politics of the Palestinian Authority. From Oslo to Al-Aqsa* (London: Routledge, 2005).
8. Nadia Nasser-Najjab, "Palestinian Political Movements: Should They be Registered?" *Palestine-Israel Journal* 12, no. 1 (2005): 13–19.
9. Notable exceptions to this general rule are Fatah, which has embraced its role as party of state in the West Bank since 1994 and in its 2009 party convention even voted representatives of the party diaspora out of office, and the PPP, which has remained affiliated with the PNA almost uninterruptedly since the its establishment. Hamas has come to embrace this ambiguity with its decision in 2006 to participate in PLC elections.
10. Amal Jamal, *The Palestinian National Movement. Politics of Contention 1967–2005* (Bloomington, IN: Indiana University Press, 2005), 141.
11. Jamil Hilal, "The Polarization of the Palestinian Political Field," *Journal of Palestine Studies* 39, no. 3 (2010): 24–39.
12. At the same time, progress in state-building policies of West Bank prime minister Salam Fayyad has repeatedly been acknowledged by international organizations. Thus, the World Bank in its September 2011 report stipulated that "Palestinian public institutions compare favorably to other countries in the region and beyond." "Sustaining Achievements in Palestinian Institution Building and Economic Growth. Economic Monitoring Report to the ad hoc Liaison Committee," World Bank, accessed May 30, 2012, http://siteresources.worldbank.org/INTWESTBANKGAZA/Resources/WorldBankAHLCReportSep2011.pdf.
13. "Presidential Decree on the postponement of presidential and legislative elections," President of the Palestinian National Authority, accessed June 1, 2012, www.elections.ps/Portals/0/pdf/Presidential_decree_on_the_postponment_of_presidential_and_legislative_elections_2010_English.pdf.
14. Asad Ghanem, *Palestinian Politics after Arafat—A Failed National Movement* (Bloomington, IN: Indiana University Press, 2010).
15. Daoud Kuttab, "Wanted: New Palestinian Political Parties," *Huffington Post*, April 21, 2011, accessed June 1, 2012, www.huffingtonpost.com/daoud-kuttab/wanted-new-palestinian-po_b_851848.html.
16. "Opinion Poll," Near East Consulting, accessed May 31, 2012, www.neareastconsulting.com/press/2012/April2012-PR-EN.pdf.
17. For a broader historical account of the development of Palestinian political life, see Yezid Sayigh, *Armed Struggle and the Search for State. The Palestinian National Movement 1949–1993* (Oxford: Oxford University Press, 1997).
18. Iyad Barghouti, *Political Secularism and the Religious Question in Palestine* (Ramallah: Ramallah Center for Human Rights Studies, 2012), 12.
19. "Opinion Poll no. 76," Jerusalem Media and Communication Center, accessed July 1, 2012, www.jmcc.org/documentsandmaps.aspx?id=855
20. Given the nature of the Israeli–Palestinian conflict, the question of what distiunguishes legal "resistance" from acts of "terrorism" is controversial. While Israeli public discourse frequently considers any Palestinian act of violence "terrorism," Palestinians often consider attacks such as suicide bombings "operations of resistance." In the text, the label "terrorism" has been used to designate the use of force by Palestinians against Israeli civilians.

21. Sayigh, *Armed Struggle*, 665.
22. Khaled Hroub, *Hamas. A Beginner's Guide* (London: Pluto Press, 2010), 24.

2 Hamas: Between Terror and Realpolitik

1. See chapter 2.4 (excerpts from Hamas Charter).
2. Ibid.
3. Azzam Tamimi, *Hamas: Unwritten Chapters* (London: Hurst & Company, 2007), 149.
4. Khaled Amayreh, "Running out of Time,"*Al Ahram Weekly*, January 29–February 4, 2004.
5. With the notable exception of a suicide bombing in 2008 in Dimona, which killed one Israeli civilian.
6. For all quotes from Hamas's 2006 election platform, see chapter 2.4 (excerpts from Election Platform of Change and Reform List).
7. "Hamas Leader Sets Conditions," *CNN World*, January 29, 2006, accessed May 30, 2012, http://articles.cnn.com/2006-01-29/world/hamas.interview_1_palestinian-prisoners-top-hamas-official-hudna?_s=PM:WORLD.
8. See chapter 2.4 (excerpts from Program of the National Unity Government).
9. See chapter 2.4 (excerpts from Hamas Charter).
10. See chapter 2.4 (Development Plan 2011–2012 Gaza Ministry of Planning).
11. Michael Bröning, "Hamas Comes in from the Cold," *Project Syndicate*, February 22, 2012, accessed June 1, 2012, www.project-syndicate.org/commentary/hamas-comes-in-from-the-cold.
12. Suggested further readings: Joren Gunning, *Hamas in Politics* (New York: Columbia University Press, 2010); Khaled Hroub, *Hamas—a Beginner's Guide* (London: Pluto Press, 2010).
13. See chapter 2.4 (excerpts from Hamas Charter).
14. "Sheikh Ahmad Yassin (1938–2004)," Ikhwanweb, accessed May 31, 2012, www.ikhwanweb.com/article.php?id=23862.
15. "Sheikh Ahmad Yassin (1936–2004)," Miftah, accessed May 31, 2012, www.miftah.org/Display.cfm?DocId=3377&CategoryId=11.
16. "Israel Defiant Over Yassin Killing," *BBC News*, March 22, 2004, accessed May 30, 2012, http://news.bbc.co.uk/2/hi/3557451.stm.
17. "Annan Strongly Condemns Israeli Assassination of Hamas Leader," United Nations News Center, accessed May 31, 2012, www.un.org/apps/news/storyAr.asp?NewsID=10155&Cr=middle&Cr1=east.
18. "Hamas Vows to Honor Palestinian Referendum on Peace with Israel," *Haaretz*, December 1, 2010.
19. Fares Akram, "At a Rally for Hamas, Celebration and Vows," *The New York Times*, December 14, 2011.
20. Mehdi Hassan, "No Kind of Martyr," *New Statesman*, 140, no. 5052 (2011): 26.
21. "Hamas' Gaza Chief: Iran Will Help Muslim World to Liberate Al Aqsa Mosque," Haaretz. February 12, 2012.
22. General Directorate of Gaza Ministry of Planning, e-mail message to FES office Gaza, April 12, 2012. Translated from Arabic by Usama Anthar and Michael Bröning.
23. Hamas Political Bureau Gaza, English language program of National Unity Government provided to FES office in Gaza, March 5, 2012.

24. Hamas Political Bureau Gaza, English language program of Change and Reform list provided to FES office in Gaza, March 5, 2012.
25. "Hamas Covenant 1988. The Covenant of the Islamic Resistance Movement," Yale Law School / The Avalon Project, accessed March 5, 2012, http://avalon.law.yale.edu/20th_century/hamas.asp.

3 From Resistance Movement to Party of State

1. See chapter 3.4 (excerpts from Political Platform of Fatah).
2. See chapter 3.4 (excerpts from Fatah Constitution).
3. Ibid.
4. "Letter from President Yasser Arafat to President Clinton," *Miftah*, accessed June 10, 2012, www.miftah.org/Display.cfm?DocId=428&CategoryId=10.
5. George Mitchell, Suleyman Demirel, Thorbjoern Jagland, Warren B. Rudman, and Javier Solana, "Sharm el-Sheikh Fact Finding Committee Report," April 30, 2001, accessed June 1, 2012, http://2001-2009.state.gov/p/nea/rls/rpt/3060.htm.
6. For quotes from Fatah's new political program see chapter 3.4 (excerpts from Political Platform of Fatah).
7. See chapter 3.4 (excerpts from Fatah Constitution).
8. Suggested further readings: "Salvaging Fatah," International Crisis Group, Middle East Report No. 91, (2009); Yezid Sayigh, *Armed Struggle and the Search for State: The Palestinian National Movement 1949–93* (Oxford: Clarendon Press, 1997).
9. See chapter 3.4 (excerpts from Fatah Constitution).
10. "The PLO's Ten Point Plan Adopted at the 12th Session of the Palestine National Council," Jewish Virtual Library, accessed June 1, 2012, www.jewishvirtuallibrary.org/jsource/Terrorism/PNCProgram1974.html.
11. "Cahier Spécial sur le Proche-Orient," *Monde Diplomatique* (Paris: Le Monde, 2006).
12. Ibid.
13. "UN Tells Israel to 'Get Out'," *The Telegraph*, March 30, 2002, accessed June 1, 2012, www.telegraph.co.uk/news/1389310/UN-tells-Israel-to-get-out.html.
14. "Bush Sees Arafat as Irrelevant," *The Telegraph*, June 6, 2002, accessed June 1, 2012, www.telegraph.co.uk/news/worldnews/middleeast/israel/1396455/Bush-sees-Arafat-as-irrelevant.html.
15. Omri Efraim, "Lieberman to Europe: Israel Has Nothing to Apologize for," *Ynet News*, December 25, 2011, accessed May 30, 2012, www.ynetnews.com/articles/0,7340,L-4166615,00.html.
16. Marwan Barghouti, "Want Security? End the Occupation," *Washington Post*, January 16, 2002.
17. Gil Friedman, "Strategic Deficiencies in National Liberation Struggles: The Case of Fatah in the Al Aqsa Intifada," *Journal of Strategic Studies* 31, no. 1 (2008): 41.
18. Khaled Amayreh, "Denouncing a Show Trial," *Al Ahram Weekly*, October 2–8, 2003.
19. Hossam Ezzedine, "Barghouti: Veto on UN Bid Tantamount to 'Terror'," *Maan News*, August 19, 2011, accessed May 30, 2012, www.maannews.net/eng/ViewDetails.aspx?ID=414284.
20. Fatah Foreign Relations Commission Ramallah, English language version of Political Platform of Fatah provided to FES office in Jerusalem, February 5, 2011.
21. Fatah Foreign Relations Commission Ramallah, English language version of Fatah Constitution provided to FES office in Jerusalem, February 5, 2011.

4 Arab Anti-Imperialists

1. See chapter 4.4 (excerpts from PFLP Platform).
2. See chapter 4.4 (excerpts from Statement on the 39th Anniversary of the Founding of the PFLP).
3. "The PLO's Ten Point Plan Adopted at the 12th Session of the Palestine National Council," Jewish Virtual Library, accessed June 1, 2012, www.jewishvirtuallibrary.org/jsource /Terrorism/PNCProgram1974.html
4. Hossam Ezzeddine, "Saadat: Qorei Govt cannot Represent Palestinians," *Middle East Online* (2003), accessed May 30, 2012, www.middle-east-online.com/english/?id=7080
5. "PFLP denounces PA economic policies, calls for popular protection and development," PFLP, accessed June 1, 2012, http://pflp.ps/english/2012/01/pflp-denounces-pa-economic -policies-calls-for-popular-protection-and-development/.
6. See chapter 4.4 (excerpts from Statement on the 39th Anniversary of the Founding of the PFLP).
7. Ibid.
8. "Political Statement on the 39th Anniversary of the founding of the PFLP," PFLP, accessed March 30, 2012, http://pflp.ps/english/2006/12/political-statement-on-the-39th-anniversary-of-the-founding-of-the-pflp.
9. Suggested further readings: Harold M. Cubert, *The PFLP's Changing Role in the Middle East* (London: Frank Cass, 1997); Matti Steinberg, "The Worldview of Habash's 'Popular Front'" *Jerusalem Quarterly*, 45–48 (1988): 3–36.
10. "Unity in Struggle—George Habash (1925–2008)," *Al Ahram Weekly* (January 31–February 6, 2008), accessed May 30, 2012, http://weekly.ahram.org.eg/2008/882/re31.htm.
11. Asad AbuKhalil, "George Habash's Contribution to the Palestinian Struggle," *Electronic Intifada* (2008), accessed June 1, 2012, http://electronicintifada.net /content/george-habashs-contribution-palestinian-struggle/7332.
12. Grace Halsell, "A Visit with George Habash: Still the Prophet of Arab Nationalism and Armed Struggle against Israel," *Washington Report on Middle East Affairs* 136 (1998): 49.
13. "Interview with Ahmad Sa'adat," *ABC Diario Español*, February 4, 2004.
14. Stephen Lendman, "Ahmad Sa'adat: A Palestinian Prisoner of Conscience," *Palestinian Chronicle* (2010), accessed June 1, 2012, http://palestinechronicle.com /view_article_details.php?id=16108.
15. "Political Statement on the 39th Anniversary of the founding of the PFLP."
16. PFLP Gaza, English language version of Election Platform of PFLP provided to the FES office in Gaza, October 17, 2011.
17. "Platform of the Popular Front for the Liberation of Palestine," PFLP, accessed July 1, 2012, http://pflp.ps/english/1969/12/platform-of-the-popular-front-for-the-liberation -of-palestine-1969/.

5 A History of Nonviolence

1. See chapter 5.4 (excerpts from The Palestinian National Initiative).
2. Ibid.
3. "Mustafa Barghouti Trails in Palestinian Polls," *Arab News* (2005), accessed June 1, 2012, http://archive.arabnews.com/services/print/print.asp?artid=57173&d=7&m=1&y=2005&hl =Mustafa%20Barghouti%20Trails%20in%20Palestinian%20Polls.

4. "Profile: Independent Palestine," al-Mubadara, accessed May 30, 2012, www.almubadara.org/new/edetails.php?id=722.
5. See chapter 5.4 (excerpts from the Political Platform).
6. "Israel Knows Apartheid Has No Future," al-Mubadara, accessed April 13, 2010, www.almubadara.org/new/edetails.php?id=6607.
7. Mustafa Barghouti, "The Slow Death of Palestinian Democracy," *Foreign Policy* (2010), accessed June 1, 2012, www.foreignpolicy.com/articles/2010/07/21/the_slow_death_of_palestinian_democracy.
8. Suggested further readings: Martin Bergsbakk Holter, *Al-Mubadara: Third Current Politics of the Second Intifada. Remobilizing Politics in a De-Powered Palestinian Authority*. Master Thesis, University of Oslo, 2007.
9. "Israel Knows Apartheid Has."
10. "Bader Boycott Campaign," al-Mubadara, accessed May 31, 2012, www.almubadara.org/details.php?id=nztjk5a1593y8zop4z1zd.
11. "The FP Top 100 Global Thinkers," *Foreign Policy* (2011), accessed May 30, 2012, www.foreignpolicy.com/articles/2011/11/28/the_fp_top_100_global_thinkers?page=0,47.
12. Edward Said, "The Morning After," *London Review of Books* 15, no. 20 (1993): 3.
13. "Interview with Edward Said," *Politics and Culture* 3 (2000), accessed May 31, 2012, www.politicsandculture.org/2010/08/10/an-interview-with-edward-said-2/.
14. Edward Said, "Emerging Alternatives in Palestine," *Al Ahram Weekly* (2002), accessed June 1, 2012, http://weekly.ahram.org.eg/2002/568/op2.htm.
15. PNI Ramallah, English language version of Political Platform of PNI provided to the FES office in Jerusalem, December 1, 2011.
16. PNI Ramallah, English language version of The Palestinian National Initiative: Leading the Palestinian People toward Freedom, Independence, Justice, Democracy, and a Life of Dignity provided to the FES office in Jerusalem, December 1, 2011.

6   The PNA's Loyal Opposition

1. Martin Bergsbakk Holter, *Al-Mubadara: Third Current Politics of the Second Intifada. Remobilizing Politics in a De-Powered Palestinian Authority*. Master Thesis, University of Oslo, 2007, 73.
2. Eric Hazan, "Palestinian Defiance," *New Left Review* 32 (March–April 2005), accessed June 5, 2012, http://newleftreview.org/II/32/mustafa-barghouti-palestinian-defiance.
3. See chapter 6.4 (excerpts from Political Program of PPP).
4. "Concluding Statement of the Fourth Party Congress," Palestinian People's Party, accessed April 15, 2012, http://solidnet.org/old/cgi-bin/agent707d.html?parties/0590=palestine,_palestinian_peoples_party/960ppp11apr08.doc.
5. See chapter 6.4 (excerpts from Political Program of PPP).
6. Suggested further readings: Musa Al-Budeiri, *The Palestine Communist Party 1919–1948: Arab & Jew in the Struggle for Internationalism* (London: Ithaca Press, 1979).
7. "Palestinian Local Poll Postponed," *Al Jazeera*, June 10, 2010, accessed June 1, 2012, www.aljazeera.com/news/middleeast/2010/06/2010610155813954648.html.
8. Amira Hass, "Public Outcry Forces Palestinian PM to Suspend Austerity Measures," *Haaretz*, February 7, 2012.
9. "The strategy to establish the independent Palestinian state and achieve the rights of our people," Palestinian People's Party, accessed March 27, 2011, www.palpeople.org/atemplate.php?id=1655.

10. Secretariat of Palestinian People's Party Ramallah, Arabic version of Political Program of PPP provided to the FES office in Jerusalem, March 1, 2012. Translated from Arabic by Usama Anthar and Michael Bröning.
11. "The Program of Al Badil's List," DFLP, accessed June 1, 2012, www.dflp-palestine.net/english/documents/the_program_of_Al-Badil-s_list.htm.
12. Secretariat of PPP Ramallah, Arabic version of PPP Election Program (1995) provided to the FES office in Jerusalem, March 1, 2012. Translated from Arabic by Usama Anthar and Michael Bröning.

7 Palestinian Marxists and their Coming of Age

1. "The Democratic Front for the Liberation of Palestine," DFLP, accessed June 1, 2012, www.dflp-palestine.net/english/about_dflp/dflp_foundation.htm.
2. "The PLO's Ten Point Plan Adopted at the 12th Session of the Palestine National Council," Jewish Virtual Library, accessed June 1, 2012, www.jewishvirtuallibrary.org/jsource/Terrorism/PNCProgram1974.html.
3. "The Democratic Front."
4. "Courts Halt Yitzhar Pullout; Hundreds Converge on Outpost," *Haaretz*, June 19, 2003.
5. "Chronological Review of Events Relating to the Question of Palestine," UNISPAL, accessed June 10, 2012, http://unispal.un.org/UNISPAL.NSF/0/17459CC48D8D397985256D750063AD52.
6. "10 Topics about the Current Situation," DFLP, accessed July 1, 2012, www.dflp-palestine.net/english/statements/10-topics-about-current-situation-finals-statement-of-central-committee-session.htm.
7. "DFLP in Damascus: Peace Talks Dangerous," *Maan News*, March 6, 2010, accessed June 1, 2012, www.maannews.net/eng/ViewDetails.aspx?ID=266464.
8. "DFLP militants claim fire on Israel," *Maan News*, April 8, 2011, accessed May 15, 2012, www.maannews.net/eng/ViewDetails.aspx?ID=376749.
9. Suggested further readings: Paul Lalor, "DFLP differences reflect the debate within the PLO," *Middle East International* no. 374 (1990): 17–19; Matti Steinberg, "The Worldview of Hawatmeh's 'Democratic Front'," *Jerusalem Quarterly* 49–52 (1989): 23–40.
10. Hugh Dellios, "Arafat, Rival Put Aside Differences," *Chicago Tribune*, August 24, 1999, accessed May 30, 2012, http://articles.chicagotribune.com/1999-08-24/news/9908240290_1_palestinian-factions-millions-of-palestinian-refugees-arafat-aide.
11. "A statement released by the Democratic Front for the Liberation of Palestine about the financial crisis of the Palestinian authority," DFLP, accessed July 4, 2012, www.dflp-palestine.net/english/statements/a-statement-released-by-the-democratic-front-f or-the-liberation-of-palestine-about-the-financial-crisis.htm.
12. "10 Topics about Current Situation."
13. Branch office of DFLP Gaza, English version of DFLP Party Platform (2007) provided to the FES office in Gaza, March 15, 2011.
14. "The Program o Al Badil's List," DFLP, accessed June 1, 2012, www.dflp-palestine.net/english/documents/the_program_of_Al-Badil-s_list.htm.
15. Branch office of DFLP Gaza, English version of DFLP Transitional Program (1975) provided to the FES office in Gaza, March 15, 2011.

BIBLIOGRAPHY

Abu Khalil, Asad. "George Habash's Contribution to the Palestinian Struggle." *Electronic Intifada*, January 30, 2008. Accessed June 5, 2012. http://electronicintifada.net/content/george-habashs-contribution-palestinian-struggle/7332.
Akram, Fares. "At a Rally for Hamas, Celebration and Vows." *The New York Times*, December 14, 2011.
Al-Budeiri, Musa. *The Palestine Communist Party 1919–1948: Arab & Jew in the Struggle for Internationalism*. London: Ithaca Press, 1979.
al-Mubadara. "Profile: Independent Palestine." Accessed May 30, 2012. http://www.almubadara.org/new/edetails.php?id=722.
———. "Bader Boycott Campaign." Accessed May 25, 2012. http://www.almubadara.org/details.php?id=nztjk5a1593y8zop4z1zd.
———. "Israel Knows Apartheid Has No Future." Accessed April 13, 2010. http://www.almubadara.org/new/edetails.php?id=6607.
Amayreh, Khaled. "Denouncing a Show Trial." *Al Ahram Weekly*, October 2–8, 2003.
———. "Running out of Time." *Al Ahram Weekly*, January 29–February 4, 2004.
Ayyad, Abdelaziz A. *Arab Nationalism and the Palestinians 1850–1939*. Jerusalem: PASSIA, 1999.
Barghouti, Iyad. *Political Secularism and the Religious Question in Palestine*. Ramallah: Ramallah Center for Human Rights Studies, 2012.
Barghouti, Marwan. "Want Security? End the Occupation." *Washington Post*, January 16, 2002.
Barghouti, Mustafa. "The Slow Death of Palestinian Democracy." *Foreign Policy* (2010). Accessed June 1, 2012. http://www.foreignpolicy.com/articles/2010/07/21/the_slow_death_of_palestinian_democracy.
Baumgarten, Helga. "The Three Faces / Phases of Palestinian Nationalism 1948–2005." *Journal of Palestine Studies* 34, no. 4 (2005): 25–48.
Branch office of DFLP Gaza, English version of DFLP Party Platform (2007) provided to FES office in Gaza, March 15, 2011.
Bröning, Michael. "Hamas Comes in from the Cold." *Project Syndicate*, February 22, 2012. Accessed June 1, 2012. http://www.project-syndicate.org/commentary/hamas-comes-in-from-the-cold.
Brown, Nathan J. *Palestinian Politics after the Oslo Accords. Resuming Arab Palestine*. Berkeley and Los Angeles: University of California Press, 2003.
———. "Evaluating Palestinian Reform." *Carnegie Papers Middle East Series* No. 59 (2005).
———."Bush Sees Arafat as Irrelevant." *The Telegraph*, June 6, 2002. Accessed May 1, 2012. http://www.telegraph.co.uk/news/worldnews/middleeast/israel/1396455/Bush-sees-Arafat-as-irrelevant.html.

Bibliography

Cubert, Harold M. *The PFLP's Changing Role in the Middle East.* London: Frank Cass, 1997.
Cubert, Harold M. "Courts Halt Yitzhar Pullout; Hundreds Converge on Outpost." *Haaretz,* June 19, 2003.
Dellios, Hugh. "Arafat, Rival Put Aside Differences." *Chicago Tribune,* August 24, 1999. Accessed May 30, 2012. http://articles.chicagotribune.com/1999-08-24/news/9908240290_1_palestinian-factions-millions-of-palestinian-refugees-arafat-aide.
DFLP. "The Democratic Front for the Liberation of Palestine." Accessed June 10, 2012. http://www.dflp-palestine.net/english/about_dflp/dflp_foundation.htm.
———. "10 Topics about Current Situation." Accessed July 1, 2012. http://www.dflp-palestine.net/english/statements/10-topics-about-current-situation-finals-statement-of-central-committee-session.htm.
———. "The Program of Al Badil's List." DFLP. Accessed June 1, 2012. http://www.dflp-palestine.net/english/documents/the_program_of_Al-Badil-s_list.htm.
———. "A Statement Released by the Democratic Front for the Liberation of Palestine about the Financial Crisis of the Palestinian authority." DFLP. Accessed July 4, 2012. http://www.dflp-palestine.net/english/statements/a-statement-released-by-the-democratic-front-for-the-liberation-of-palestine-about-the-financial-crisis.htm.
———. "DFLP Militants Claim Fire on Israel." *Maan News.* Accessed May 15, 2012. http://www.maannews.net/eng/ViewDetails.aspx?ID=376749.
———. "DFLP in Damascus: Peace Talks Dangerous." *Maan News,* March 6, 2010. Accessed June 5, 2012. http://www.maannews.net/eng/ViewDetails.aspx?ID=266464.
Efraim, Omri. "Lieberman to Europe: Israel Has Nothing to Apologize for." *Ynet News,* December 25, 2011. Accessed May 25, 2012. http://www.ynetnews.com/articles/0,7340,L-4166615,00.html.
Ezzedine, Hossam. "Barghouti: Veto on UN Bid Tantamount to ´Terror´." *Maan News,* August 19, 2011. Accessed May 30, 2012. http://www.maannews.net/eng/ViewDetails.aspx?ID=414284.
———. "Saadat: Qorei Govt Cannot Represent Palestinians." *Middle East Online* (2003). Accessed May 30, 2012. http://www.middle-east-online.com/english/?id=7080.
Fatah Foreign Relations Commission Ramallah. English language version of Political Platform of Fatah provided to FES office in Jerusalem, February 5, 2011.
Fatah Foreign Relations Commission Ramallah. English language version of Fatah Constitution provided to FES office in Jerusalem, February 5, 2011.
Friedman, Gil. "Strategic Deficiencies in National Liberation Struggles: The Case of Fatah in the Al Aqsa Intifada." *Journal of Strategic Studies* 31, no. 1 (2008): 41–67.
General Directorate of Gaza Ministry of Planning, e-mail message to FES office Gaza, April 12, 2012. Translated from Arabic by Usama Anthar.
Ghanem, Asad. *Palestinian Politics after Arafat – a Failed National Movement.* Bloomington, IN: Indiana University Press, 2010.
Gunning, Joren. *Hamas in Politics.* New York: Columbia University Press, 2010.
Halsell, Grace. "A Visit with George Habash: Still the Prophet of Arab Nationalism and Armed Struggle against Israel." *Washington Report on Middle East Affairs* 136 (1998): 49.
Halsell, Grace. "Hamas' Gaza Chief: Iran Will Help Muslim World to Liberate Al Aqsa Mosque." *Haaretz,* February 12, 2012.
Halsell, Grace. "Hamas Leader Sets Conditions for Truce." *CNN World,* January 29, 2006. Accessed May 30, 2012. http://articles.cnn.com/2006-01-29/world/hamas.interview_1_palestinian-prisoners-top-hamas-official-hudna?_s=PM:WORLD.
Hamas Political Bureau Gaza, English language program of National Unity Government provided to FES office in Gaza, March 5, 2012.

———. "Hamas Vows to Honor Palestinian Referendum on Peace with Israel." *Haaretz*. December 1, 2010.
Hamas Political Bureau Gaza, English language program of Change and Reform list provided to FES office in Gaza, March 5, 2012.
Hass, Amira. "Public Outcry Forces Palestinian PM to Suspend Austerity Measures." *Haaretz*. February 7, 2012.
Hassan, Mehdi. "No Kind of Martyr." *New Statesman* 140, no. 5052 (2011): 26.
Hazan, Eric. "Palestinian Defiance." *New Left Review* 32 (March–April 2005). Accessed June 5, 2012. http://newleftreview.org/II/32/mustafa-barghouti-palestinian-defiance.
Hilal, Jamil. "The Polarization of the Palestinian Political Field." *Journal of Palestine Studies* 39, no. 3 (2010): 24–39.
Holter, Martin B. *Al-Mubadara: Third Current Politics of the Second Intifada. Remobilizing Politics in a De-Powered Palestinian Authority.* Master Thesis, University of Oslo, 2007.
Hroub, Khaled. *Hamas. A Beginner's Guide.* London: Pluto Press, 2010.
Ikhwanweb. "Sheikh Ahmad Yassin (1938–2004)." Accessed May 31, 2012. http://www.ikhwanweb.com/article.php?id=23862.
International Crisis Group. "Salvaging Fatah." *Middle East Report* no. 91 (November 2009).
"Interview with Ahmad Sa'adat." *ABC Diario Español*, February 4, 2004.
"Interview with Edward Said." *Politics and Culture*, 3 (2000). Accessed May 31, 2012. http://www.politicsandculture.org/2010/08/10/an-interview-with-edward-said-2/.
"Israel Defiant Over Yassin Killing." *BBC News*, March 22, 2004. Accessed May 30, 2012. http://news.bbc.co.uk/2/hi/3557451.stm.
Jamal, Amal. *The Palestinian National Movement. Politics of Contention 1967–2005.* Bloomington, IN: Indiana University Press, 2005.
Jerusalem Media and Communication Center. "Opinion Poll no. 76." Accessed July 1, 2012. http://www.jmcc.org/documentsandmaps.aspx?id=855.
King, Mary Elizabeth. *A Quiet Revolution: The First Palestinian Intifada and Nonviolent Resistance.* New York: Nation Books, 2007.
Kuttab, Daoud. "Wanted: New Palestinian Political Parties." *Huffington Post*, April 21, 2011. Accessed June 1, 2012. http://www.huffingtonpost.com/daoud-kuttab/wanted-new-palestinian-po_b_851848.html.
Lalor, Paul. "DFLP Differences Reflect the Debate Within the PLO." *Middle East International* No 374 (1990): 17–19.
Lendman, Stephen. "Ahmad Sa'adat: A Palestinian Prisoner of Conscience." *Palestinian Chronicle*, May 7, 2010. Accessed June 1, 2012. http://palestinechronicle.com/view_article_details.php?id=16108.
Miftah. "Sheikh Ahmad Yassin (1936–2004)." Accessed May 31, 2012. http://www.miftah.org/Display.cfm?DocId=3377&CategoryId=11.
Miftah. "Letter From President Yasser Arafat to President Clinton." Accessed June 10, 2012, http://www.miftah.org/Display.cfm?DocId=428&CategoryId=10.
Mitchell, George, Suleyman Demirel, Thorbjoern Jagland, Warren B. Rudman, Javier Solana, "Sharm el-Sheikh Fact Finding Committee Report." April 30, 2001, accessed June 1, 2012. http://2001-2009.state.gov/p/nea/rls/rpt/3060.htm.
Monde Diplomatique. *Cahier Spécial sur le Proche-Orient.* Paris: Le Monde, 2006.
"Mustafa Barghouti Trails in Palestinian Polls." *Arab News*, January 7, 2005. Accessed June 1, 2012. http://archive.arabnews.com/services/print/print.asp?artid=57173&d=7&m=1&y=2005&hl=Mustafa%20Barghouti%20Trails%20in%20Palestinian%20Polls.
Nasser-Najjab, Nadia. "Palestinian Political Movements: Should They be Registered?" *Palestine-Israel Journal* 12, no. 1 (2005): 13–19.

Near East Consulting. "Opinion Poll." Accessed May 31, 2012. http://www.neareastconsulting.com/press/2012/April2012-PR-EN.pdf.
"Palestinian Local Poll Postponed." *Al Jazeera*, June 10, 2010. Accessed June 1, 2012. http://www.aljazeera.com/news/middleeast/2010/06/2010610155813954648.html.
Palestinian People' s Party. "Concluding Statement of the Fourth Party Congress." Accessed April 15, 2012. http://solidnet.org/old/cgi-bin/agent707d.html?parties/0590=palestine,_palestinian_peoples_party/960ppp11apr08.doc.
Palestinian People' s Party. "The Strategy to Establish the Independent Palestinian State and Achieve the Rights of Our People." Accessed March 27, 2011. http://www.palpeople.org/atemplate.php?id=1655.
Parsons, Nigel. *The Politics of the Palestinian Authority. From Oslo to Al-Aqsa*. London: Routledge, 2005.
PFLP. "PFLP Denounces PA Economic Policies, Calls for Popular Protection and Development." Accessed June 1, 2012. http://pflp.ps/english/2012/01/pflp-denounces-pa-economic-policies-calls-for-popular-protection-and-development/.
———. "Platform of the Popular Front for the Liberation of Palestine." PFLP. Accessed July 1, 2012. http://pflp.ps/english/1969/12/platform-of-the-popular-front-for-the-liberation-of-palestine-1969/.
———. Gaza. English language version of "Election Platform of PFLP" provided to FES office in Gaza, October 17, 2011.
PNI Ramallah. English language version of "Political Platform of PNI" provided to FES office in Jerusalem, December 1, 2011.
PNI Ramallah. English language version of "The Palestinian National Initiative: Leading the Palestinian People toward Freedom, Independence, Justice, Democracy, and a Life of Dignity" provided to FES office in Jerusalem, December 1, 2011.
President of the Palestinian National Authority. "Presidential Decree on the postponement of presidential and legislative elections." January 23, 2010. Accessed June 1, 2012. http://www.elections.ps/Portals/0/pdf/Presidential_decree_on_the_postponment_of_presidential_and_legislative_elections_2010_English.pdf.
Said, Edward. "Emerging Alternatives in Palestine." *Al Ahram Weekly* (2002). Accessed June 1, 2012. http://weekly.ahram.org.eg/2002/568/op2.htm.
———. "The Morning After." *London Review of Books* 15, no. 20 (1993): 3–5.
Sayigh, Yezid. *Armed Struggle and the Search for State. The Palestinian National Movement 1949–1993*. Oxford: Oxford University Press, 1997.
Secretariat of Palestinian People's Party Ramallah. Arabic version of Political Program of PPP provided to FES office in Jerusalem, March 1, 2012. Translated from Arabic by Usama Anthar and Michael Bröning.
Secretariat of PPP Ramallah. Arabic version of PPP Election Program (1995) provided to FES office in Jerusalem, March 1, 2012. Translated from Arabic by Usama Anthar and Michael Bröning.
Steinberg, Matti. "The Worldview of Habash's 'Popular Front'." *Jerusalem Quarterly* 45–48 (1988): 3–36.
———. "The Worldview of Hawatmeh's 'Democratic Front'." *Jerusalem Quarterly* 49–52 (1989): 23–40.
Tamimi, Azzam. *Hamas: Unwritten Chapters*. London: Hurst & Company, 2007.
"The FP Top 100 Global Thinkers." *Foreign Policy* (2011). Accessed May 30, 2012. http://www.foreignpolicy.com/articles/2011/11/28/the_fp_top_100_global_thinkers?page=0,47.
"UN Tells Israel to 'Get Out'." *The Telegraph*, March 30, 2002. Accessed June 1, 2012. http://www.telegraph.co.uk/news/1389310/UN-tells-Israel-to-get-out.html.

Bibliography

UNISPAL. "Chronological Review of Events Relating to the Question of Palestine." Accessed June 10, 2012. http://unispal.un.org/UNISPAL.NSF/0/17459CC48D8D397985256D750063AD52.
United Nations News Center. "Annan Strongly Condemns Israeli Assassination of Hamas Leader." Accessed May 31, 2012. http://www.un.org/apps/news/storyAr.asp?NewsID=10155&Cr=middle&Cr1=east.
"Unity in Struggle—George Habash (1925–2008)." *Al Ahram Weekly*, January 31–February 6, 2008. Accessed May 30, 2012. http://www.weekly.ahram.org.eg/2008/882/re31.htm.
World Bank. "Sustaining Achievements in Palestinian Institution Building and Economic Growth. Economic Monitoring Report to the ad hoc Liaison Committee." Accessed May 30, 2012. http://siteresources.worldbank.org/INTWESTBANKGAZA/Resources/WorldBankAHLCReportSep2011.pdf.
Yale Law School / The Avalon Project. "Hamas Covenant 1988. The Covenant of the Islamic Resistance Movement." Accessed March 5, 2012. http://www.avalon.law.yale.edu/20th_century/hamas.asp

INDEX

Abbas, Mahmoud
  Arab Spring and, 67–68
  Barghouthi and, 78, 123, 128
  bio, 73–75
  Cairo Agreement and, 25–26
  DFLP and, 180, 183, 185–86
  Doha Declaration and, 31, 38, 202
  Fatah and, 59, 64–65, 78, 86
  General Conference and, 67–68
  Hamas and, 67, 180
  Haniya and, 33
  intifada and, 64
  Mecca Agreement and, 201
  National Unity Government and, 202
  Oslo Accords and, 71
  PFLP and, 102–3
  PLO and, 71–72
  PNI and, 125
  as prime minister, 21, 64, 201
  role within Fatah, 59
al-Aqsa Martyrs' Brigade, 59, 63–64, 77
al-Aqsa Mosque, 47
al-Mubadara
  see Palestinian National Initiative (PNI)
al-Qaeda, 34
Ali, Said Abu, 65, 68
Amirah, Hanna, 148–49
Annan, Kofi, 29
Apartheid, 80, 88, 126

Apartheid Wall, 114, 116, 123, 133, 139
Arab Nationalist Movement (ANM), 97, 105–6, 179
Arab Spring, 5–6, 12, 24, 38, 40–41, 67, 80, 126, 187–88
Arafat, Yasir, 28, 57–58, 60–65, 68–74, 76, 79, 85, 106–7, 130–31, 176–77, 180, 201–2
Ashrawi, Hanan, 6
Ayyash, Yahya, 19

Barak, Ehud, 72, 131, 180, 200
Barghouthi, Bashir, 148–49, 156–57, 160
Barghouthi, Marwan, 64, 75–78
Barghouthi, Mustafa
  Anti-Apartheid Wall Campaign and, 123–27
  bio, 128–29
  Hamas and, 127
  PFLP and, 102
  PNI and, 121, 123, 131–36, 149–50
  Yaghi and, 136–38
Battle of Karameh, 60, 69, 199
Black September, 60, 70, 99, 176, 199
Bush, George W., 72

Cairo Agreement, 25–27, 31, 67, 75, 82, 85, 202
Cairo Dialogue, 118

Cairo Unity Paper, 155
Camp David peace talks, 9, 63, 72, 131, 149, 200
Change and Reform list, 16, 20, 33, 35, 43, 45–46, 49–50, 54, 64, 201
Clinton, Bill, 72, 178, 200
communism
    DFLP and, 184
    Hamas and, 41
    Israel and, 154, 163
    Jordan and, 147
    PCP, 147–48, 200
    see also Palestinian People's Party (PPP)

Dahlan, Mohammad, 64, 73, 78–79, 81
Dakkak, Ibrahim, 121
Declaration of Independence (Palestinian), 100, 168, 200
Declaration of Principles (DoP), 66, 73, 155, 177
Democratic Front for the Liberation of Palestine (DFLP)
    Abbas and, 180, 183, 185–86
    Arab Spring and, 188
    economic development and, 193–95
    excerpts from party documents, 191–98
    Fatah and, 174, 176–77, 180–81, 183–84
    Fayyad and, 173, 178, 181, 184, 187–88
    Gaza and, 188–89
    Hawatmeh, 179–81
    history, 173–79
    internal dynamics of, 183–84
    interviews with party decision-makers, 181–90
    intifada and, 182–84
    Israel and, 191–93
    Marxism and, 184
    organizational structure, 175
    Oslo Accords and, 173, 177, 179–80, 183–86
    overview, 174
    PFLP and, 182
    PLO and, 184
    PNA and, 186–87
    politics and, 181–82, 189–90
    PPP and, 187
    religion and, 195–96
    Syria and, 190
    terrorism and, 182–83, 186
    Transitional Program, 176, 180, 182, 191–93, 195, 197
    two-state solution and, 175–77, 179–80, 182, 187, 189
    vision of state and society, 196–98
Doha Declaration, 26–27, 31, 38, 67, 75, 202

Egypt
    Arab Spring and, 5, 38, 80
    Arafat and, 69
    Fatah and, 60, 80, 85, 90, 93
    Gaza Strip and, 22, 24, 33–34, 85, 202
    Hamas and, 16, 37–38, 50
    Muslim Brotherhood and, 15–16, 28, 38
    NLL and, 147
    PFLP and, 111
    Yassin and, 28

Fatah (Palestinian National Liberation Movement)
    1996 elections and, 4
    2009 party platform, 8, 57, 66, 79, 86–91, 93–96
    Abbas and, 73–75
    activism, 11–12, 80
    Arab Spring and, 80
    Arafat and, 68–72
    Barghouthi and, 75–78
    Cairo Agreement and, 25–26
    charting transition of, 57–68
    corruption charges, 79–80
    DFLP and, 174, 176–77, 180–81, 183–84
    economic development and, 93
    exiled politicians and, 82
    Fayyad and, 82–83

FES and, 9
founding of, 1, 199
General Conference and, 74, 81, 84–85
Hamas and, 4–5, 15, 17–27, 33, 85
internal divisions, 81
interviews with party decision-makers, 78–86
Israel and, 81, 84, 86–92
Meshal and, 29, 31
nonviolence and, 11–12, 80, 82
organizational structure, 59
overview, 58
PFLP and, 97–98, 102–3, 105, 111, 113
PNI and, 121–23, 125–29, 131–33, 136–37
political role, 1–2, 79, 81, 83
PPP and, 148–49, 153, 155, 158, 160
programmatic documents, 86–96
state's role vis-à-vis religion and, 93–94
two-state solution and, 10, 80
views of, 7
vision of state and society, 94–96
women and, 83–86
Fatah al-Intifada, 61
Fayyad, Salam
  appointment as Prime Minister, 33, 202
  Barghouthi and, 128
  DFLP and, 173, 178, 181, 184, 187–88
  Fatah and, 82–84, 203
  PFLP and, 103
  PNA and, 111, 151
  PNI and, 135, 137
  PPP and, 153–55, 159
  Salhi and, 153
  statebuilding, 103, 111–12, 135, 155, 184, 186–87, 202
  taxes and, 83, 111, 135, 151, 155, 167
  Third Way list and, 6–7, 126
  views of, 43, 82–84, 135
  West Bank and, 67–68
FIDA
  see Palestinian Democratic Union (FIDA)
Friedrich-Ebert-Stiftung (FES), 9

Gaza Strip
  DFLP and, 174–75, 177, 179–81, 183, 188–90, 194, 197
  Fatah and, 58, 61–66, 68–70, 74–75, 78, 81–85, 89–90
  Hamas and, 4, 12, 15–17, 19, 21–35, 37–38, 42–43, 48–51
  NLL and, 147
  Oslo Accords and, 3, 5
  political factions and, 3–5, 8–9
  PFLP and, 97–98, 100–5, 108–15
  PNI and, 122–24, 127–28, 130–31, 133–38
  PPP and, 147–54, 158–62, 167, 170
General Conference, 149–51, 161, 174, 182, 187, 190
  DFLP, 187, 190
  Fatah, 59, 62, 65, 74, 76, 78, 80–84, 86
  PNI, 135
  PPP, 161
  UNESCO, 202
General Union of Palestinian Students, 69
Ghoul, Kayed al, 109, 112–14

Habash, George, 97, 99–101, 105–7
Haddad, Wadie, 105
Hamas
  Arab Spring and, 38, 40–41
  Barghouthi and, 127
  Charter, 36, 41
  Doha Declaration and, 38
  economic development and, 48–49
  excerpts from programmatic documents, 43–50
  Fatah and, 4–5, 15, 17–27, 33, 85
  Fayyad and, 43
  Gaza and, 37, 42, 48–50
  Haniya and, 31–34
  history, 15–27
  interviews with party decision-makers, 34–43
  Islamic Jihad and, 37, 41

Hamas—*Continued*
  Israel and, 35–40, 42, 43–45
  Meshal and, 29–31
  Oslo Accord and, 15, 18, 20, 29, 62
  overview, 16
  organizational structure, 25
  Palestinian state and, 36, 41
  religion and, 41, 50–51
  two-state solution and, 11, 38–39
  violence and, 36–37
  vision of state and society, 51–56
  West Bank and, 42
  women and, 42

Hamdan, Abdel Majid, 149
Haniya, Ismail, 22, 25, 27, 31–36, 38, 202, 203
Hawatmeh, Nayef, 174–75, 177–81
Health, Development Information and Policy Institute (HDIP), 128
Hezbollah, 104, 131, 201
Hijla, Lana Abu, 84
Hizb ut-Tahrir, 7
Hroub, Khaled, 12
Hussein, Saddam, 71, 200
Husseini, Adnan, 68
Husseini, Amin al, 16

intifada
  first, 15–16, 28, 30, 32, 61–62, 148, 152, 159, 176, 200
  DFLP and, 182–84
  PFLP and, 115
  PLO and, 130
  PPP and, 162, 166
  second, 19, 29, 63–64, 67, 72–77, 101–2, 121, 123, 129, 151, 177–79, 201
Interim Agreement, 155
Iran, 18, 25–26, 30, 34, 38, 85, 158
Israel
  communism and, 154, 163
  DFLP and, 173, 176–82, 185–97
  establishment of, 1, 147

  Fatah and, 57–94
  Hamas and, 15–45, 48, 50
  Israeli-Palestinian conflict, 7–12
  Jordan and, 19
  Lebanon and, 17, 61, 200
  NLL and, 147
  Olso Accords and, 3, 61–62, 71
  PFLP and, 97–119
  PNA and, 202
  PNI and, 127–44
  PPP and, 147–68
  restrictions on Palestinians, 4
  settlements, 11, 29, 38–39, 44, 62, 67, 74, 76–77, 81–82, 85–91, 93, 114, 116, 129–30, 134, 139–41, 145, 154, 156, 162–64, 167, 177–79, 183, 185, 189, 191–92, 194
  terrorism and, 29–31, 42
  United States and, 2
  see also Gaza Strip; West Bank

Jarrar, Khalida, 102, 108–12
Jawad, Nasser Abdel, 35, 41–43
Jerusalem, 9, 19, 21, 29, 31, 33, 36–37, 41, 44–45, 47, 56, 68–69, 72, 74, 83–84, 86–91, 97, 103, 107, 114–15, 121, 124, 128–30, 139–40, 144, 151–52, 154, 161–64, 166–68, 170, 185, 191–92, 195–97
Jibril, Ahmad, 99
Jordan
  Arafat and, 69–70
  Barghouthi and, 75
  Battle of Karameh and, 60, 69, 199
  Communist Party, 147
  DFLP and, 175–76, 179–81, 195
  Fatah and, 59–61, 69, 82, 87, 90, 93
  Hamas and, 17, 29–30, 50
  Israel and, 19
  PFLP and, 97, 99, 104–6, 117
  PPP and, 147

Karim, Qais Abd al, 178–79, 181–84
Khaled, Taysir, 178, 180, 183

Khatib, Ghassan al, 149, 153–58
King Hussein, 30, 60, 69–70, 180

Lebanon
  Civil War, 199
  DFLP and, 174–77, 180, 183, 192
  Fatah and, 60–61, 85, 87
  Hamas and, 17–18
  Haniya and, 32
  Hezbollah and, 131
  Israel and, 17, 61, 200
  PFLP and, 99–100, 104, 106
  PLO and, 61, 70, 200
  Said and, 131

Madrid Peace Conference, 61, 71, 128, 153, 155, 159, 176–78, 185, 200
Majdalawi, Jamil, 102
Marxism, 97–100, 107, 109, 112, 148–49, 152, 154, 157–59, 173–75, 181, 184–85
Marzouk, Musa Abu, 30–31
Mashal, Khaled, 17–19, 21, 25, 27, 29–33, 38, 75, 78, 200, 201
Masri, Majida al, 178, 181, 184–88
Mecca Agreement, 21, 201
Middle East Quartet, 20–21, 33, 115, 201
Mubarak, Hosni, 38, 111
Mughrabi, Dalal, 78
Muslim Brotherhood, 15–16, 22, 28, 30–31, 35, 37–38, 46, 69, 79, 85

Naji, Jawad al, 68
Nasser, Gamal Abdel, 28, 60, 69, 106
National Guidance Committee (NGC), 152
National Liberation League (NLL), 147
National Resistance Brigades, 175–77, 190
National Unity Document, 10, 21
National Unity Government, 23, 33, 43–45, 49, 52–54, 125, 128, 137, 152, 156, 197, 202

nonviolence
  Barghothi and, 77
  DFLP and, 182, 186–87, 190
  Fatah and, 65–66, 77, 80, 82, 84, 88
  Hamas and, 36
  nonviolent activism, 11–12, 126–27
  PNI and, 121, 123, 125–29, 133, 137–39, 144
  PPP and, 147, 149, 151–52, 158
  Yassin and, 28

Obama, Barack, 38
one-state solution, 10–11, 36, 98, 101, 112, 133, 154
Oslo Accords
  Abbas and, 73
  Arafat and, 71, 106
  Barghouthi and, 76, 149
  DFLP and, 173, 177, 179–80, 183–86
  Fatah and, 79
  Hamas and, 15, 18, 20, 29, 62
  Israeli–Palestinian relations and, 61–62, 71
  PFLP and, 97, 100–2, 109, 112, 116
  PNA and, 3, 5, 61, 155–56, 200
  PNI and, 126, 132, 139
  political parties and, 3
  PPP and, 149, 155, 159
  rejection of, 15, 18, 130
  Sa'adat and, 107
  Said and, 130
  Salhi and, 152
  signing of, 61–62, 200, 205
  Yassin and, 29
Oslo II, 155–56

Palestine Liberation Organization (PLO)
  Abbas and, 71–72
  DFLP and, 174, 176–77, 179–80, 183–85, 187–90, 192, 197–98
  Executive Committee, 73, 99–102, 106, 118, 148, 152, 180
  Fatah and, 57–63, 66–73, 77, 82

Palestine Liberation
Organization—*Continued*
  Hamas and, 15–19, 24–25, 31, 39, 44
  intifada and, 130
  Lebanon and, 61, 70, 200
  PFLP and, 97–102, 106–7, 109–10, 118
  PNA and, 4
  PNI and, 122, 126–27, 130, 136–37
  political parties and, 1–2, 4, 10–11
  PPP and, 148–49, 151–53, 155, 170–71
  UN and, 70, 202
Palestine Papers, 67, 74, 109, 202
Palestinian Democratic Union (FIDA), 7, 150, 177–78, 187
Palestinian General Federation of Trade Unions (PGFTU), 59
Palestinian National Authority (PNA)
  Abbas and, 201
  authority of, 2–5
  DFLP and, 177–79, 181, 184–88, 190, 193
  election law, 6
  Fatah and, 57, 59, 61–65, 67–68, 71–76, 78, 82, 94
  Fayyad and, 111, 151
  Hamas and, 16, 18–19, 21–25, 29, 31–35, 39, 45
  Israel and, 202
  Oslo Accords and, 3, 5, 61, 155–56, 200
  PFLP and, 100–3, 107–8, 110–11, 113
  PNI and, 122–24, 126–27, 130–32, 134–35
  PPP and, 147, 149–57, 159, 164, 170–71
Palestinian National Initiative (PNI)
  Abbas and, 125
  Barghouthi and, 121, 123, 128–29, 131–36, 149–50
  boycotts, 134
  economic development and, 140–42
  excerpts from party documents, 139–46
  Fatah and, 121–23, 125–29, 131–33, 136–37
  Fayyad and, 135, 137
  Gaza and, 137–38
  history, 121–27
  interview with party decision-makers, 131–38
  Israel and, 134, 139–40
  nonviolence and, 133
  as "one man show," 134, 138
  organizational structure of, 124
  Oslo Accords and, 126, 132, 139
  overview, 122
  PNA and, 134–35
  politics and, 131–32, 134, 136–37
  Said and, 129–31
  two-state solution and, 10, 132–33
  vision of state and society, 142–46
  West Bank and, 137–38
Palestinian National Liberation Movement
  see Fatah
Palestinian People's Party (PPP)
  current ideological outlook, 158–59
  economic development and, 164–67
  excerpts of programmatic documents, 161–71
  Fatah and, 148–49, 153, 155, 158, 160
  Fayyad and, 153–55, 159
  Gaza and, 154, 160–61
  grassroots efforts, 157–58
  history, 147–51
  interviews with party decision-makers, 153–61
  intifada and, 162, 166
  Israel and, 143, 158, 161–64
  Marxism and, 154–55, 157
  nonviolence and, 158
  oppositional role, 156–57
  organizational structure, 150
  Oslo Accords and, 149, 155, 159
  overview, 148
  PNA and, 154–55
  politics and, 153–54, 160–61
  religion and, 168
  Salhi and, 152–53

two-state solution and, 147, 151, 153–54, 157–59
vision of state and society, 168–71
West Bank and, 161
PFLP
   see Popular Front for the Liberation of Palestine
PGFTU
   see Palestinian General Federation of Trade Unions
PNI
   see Palestinian National Initiative
Popular Front for the Liberation of Palestine (PFLP)
   Abbas and, 102–3
   alternative strategy of, 112–13
   Barghouthi and, 102
   changes since founding of, 112
   economic development and, 117–18
   excerpts from party documents, 114–19
   Fatah and, 97–98, 102–3, 105, 111, 113
   Fayyad and, 103
   Gaza and, 111, 113–14
   Habash and, 105–6
   history, 97–105
   interviews with party members, 108–14
   intifada and, 115
   Israel and, 110–11, 114–17
   organizational structure, 104
   Oslo Accords and, 97, 100–2, 109, 112, 116
   overview, 98
   PNA and, 111–12
   politics and, 109–11
   religion and, 118
   Sa'adat and, 106–8
   terrorism and, 110–11, 113
   two-state solution and, 97–105, 108–9
   vision of state and society, 118–19
Popular Resistance Committee, 23–24
PPP
   see Palestinian People's Party

Qasim, Abd al-Karim, 179
Qassam Brigades, 18–19, 25, 27
Qawasmeh, Khaled al, 65, 68
Qurei, Ahmad, 64, 74, 201

Rabbo, Yasser Abed, 7, 150, 177, 187
Rabin, Yitzhak, 61, 71, 200
Rantisi, Abdel Aziz al, 19, 30, 32, 34
Road Map for Peace, 73, 108, 115–16, 126, 154, 178, 201

Sa'adat, Ahmad, 101–2, 104, 106–8, 110
Said, Edward, 121, 123, 129–32, 134, 136
Saidam, Sabri, 78, 81–84
Salhi, Bassam, 150–53
Shaath, Nabil, 78–80
Shafi, Haider Abdel, 121, 132, 134, 136
Shalit, Gilad, 21, 26, 39, 78, 108, 194, 202
Sharon, Ariel, 29, 63, 72, 138, 160, 163, 191, 201
Shukairy, Ahmad, 60
Six Day War, 30, 58, 69, 106–7, 180, 199
Social Democratic Party (SPD), 9
Socialist International, 57–58, 122, 125, 136
Suez Crisis, 69

terrorism
   Abbas and, 73
   Arafat and, 68
   DFLP and, 173, 177, 182–83, 186, 190
   Fatah and, 59, 64, 70, 77, 82, 89
   Hamas and, 15, 25, 29–31, 42, 51
   Israel and, 29–31, 42
   labeling of political groups as terrorists, 9
   PFLP and, 97, 99, 104–5, 108, 110–11, 113, 119
   PNI and, 121, 130
   political parties and, 2, 7

terrorism—*Continued*
  Qassam Brigades and, 18–19
  Yassin and, 29
  Third Way list, 6–7, 43, 126
two-state solution
  DFLP and, 175–77, 179–80, 182, 187, 189
  Fatah and, 10, 61, 71, 76, 80
  Hamas and, 11, 38–39
  PFLP and, 97–105, 108–9
  PNI and, 10, 132–33
  politics surrounding, 10–11
  PPP and, 147, 151, 153–54, 157–59

UN General Assembly, 70–71, 191, 200
United National Leadership of the Uprising (UNLU), 61, 148, 152, 176
United Nations
  Abbas and, 73
  Arafat and, 70–71, 200
  DPLP and, 180, 183, 185
  Fatah and, 73–74, 77, 81, 85–89, 91
  Hamas and, 29, 32, 36
  Middle East Quartet and, 20, 201
  Partition Plan, 147
  PFLP and, 101, 109, 112, 115
  PLO and, 70, 202
  PNI and, 130
  PPP and, 164
  Resolution 194, 86, 163
  Resolution on Settlements, 38
  Road Map for Peace and, 154
  Security Council, 85

UNESCO, 191
UNRWA (Relief and Works Agency), 22, 32

Weizmann, Ezer, 180
West Bank
  DFLP and, 174–75, 177–78, 180, 183, 187–90, 197
  Fatah and, 4, 61–62, 65–70, 73–77, 83–85, 89
  FES and, 9
  Hamas and, 17, 19, 21–31, 33–35, 37, 42–43
  Israeli settlements in, 11
  Oslo Accords and, 3
  PFLP and, 97, 100–4, 107, 110–11, 113, 115
  PNI and, 122–23, 126–27, 130, 135, 137–38
  political factions and, 5
  PPP and, 147–48, 150–52, 154, 158–62, 167, 170
  terrorism and, 19
West Bank Fatah Higher Committee, 76
West Bank Steering Committee, 77
World Bank, 160, 206

Yaghi, Ayed, 131, 136–38
Yassin, Ahmed, 16–19, 28–30, 32, 34, 37, 200, 201

Zedan, Saleh, 181, 188–90
Zionism, 21, 47, 49, 51, 55, 59, 66, 73, 91–92, 97, 104, 108, 114–17, 147, 163, 176, 192–93, 197

Lightning Source UK Ltd.
Milton Keynes UK
UKHW022240011121
393214UK00003B/203